P9-DER-279

Ecuador
a country study

Federal Research Division
Library of Congress
Edited by
Dennis M. Hanratty
Research Completed
December 1989

On the cover: Inca gold sun pendant

Third Edition, First Printing, 1991.

Library of Congress Cataloging-in-Publication Data

Ecuador : a country study / Federal Research Division, Library of
    Congress ; edited by Dennis M. Hanratty.—3rd ed.
        p.   cm. — (Area handbook series, ISSN 1057-5294) (DA
pam ; 550-52)
        "Research completed December 1989."
        Rev. ed. of: Area handbook for Ecuador / co-authors,
    Thomas E. Weil . . . [et al.]. 1973.
        Includes bibliographical references (pp. 265-282) and index.
        ISBN 0-8444-0730-5
        1. Ecuador.   I. Hanratty, Dennis Michael, 1950-   .
    II. Library of Congress. Federal Research Division.   III. Area
    handbook for Ecuador.   IV. Series.   V. Series: DA pam ;
    550-52.
    F3708.E383   1991   91-9494
    986.6—dc20   CIP

Headquarters, Department of the Army
DA Pam 550-52

For sale by the Superintendent of Documents, U.S. Government Printing Office
Washington, D.C. 20402

Foreword

This volume is one in a continuing series of books prepared by the Federal Research Division of the Library of Congress under the Country Studies—Area Handbook Program sponsored by the Department of the Army. The last page of this book lists the other published studies.

Most books in the series deal with a particular foreign country, describing and analyzing its political, economic, social, and national security systems and institutions, and examining the interrelationships of those systems and the ways they are shaped by cultural factors. Each study is written by a multidisciplinary team of social scientists. The authors seek to provide a basic understanding of the observed society, striving for a dynamic rather than a static portrayal. Particular attention is devoted to the people who make up the society, their origins, dominant beliefs and values, their common interests and the issues on which they are divided, the nature and extent of their involvement with national institutions, and their attitudes toward each other and toward their social system and political order.

The books represent the analysis of the authors and should not be construed as an expression of an official United States government position, policy, or decision. The authors have sought to adhere to accepted standards of scholarly objectivity. Corrections, additions, and suggestions for changes from readers will be welcomed for use in future editions.

Louis R. Mortimer
Chief
Federal Research Division
Library of Congress
Washington, D.C. 20540

Acknowledgments

The authors wish to acknowledge the contributions of Thomas E. Weil, Jan Knippers Black, Howard I. Blutstein, David S. McMorris, Mildred Gill Mersereau, Frederick P. Munson, and Kathryn E. Parachini, who wrote the 1973 edition of the *Area Handbook for Ecuador*. Portions of their work were incorporated into the present volume.

The authors are grateful to individuals in various agencies of the United States government and private institutions who gave their time, research materials, and special knowledge to provide information and perspective. These individuals include Ralph K. Benesch, who oversees the area handbook program for the Department of the Army. None of these individuals is in any way responsible for the work of the authors, however.

The authors also wish to thank those who contributed directly to the preparation of the manuscript. These include Sandra W. Meditz, who reviewed all drafts and served as liaison with the sponsoring agency; Ruth Nieland, who edited the chapters; Martha E. Hopkins and Marilyn Majeska, who managed editing and production; and Barbara Edgerton, Janie L. Gilchrist, and Izella Watson, who did the word processing. Cissie Coy performed the final prepublication editorial review, and Joan C. Cook compiled the index. Malinda B. Neale of the Library of Congress Printing and Processing Section performed phototypesetting, under the supervision of Peggy Pixley.

David P. Cabitto, who was assisted by Sandra K. Ferrell and Wayne Horne, provided invaluable graphics support. Harriet R. Blood, David P. Cabitto, and Greenhorne and O'Mara prepared the maps. David P. Cabitto also deserves special thanks for designing the illustrations for the book's cover and the title page of each chapter.

The authors also would like to thank several individuals who provided research support. Arvies J. Staton supplied information on military ranks and insignia, and Karen M. Sturges-Vera wrote the section on geography in chapter 2.

Finally, the authors acknowledge the generosity of the individuals and the public and private agencies who allowed their photographs to be used in this study. We are indebted especially to those who contributed original work not previously published.

Contents

Chapter 3. The Economy 101
Edmundo Flores and Tim Merrill

List of Figures

Preface

Like the 1973 *Area Handbook for Ecuador,* this study is an attempt
to treat in a compact and objective manner the dominant social,
political, economic, and military aspects of contemporary Ecuador. Sources of information included scholarly books, journals, and
monographs; official reports of governments and international organizations; numerous periodicals; and interviews with individuals having special competence in Ecuadorian and Latin American
affairs. Chapter bibliographies appear at the end of the book; brief
comments on sources recommended for further reading appear at
the end of each chapter. Measurements are given in the metric system; a conversion table is provided to assist readers unfamiliar with
metric measurements (see table 1, Appendix). A glossary is also included.

Although there are numerous variations, Spanish surnames
generally consist of two parts: the patronymic name followed by
the matronymic. In the instance of Rodrigo Borja Cevallos, for
example, Borja is his father's name, Cevallos, his mother's maiden
name. In informal use, the matronymic is often dropped. Thus,
after the first mention, we have usually referred simply to Borja.
A minority of individuals use only the patronymic. For purposes
of clarity, some individuals with common patronymics, such as
Gabriel García Moreno, are referred to with both patronymics and
matronymics. Special rules govern discussion of Galo Plaza Lasso,
who is referred to by Ecuadorian historians and throughout this
book as Galo Plaza to differentiate him from his father, Leónidas
Plaza Gutiérrez.

Country Profile

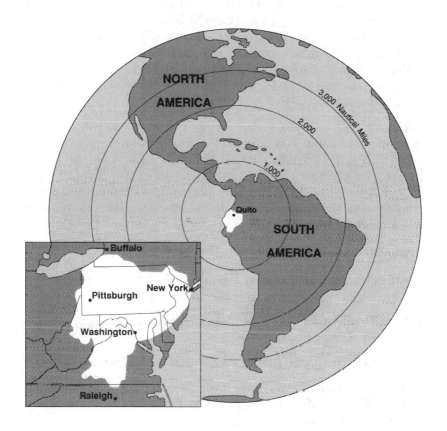

Country

Formal Name: Republic of Ecuador (República del Ecuador).

Short Form: Ecuador.

Term for Citizens: Ecuadorian(s).

Capital: Quito.

Geography

Size: Approximately 280,000 square kilometers.

Topography: Divided into three continental regions—the Costa, Sierra, and Oriente—and one insular region—the Galápagos Islands. Costa, located between Pacific Ocean and Andes Mountains, consists of coastal lowlands and mountains. Sierra composed of two major chains of Andes Mountains—Cordillera Occidental (Western Chain) and Cordillera Oriental (Eastern Chain)—and intermontane basin or plateau between the two chains. Cordillera Occidental contains Ecuador's highest peak, 6,267-meter Mount Chimborazo. Oriente consists of Andean piedmont and eastern lowlands. Galápagos are islands of varied size located 1,000 kilometers west of Ecuadorian coast.

Climate: Tropical climate throughout Costa, although variations in temperature and rainfall result from proximity to warm or cool ocean currents. Sierra climate ranges from tropical to frozen, depending on altitude; notable rainfall variations also occur. Tropical climate and abundant rainfall prevail in Oriente. Galápagos climate varies from tropical and desert-like at sea level to cold and wet at highest point.

Society

Population: Estimates of total population in 1989 ranged from 10.8 to 11 million; annual growth rate estimated at 2.3 to 2.8 percent.

Ethnic Groups: Indians and mestizos, 40 percent each; whites, 10 to 15 percent; blacks, 5 percent.

Languages: Spanish (official) and Quichua (a Quechua dialect).

Religion: Approximately 94 percent Roman Catholic. Beginning in late 1960s, significant gains made by Protestant evangelical and Pentecostal churches.

Education and Literacy: School attendance theoretically compulsory for children between ages six and fourteen. Primary and secondary schools each offered six-year programs. Higher education consisted of twelve state and five private universities as well as various polytechnic schools and teachers' colleges. Estimated 85 percent literacy rate in mid-1980s.

Health: Infant mortality rate estimates in early 1980s ranged from 70 to 76 per 1,000 live births; the infant mortality rate was approximately 63 per 1,000 live births in 1985. Infant mortality varied significantly by region and socioeconomic status. Life expectancy at birth in mid-1980s sixty-four years. Ministry of Public Health operated four-tiered system of health care, but lack of trained professionals hampered public health care. Maternal mortality remained high, especially in rural areas. Some tropical diseases, including malaria, continued to be of concern to health officials.

Economy

Gross Domestic Product (GDP): US$9.4 billion in 1989, or US$940 per capita. Substantial economic growth in 1970s following discovery of new petroleum fields in Oriente and international price increases for petroleum. Increased external debt, lowered petroleum prices, devastation from floods and earthquake, and economic mismanagement combined to produced serious economic problems during 1980s. GDP declined by 5.2 percent in 1987, increased by 8 percent in 1988, and grew by only 1 percent in 1989.

Agriculture: Including livestock raising, forestry, and fishing, almost 18 percent of GDP in 1987. Sector employed about 35 percent of nation's workforce in 1987.

Natural Resources and Energy: Petroleum and mining accounted for 8 percent of GDP in 1987. Nation had 1.6 million barrels of proven oil reserves, vast majority of which found in Oriente. Abundant natural gas reserves in Oriente and in Gulf of Guayaquil.

Industry: About 17 percent of GDP in 1987. Food processing and textile manufacturing most important components of industry sector. Nearly 10 percent of labor force employed in industry in 1987. Vast majority of firms had fewer than five workers.

Services: Accounted for nearly 50 percent of GDP and 24 percent of labor force in 1987. Wholesale and retail trade, financial services, and transportation and communications most important segments.

Imports: Totalled almost US$2.1 billion in 1987. Imports consisted primarily of raw materials and capital goods for industry, foods and lubricants, transportation equipment, durable consumer goods, and non-durable consumer goods. Major suppliers of imports were United States, Japan, the Federal Republic of Germany (West Germany), and Brazil.

Exports: Totalled US$2.3 billion in 1989. Petroleum generated half of all export revenues; other major exports included shrimp, bananas, coffee, and cocoa. Over 60 percent of exports in 1987 destined for United States.

Balance of Payments: Chronic current-account deficits during late 1980s, although deficit reduced from nearly US$1.2 billion in 1987 to US$500 million in 1989. External debt reached US$11.3 billion in 1989.

Exchange Rate: Sucre (S/) pegged to United States dollar during 1980s but devalued numerous times during 1980s. Official rate averaged S/526 = US$1 in 1989.

Fiscal Year: Calendar year.

Fiscal Policy: Upon assuming presidency in 1988, Rodrigo Borja Cevallos (1988–) inherited a rapidly deteriorating economy characterized by growing fiscal deficit, rapid monetary expansion, capital flight, and excessive government spending. Borja implemented economic austerity measures that included sharp currency devaluation, tax increases, import restrictions, government spending reductions, and substantial increases in fuel prices and electricity rates.

Transportation and Communications

Roads: Approximately 28,000 kilometers of roads in 1989, of which 3,600 paved, 17,400 gravel and improved earth, and 7,000 dirt roads. Pan American Highway most heavily traveled route. Few all-weather highways located in Oriente.

Railroads: Totalled 965 kilometers in 1989. Service on principal line between Quito and Guayaquil only partially restored following floods in early 1980s.

Airports: One hundred seventy-nine airports, of which forty-three had permanent surface runways. Quito and Guayaquil only international airports and handled largest volume of air traffic.

Ports: Country's five ports carried 95 percent of all imports and exports in late 1980s. Sixty percent of this trade passed through two Guayaquil ports. The national merchant marine consisted of 130 vessels.

Government and Politics

Government: Democratic and unitary state with republican, presidential, elective, and representative government. Under 1979 Constitution, chief executive is president of republic, elected to four-year term by majority popular vote. Reelection of incumbent not permitted. President's varied executive duties include enforcement of Constitution; approval of laws; maintenance of domestic order and national security; determination of foreign policy; and assumption of emergency powers during times of crisis. Principle of "legislative coparticipation" also allows president to share in formation of laws as well as in the execution and application of laws. Unicameral

National Congress enacts legislation; reforms and interprets Constitution; establishes revenues; approves public treaties; appoints high-level government officials from lists submitted by president; and reviews executive branch budget. Judiciary is responsible for technical matters.

Politics: Political parties suffered from factionalism and weak organization; were often overshadowed by personalist movements. Persistent regional rivalries between Quito and Guayaquil also contributed to contentious political debates. In May 1988, Borja, leader of Social Democratic party, the center-left Democratic Left (Izquierda Democrática-ID), defeated Abdalá Bucaram Ortiz of populist Ecuadorian Roldosist Party (Partido Roldosista Ecuatoriano-PRE) in second round of presidential elections and assumed presidency in August 1988, succeeding longtime rival and conservative-turned-populist León Febres Cordero Ribadeneyra (1984–88).

International Relations: Borja administration maintained good relations with United States. In contrast to Febres Cordero administration, also pursued more active relations with Third World, multilateral organizations, Western Europe, and socialist countries. Protracted border dispute with Peru strained relations between the two countries.

International Agreements and Membership: Party to Inter-American Treaty of Reciprocal Assistance of 1947 (Rio Treaty). Member of numerous regional and international organizations, including Organization of American States, United Nations and its specialized agencies, International Monetary Fund, World Bank, Inter-American Development Bank, Andean Pact, Latin American Economic System, Latin American Energy Organization, Latin American Integration Association, Nonaligned Movement, and Organization of Petroleum Exporting Countries.

National Security

Armed Forces: Included army, navy, and air force with total strength estimated at 49,000 in 1988. Country divided into four army theaters of operation (defense zones), three naval zones, and two air zones. Army operational zones consisted of five infantry brigades, two jungle brigades, one special forces brigade, and armored, logistics, engineering, and army aviation commands. Navy organized into destroyer division; fast-missile craft, corvette, and submarine squadrons; auxiliary vessels and transports; a naval aviation unit; coast guard; and marines. Air Force operations consisted of fighter and fighter-ground attack squadrons; light attack squadron; and air defense group.

Equipment: Major ground forces armaments included French-origin light tanks, four-wheeled reconnaissance vehicles, and armored personnel carriers; Brazilian armored cars and wheeled personnel carriers; and tracked personnel carriers from the United States. Naval equipment included West German missile attack craft and two small submarines; Italian corvettes equipped with Exocet missiles; and one Gearing-class destroyer from United States. Air Force equipment included British Jaguars; United States Cessnas; and Israeli Kfirs.

Police: Subordinate to Ministry of Government and Justice. Estimated 18,000 members organized into technical operations and support directorates and four operational units.

Figure 1. Administrative Divisions of Ecuador, 1989

Introduction

AS THE 1990s began, deep-rooted sociological, geographical, economic, and political features continued to define Ecuador. Despite such post-World War II developments as widespread migration, the growth of import-substitution (see Glossary) industrialization, and the emergence of an urban middle class, Ecuador remained strongly influenced by its history. Four key themes dominated the historical landscape and remained essential to an understanding of contemporary Ecuador. First, the nation had a highly skewed social structure that could be traced to its colonial past. Second, persistent regional rivalries often determined the outcome of key national issues. Third, the economy continued to be subject to the fortunes of a single commodity. Finally, the political system lacked strong, stable institutions.

Spanish social structures and values took hold most completely in the sixteenth century in the Sierra (Andean highlands). Not coincidentally, the Sierra was also that Ecuadorian region where the Inca conquerors had been most successful fifty years earlier. Spanish officials adapted the prevailing Inca hierarchical social system and established a tripartite, semifeudal structure consisting of small numbers of white elites, (both *peninsulares*—Spanish-born persons residing in the New World—and criollos—persons of pure Spanish descent born in the New World), a somewhat larger group of mestizo artisans, and a large Indian underclass. Since Ecuador lacked the mineral riches found in other Spanish colonies, such as Peru and Mexico, land became the critical commodity. Through the *encomienda* system, elites received tracts of Sierra land along with the right to extract labor from Indians living on that land. Colonists also adapted the Inca concept of obligatory public service (*mita*) and required Indians to toil in textile sweatshops scattered through the highlands. Debts incurred through the Spanish *mita* often transformed what was supposed to be a transitory labor obligation into a peonage system passed across generations.

The successful struggle for independence in the 1820s resulted in the transfer of power from *peninsulares* to criollos. It did little, however, to change other aspects of the social system, which by then had become dominated by haciendas with a resident Indian labor force. These residents, known as *huasipungueros,* typically worked the hacienda fields for four days per week in exchange for the right to own a small plot of land (*minifundio*).

The *huasipungo* system survived in isolated pockets of the Sierra until finally being abolished by the 1964 Agrarian Reform Law. This law and a successor measure in 1973, however, did not affect the basic distribution of landownership, which remained highly inequitable. In the 1980s, only 5 percent of all farms exceeded fifty hectares, yet these same farms represented over 55 percent of land under cultivation. By contrast, 80 percent of all farms encompassed fewer than ten hectares and accounted for only 15 percent of farmland.

Until the 1970s, landless Sierra peasants in search of work typically migrated to the Costa (coastal region). At independence, the Costa contained less than 20 percent of the national population. Nonetheless, it represented the most dynamic force in Ecuador's economy. This dynamism was centered in the port city of Guayaquil, which had established itself during the colonial period as an important shipbuilding and trade center.

An intense rivalry between Guayaquil and Quito—the national capital and most important Sierra city—dominated nineteenth-century Ecuadorian politics. By the 1850s, a clear dichotomy had emerged between the Catholic, conservative Sierra and the anticlerical, liberal Costa, with regional leadership in the hands of Gabriel García Moreno and José María Urbina, respectively. García Moreno played a critical role in the late 1850s and early 1860s in pulling Ecuador back from the brink of permanent dissolution. However, during a rule that lasted until his assassination in 1875, García Moreno polarized the religious issue through the enactment of legislation granting broad powers to the Roman Catholic Church. Following a twenty-year transitional period, José Eloy Alfaro Delgado seized power on behalf of Guayaquil Liberals and established a permanent separation of church and state.

The removal of the religious issue from the national agenda did little to alter regional tensions. Costa elites long resented what they perceived to be a transfer of their wealth to the less industrious Sierra. In addition, economic stagnation in the Sierra and dynamism in the Costa combined to produce a massive population shift in the twentieth century. By the early 1980s, the population of Guayaquil easily outdistanced that of Quito. Despite the presence of large squatter communities in both cities, regional rather than class identification remained the most important determinant of voting behavior. For example, a majority of Costa voters supported the second-round presidential candidates from their region in both the 1984 and 1988 elections, even though the political ideologies of these candidates varied widely.

On three separate occasions over the last hundred years, a single export product offered the prospect of a solid financial future. In each case, however, Ecuadorian hopes were dashed by a cruel dose of fiscal reality. Ideal growing conditions north of Guayaquil and the latter's excellent port facilities enabled Ecuador by 1900 to become the world's leading exporter of cocoa. Customs duties from cocoa exports filled government coffers. The cocoa boom also had an important sociological impact as Costa growers sought to attract Sierra peasants through sharecropping and wage-labor arrangements. By the mid-1920s, however, crop disease and competition from other producing nations had devastated Ecuadorian cocoa production. Lowered world demand resulting from the Great Depression dealt a further crushing blow to Ecuador's export effort. From 1928 to 1932, the total value of Ecuadorian exports declined by two-thirds.

Following World War II, Ecuador had a second commodity bonanza, this time in the form of bananas. Taking advantage of crop diseases in Central America and the unleashing of pent-up demands in the United States after the war, the value of Ecuador's banana exports grew tenfold from 1948 to 1952. Once again, customs duties allowed ambitious public works spending. As was the case with cocoa, bananas were grown in the Costa. Besides stimulating the regional economy, the banana boom set off another migration wave from the Sierra. By the mid-1960s, however, Ecuador experienced a substantial drop in the volume and value of banana exports. Economic stagnation once more became the order of the day.

The discovery in 1967 of vast amounts of petroleum in the sparsely populated Oriente (eastern region) created conditions for a third economic boom. Five years later, petroleum began flowing through the 503-kilometer Trans-Ecuadorian Pipeline, bound for foreign industrialized markets. Largely as a result of petroleum exports, Ecuador's foreign exchange earnings climbed eightfold between 1971 and 1974.

Several noteworthy features distinguished the petroleum boom from the earlier cocoa and banana booms. First of all, the locus of economic activity occurred outside of the Costa. Nevertheless, although the Oriente was the actual source of the petroleum wealth and received important infrastructure development, the bulk of the revenues flowed directly to the national treasury in Quito. The government used these revenues to finance an unprecedented level of public spending, creating numerous state enterprises and expanding the scope and activities of previously established national agencies. Government funding also supported industrial growth in Quito. Finally, industrialization and public-sector expansion allowed for the emergence of an urban middle class.

Unfortunately, petroleum proved to be as illusive a treasure as the earlier golden commodities. In the first half of the 1970s, the income from petroleum made possible the purchase of a wide range of imports. When revenues stagnated around 1975, the military government that had assumed power three years earlier resorted to massive foreign borrowing. Between 1976 and 1979, Ecuador's foreign debt increased by over 400 percent. Although the civilian administrations that came to power in 1979 succeeded in slowing the debt growth rate, it still had doubled by 1986 and totalled nearly US$9 billion.

Ecuador was unprepared for the economic calamities that befell it in the 1980s. During that decade, Ecuador experienced two sharp drops in the market price for petroleum, a global recession, a dramatic increase in international interest rates, widespread crop damage resulting from flooding, and an earthquake that severed the oil pipeline for five months and cost the nation US$700 million in lost revenues. In order to qualify for additional loans and renegotiation of scheduled interest payments, Ecuadorian governments adopted various austerity packages that included reductions in public expenditures, currency devaluations, and increases in interest rates. Although necessary, these measures increased unemployment and underemployment nationwide.

Stronger political institutions might have enabled Ecuador to weather its varied economic storms. Unfortunately, national political structures historically exacerbated rather than ameliorated the fiscal picture. Except for a brief period during the 1880s and early 1890s, nineteenth-century Ecuadorian governments were authoritarian rather than democratic. Most of the heads of those governments were forcibly removed from office. Although the Liberal Party held power from 1895 to 1925, those years were hardly a model of stability. For the first half of that period, Alfaro and Leónidas Plaza Gutiérrez waged a bitter rivalry that only ended when the former unsuccessfully staged a coup and was murdered by a government-sponsored mob. In the second half, liberal politicians surrendered key financial decisions to Guayaquil banking interests. The printing of national currency by private banks generated runaway inflation and contributed heavily to the economic chaos of the late 1920s.

On three occasions in the twentieth century—1925, 1963, and 1972—the military seized direct political control. In each case, it was unsuccessful in carrying out espoused socioeconomic reforms. The last period of military rule—1972 to 1979—was both the most ambitious and disappointing of the three. Although one of the motivations for intervention was to prevent civilian politicians from dissipating the new-found petroleum wealth, the military's principal legacy was that of ever-increasing foreign debt obligations.

The 1979 Constitution is the seventeenth such document since independence in 1830. It is both an impressive and hopeful sign that as of the early 1990s Ecuador had had democratically elected governments since the inception of this Constitution and two nonviolent transfers of power. Nonetheless, the maturation of Ecuador's political institutions remained open to debate. Ecuador had a staggering number of political parties, most of which had rather shallow roots and were often little more than electoral labels for their leaders. Party identification and ideology remained weak, whereas personalism remained strong.

Perhaps most disturbing was the deteriorating level of political discourse. This was particularly true during the presidency of León Febres Cordero Ribadeneyra (1984–88). Febres Cordero's disdain for the give and take of the democratic process led to his adoption of an authoritarian style that resulted in acrimonious debates with the National Congress and threats of impeachment. In an incident that both typified the tumultuous years of the Febres Cordero administration and painfully exposed the potential threats to the democratic process, paratroop commandos kidnapped the president in 1987 and forced him to honor a congressional amnesty previously granted to Lieutenant General Frank Vargas Pazzos. Febres Cordero had dismissed Vargas as armed forces chief of staff after the latter had accused both the defense minister and an army commander of corruption. Following his dismissal, Vargas attempted two unsuccessful revolts against the government. In the bewildering interplay of Ecuadorian politics, Vargas ran for the presidency in 1988 and received over 12 percent of the vote.

Ecuador thus faced many challenges in the years ahead. Observers believed that it needed to design social structures that would allow a more equitable distribution of income and opportunities. It also needed to identify creative strategies of economic growth. Most important, Ecuador required strong, democratic political leadership.

August 1, 1991   Dennis M. Hanratty

Chapter 1. Historical Setting

Winged god cast in gold and platinum (La Tolita culture)

THROUGHOUT ITS HISTORY, Ecuador has displayed a continuity in traditional cultural and economic patterns as well as in social and political interaction among the country's highly heterogeneous social groupings. Modern patterns overlay the traditional, making present-day Ecuador a veritable living museum of its varied, rich heritage. Pre-Columbian Ecuador is reflected in the persistence of native languages, customs, and economic activities among a considerable, though diminishing, number of communities in the Sierra (Andean highlands) and the Oriente (eastern region). The legacy of three centuries of Spanish colonial rule is also pervasive and includes a social inequality that largely coincides with race, rural land tenure patterns, and the nation's dominant European cultural expressions.

Analysts of Ecuador's postindependence political history have pointed to a number of persistent ingredients. Regionalism is especially prominent, particularly as expressed in the struggle for power between the Sierra, represented by Quito, and the Costa (coastal region), represented by Guayaquil. Regionalism has coincided with the party struggle between the Quito-based Conservatives and the Guayaquil-based Liberals. Personalism, from the political prominence of military caudillos in the early years of the republic to the civilian dictators and the populists of more recent times, has been another persistent theme since independence.

Perhaps the most consistent element of Ecuador's republican history has been its political instability. In just over a century and a half, there have been no fewer than eighty-six changes of government, making for an average of 1.75 years in power for each regime. The 1979 Constitution is Ecuador's seventeenth national charter. Ecuador's political instability is a product of the struggles mentioned above combined with the important political role maintained by the nation's armed forces. The longest periods of civilian, constitutional rule were between 1912 and 1925 and again between 1948 and 1961. Governmental institutions, as a result, have had little opportunity to mature into established expressions of civilian, democratic rule.

Ecuadorian economic history has displayed marked cycles of "boom" and "bust" based on the rise and fall of particular export products. The longest-lasting "boom," between the last years of the nineteenth century and the early 1920s, resulted from Ecuador's near monopoly on the production and exportation of

3

cocoa. An on-again, off-again banana boom punctuated the decades of the 1950s and 1960s, whereas the oil boom—the most pronounced as well as the shortest of all the boom periods—lasted from 1972 until 1979. The sudden end of the oil expansion coincided with the onset of a foreign debt crisis bred by massive foreign borrowing by two successive military governments (1972–79) and by Jaime Roldós Aguilera's regime (1979–81).

Although petroleum revenues brought about significant social change by generating a sizable middle class, the widely anticipated political changes were less apparent. The populist Roldós and Conservative León Febres Cordero Ribadeneyra (1984–88) represented traditional elements, although other prominent postboom personalities, such as President Osvaldo Hurtado Larrea (1981–84), did espouse more modern, center-leftist ideologies. Still, prosperity from petroleum strengthened the state's traditionally weak fiscal hand and promised to tilt the regional balance of power significantly toward the nation's capital.

The intensity of the political struggle, commonly played out between the president and Congress during periods of civilian rule, did not seem to diminish after 1979. Perhaps the central unanswered question of the 1980s, however, was whether the armed forces would persist in their historically active political role, or would be content to operate from the sidelines without directly intervening in the political process.

Pre-Hispanic Era

Ecuador offers little archeological evidence of its pre-Hispanic civilizations. Nonetheless, its most ancient artifacts—remnants of the Valdivia culture found along the coast north of the modern city of Santa Elena in Guayas Province—date from as early as 3500 B.C. (see fig. 1). Other major coastal archaeological sites are found in the provinces of Manabí and Esmeraldas; major sites in the Sierra are found in Carchi and Imbabura provinces in the north, Tungurahua and Chimborazo provinces in the middle of the Andean highlands, and Cañar, Azuay, and Loja provinces in the south. Nearly all of these sites are dated in the last 2,000 years. Large parts of Ecuador, including almost all of the Oriente, however, remain unknown territory to archaeologists.

Knowledge of Ecuador before the Spanish conquest is limited also by the absence of recorded history within either the Inca or pre-Inca cultures as well as by the lack of interest taken in Ecuador by the Spanish chroniclers. Before the Inca conquest of the area that comprises modern-day Ecuador, the region was populated by a number of distinct tribes that spoke mutually unintelligible

languages and were often at war with one another. Four culturally related Indian groups, known as the Esmeralda, the Manta,
the Huancavilca, and the Puná, occupied the coastal lowlands in
that order from north to south. They were hunters, fishermen,
agriculturalists, and traders. Trade was especially important among
different coastal groups, who seem to have developed considerable
oceanic travel, but the lowland cultures also traded with the peoples of the Sierra, exchanging fish for salt.

The Sierra was populated by elements, from north to south, of
the Pasto, the Cara, the Panzaleo, the Puruhá, the Cañari, and
the Palta cultures. These people lived mostly on mountainsides and
in widely dispersed villages located in the fertile valleys between
the Cordillera Occidental (Western Chain) and the Cordillera
Oriental (Eastern Chain) of the Andes. The Sierra natives were
a sedentary, agricultural people, cultivating corn, quinoa, beans,
and many varieties of potatoes and squashes. The use of irrigation was prevalent, especially among the Cañari. A wide variety
of fruits, including pineapples and avocados, was grown in the
lower, warmer valleys. Historians believe that political organization centered around local chieftains who collaborated with one
another in confederations or were subjected to "kings." Such local
chiefs had considerable authority; they could raise armies, for example, and administer communal lands.

The Inca expansion northward from modern-day Peru during
the late fifteenth century met with fierce resistance by several Ecuadorian tribes, particularly the Cañari, in the region around modern-
day Cuenca; the Cara in the Sierra north of Quito; and the Quitu,
occupants of the site of the modern capital, after whom it was to
be named. The conquest of Ecuador began in 1463 under the leadership of the ninth Inca, the great warrior Pachacuti Inca Yupan-
qui. In that year, his son Topa took over command of the army
and began his march northward through the Sierra. After defeat-
ing the Quitu, he moved southward along the coast, and from there
he launched an extensive ocean journey that took him, depending
on the account, to the Galápagos Islands or to the Marquesas Islands in Polynesia. Upon his return, he tried unsuccessfully to sub-
due the populations around the Gulf of Guayaquil and the island
of Puná. By 1500 Topa's son, Huayna Cápac, overcame the resistance of these populations and that of the Cara, and thus incorporated all of modern-day Ecuador into Tawantinsuyu, as the Inca
empire was known.

The influence of these conquerors based in Cuzco (modern-day
Peru) was limited to about a half century, or less in some parts
of Ecuador. During that period, some aspects of life remained

unchanged. Traditional religious beliefs, for example, persisted throughout the period of Inca rule. In other areas, however, such as agriculture, land tenure, and social organization, Inca rule had a profound effect despite its relatively short duration. Farming remained the major form of subsistence, but the Inca introduced a variety of new crops, including yucca, sweet potatoes, coca, and peanuts. The use of llamas and irrigation was expanded considerably. Largely in private hands previously, land became, in theory at least, the property of the Inca emperor. In practice, most land was held collectively by the *ayllu,* an agrarian community group headed by a *curaca,* which was the basic social grouping under the Inca. Within the *ayllu,* each domestic family unit was allotted a small plot of arable land to grow food for its own consumption. The state and the clergy also held a substantial amount of land, which was worked by the emperor's subjects as part of their obligatory public service.

Emperor Huayna Cápac became very fond of Quito, making it a secondary capital of Tawantinsuyu and living out his elder years there before his death in about 1527. He preferred to rule through local *curacas* as long as they were willing to accept the divine authority of the Inca and to pay tribute. When he met opposition, the emperor dispersed large parts of local populations to other areas of the empire and replaced them with colonists who were brought from as far away as Chile. This wholesale movement of populations helped spread Quechua, the language of Cuzco, into Ecuador. A standing army, a large bureaucracy, and a temporally important clergy further enforced the rule of the emperor.

Huayna Cápac's sudden death from a strange disease, described by one Spanish chronicler as "probably smallpox or measles," precipitated a bitter power struggle between Huáscar, a son borne by Huayna Cápac's sister and thus the legitimate heir, and Atahualpa, a son who, although borne by a lesser wife, was reputedly his father's "favorite." This struggle raged during the half-decade before the arrival of Francisco Pizarro's conquering expedition in 1532. The key battle of this civil war was fought on Ecuadorian soil, near Riobamba, where Huáscar's northbound troops were met and defeated by Atahualpa's southbound troops. Atahualpa's final victory over Huáscar in the days just before the Spanish conquerors arrived resulted in large part from the loyalty of two of Huayna Cápac's best generals, who were based in Quito along with Atahualpa. The victory remains a source of national pride to Ecuadorians as a rare case when "Ecuador" forcefully bettered a "neighboring country."

Ruins of Ingapirca, an Inca sun temple in Cañar Province
Courtesy Embassy of Ecuador, Washington

Discovery and Conquest

The discovery and conquest of Ecuador by Spanish forces in the early sixteenth century are adjuncts to the history of the conquest of Peru, the richest of the New World prizes won for the Spanish crown. The central figure of that history is Pizarro, an illiterate adventurer from Trujillo in the Spanish region of Extremadura, who had accompanied Vasco Núñez de Balboa in his crossing of the Isthmus of Panama to discover the Pacific in 1513. Eleven years later, Panamanian governor Pedro Arias de Avila ("Pedrarias") authorized Pizarro, in partnership with an equally questionable character, a Castilian named Diego de Almargo, and a priest named Fernando de Luque, to explore southward down the west coast of South America. Their first two voyages, in 1524 and 1526, ended in failure; not until the third voyage, launched in 1531, would the Peruvian prize be won and the Inca be conquered.

The first European to set foot on the territory of modern-day Ecuador was probably Bartolomé Ruiz de Estrada, the pilot for Pizarro on his second voyage, who pushed southward while Pizarro explored the Colombian coast and Almargo returned to Panama for supplies. Pizarro himself landed on the Ecuadorian coast later

7

during his exploratory voyage and traveled as far as Tumbes in the extreme north of present-day Peru, in defiance of official orders to return to Panama.

Having thus lost the favor of the king's representatives in Panama, Pizarro was forced to return to the royal court in Spain to petition King Charles I personally for authorization of a third voyage. Flush with the success of Hernán Cortés in Mexico and tantalized by the gold pieces brought by Pizarro from Tumbes and growing fables of great wealth in the South American interior, Charles granted Pizarro authorization and much more: the titles of governor and captain-general of Peru, a generous salary, and extensive territorial concessions. Almargo was granted important, although less generous, titles and privileges; his resentment of this slight would affect relationships for the rest of the conquest. At the time that Charles granted various titles to Pizarro and Almargo, he named de Luque Bishop of Tumbes. Before returning to Panama in 1530, Pizarro recruited for the conquest several immediate family members, including two full brothers named Gonzalo and Juan as well as two half-brothers. The participation of so many of Pizarro's relatives further strained relations between the two partners in conquest.

Pizarro then embarked from Panama with some 180 men while Almargo remained there to gather additional recruits. After thirteen days at sea, Pizarro landed once again on the coast of Ecuador, where he procured some gold, silver, and emeralds, which were dispatched to Panama and put to good use in Almargo's efforts. Although the capture of the Inca stronghold of Tumbes was Pizarro's first objective, he was forced to spend several months in Ecuador, first nursing a rash of ulcers and then fighting the fierce warriors of the island of Puná. By the time the conquerors arrived in Tumbes, it had been destroyed by the Puná warriors and its population dispersed. Just to the south, they founded the first Spanish settlement in Peru, San Miguel de Tangarará. Upon their fateful departure to Cajamarca on September 24, 1532, Pizarro left a lieutenant, Sebastián de Benalcázar, in charge of protecting and developing San Miguel as a Spanish base of operations. Two years later, Benalcázar would lead the conquering forces that moved northward into Ecuador.

Meanwhile, Atahualpa was resting near Cajamarca, in the Sierra of northern Peru, following the defeat and capture of his brother. He had known of the arrival of foreign invaders for several months; it is not clear why he did not order their obliteration before they could penetrate into the heart of the empire. After a march of almost two months, Pizarro arrived in Cajamarca and summoned

Atahualpa from the nearby thermal baths known today as the Baños del Inca. Reluctantly, accompanied by several thousands of his best troops, Atahualpa went to Cajamarca's central plaza, where he was met, not by the conquistadors, but by their chaplain, Fray Vicente de Valverde, who called upon the Inca emperor to submit to the representatives of the Spanish crown and the Christian god. Atahualpa replied disparagingly, and, upon his throwing a Christian prayer book to the ground in contempt, concealed Spanish soldiers opened fire, killing thousands of Atahualpa's defenders and taking the Inca emperor captive. This slaughter, called "the decisive battle" of the conquest of Peru by historian Hubert Herring, took place on November 16, 1532.

A panic-stricken Atahualpa, fearing that Pizarro might be planning to depose him in favor of his rival brother, summoned Huáscar, at this time imprisoned in Cuzco, to Cajamarca, then ordered him to be executed along with hundreds of Huáscar's nearest of kin. It served the Spaniards' purposes to allow Atahualpa the freedom, from his cell, to command his forces. Thus continued the rapid annihilation, through a vicious civil war that now overlapped with the Spanish conquest, of the army and leadership of one of the great polities of modern history. Pizarro was not planning to depose Atahualpa, of course, but to execute him. First, however, he had Atahualpa fill his cell, once with gold, then twice with silver (estimated at 4,850 kilograms of gold and 9,700 kilograms of silver), supposedly as ransom for his release. Instead the Spaniards garrotted Atahualpa on August 29, 1533, following a mock trial at which he was convicted of every charge that Pizarro could invent for the occasion. Having deprived the Inca empire of leadership, Pizarro and another conquistador, Hernando de Soto, moved south to Cuzco, the heart of Tawantinsuyu, which they captured in November 1533; they then led their men in an orgy of looting, pillaging, and torture in search of more precious metals.

Benalcázar, Pizarro's lieutenant and fellow Extremaduran, had already departed from San Miguel with 140 foot soldiers and a few horses on his conquering mission to Ecuador. At the foot of Mount Chimborazo, near the modern city of Riobamba, he met and defeated the forces of the great Inca warrior Rumiñahui with the aid of Cañari tribesmen who, happy to throw off the yoke of their Inca rulers, served as guides and allies to the conquering Spaniards. Rumiñahui fell back to Quito, and, while in pursuit of the Inca army, Benalcázar encountered another, quite sizable, conquering party led by Guatemalan Governor Pedro de Alvarado. Bored with administering Central America, Alvarado had set sail for the south without the crown's authorization, landed on the Ecuadorian coast, and marched inland to the Sierra. Pizarro had heard of this competing expedition some time earlier and had sent Almargo north to reinforce Benalcázar. Together, Pizarro's two representatives managed to convince Alvarado, with the help of a handsome amount of gold, to call off his expedition and allow the "legal" conquest to proceed as planned. Most of Alvarado's men joined Benalcázar for the siege of Quito.

Rumiñahui left Quito in flames for the approaching conquistadors. It was mid-1534, and, after the customary orgy of violence, in December the Spanish established the city of San Francisco de Quito on top of the ruins of the secondary Inca capital. Benalcázar was soon off on more conquests in Colombia to the north; it was not until December 1540 that Quito received its first captain-general in the person of Gonzalo Pizarro, the brother of Francisco.

Benalcázar had also founded the city of Guayaquil in 1533, but it had subsequently been retaken by the local Huancavilca tribesmen. Francisco de Orellana, yet another lieutenant of Francisco Pizarro from the Spanish city of Trujillo, put down the native rebellion and in 1537 reestablished this city, which a century later would become one of Spain's principal ports in South America.

Orellana is chiefly remembered, however, for being the first European to travel the length of the Amazon River. This journey, one of the great adventure tales of Spain's conquest of America, began in February 1541, when the lure of spices, particularly cinnamon, led Pizarro's brother Gonzalo to set off from Quito to the eastern jungle with a party that included 210 Spaniards and some 4,000 Indians. Orellana was second in command. After several months of hardship and deprivation during a crossing of the Cordillera Oriental of the Andes that cost the lives of nearly half the party, Gonzalo Pizarro placed Orellana in charge of building a brigantine in the Coca River in present-day Ecuador. Together with fifty-seven Spaniards and several hundred Indians, Orellana sailed downstream in search of food and friendly natives. The explorers never rejoined Pizarro, however, but set out on their own in search of neither food nor spices, but gold. "Having eaten our shoes and saddles boiled with a few herbs," wrote Orellana in a caricature of the ruggedness for which the Extremaduran conquerors were noted, "we set out to reach the Kingdom of Gold." The group reached the mouth of the Amazon, a name given by Orellana because he believed that they had been attacked by the legendary giant female warriors at a point below the Negro River, and sailed northward along the Atlantic coast as far as Venezuela, then back to Spain. The journey completed by the expedition headed by Orellana was not to be repeated for 100 years.

In the same August 1542, as Orellana reached the Atlantic, Gonzalo Pizarro was stumbling back to Quito with the few surviving members of his party. He found Peru in political chaos. Several years earlier, Almargo had entered into open rebellion against Francisco Pizarro and been defeated in battle, tried, and executed in his newly founded capital city of Lima. The resentment among Almargo's followers did not end, however, and in June 1541, Francisco Pizarro had been assassinated by the remnants of Almargo's army. In an attempt to try to control the unruly conquistadors and to end the enslavement of the native population of America, the Spanish crown had promulgated the New Laws in 1542, which in theory though not in practice abolished *encomiendas,* and two years later it sent its first viceroy to head a newly created colonial administrative system.

Gonzalo, who had little interest in being controlled by anyone, defeated and killed the first viceroy on a battlefield near Quito. After a brief period of glory, however, the younger Pizarro was himself defeated by the forces of a subsequent royal emissary, and in 1548 he was tried and hung for treason. It was the end of the tumultuous era of the conquistadors and the beginning of two and a half centuries of relatively pacific colonial rule.

Spanish Colonial Era

Spain's colonies in the New World were, legally, the personal patrimony of the king, and he held absolute control over all matters in Ecuador. Colonial administration at all levels was carried out in the name of the monarch. The king's chief agency in Madrid was the Council of the Indies, which devoted most of its energies to formulating legislation designed to regulate virtually every aspect of colonial life. The House of Trade, seated in Seville, was placed in charge of governing commerce between Spain and the colonies. In America, the king's major administrative agents were the viceroyalty, the *audiencia* (court), and the municipal council (*cabildo*).

Between 1544 and 1563, Ecuador was an integral part of the Viceroyalty of Peru, having no administrative status independent of Lima. It remained a part of the Viceroyalty of Peru until 1720, when it joined the newly created Viceroyalty of Nueva Granada; within the viceroyalty, however, Ecuador was awarded its own *audiencia* in 1563, allowing it to deal directly with Madrid on certain matters. The Quito *audiencia,* which was both a court of justice and an advisory body to the viceroy, consisted of a president and several judges (*oidores*). The territory under the jurisdiction of Quito considerably exceeded that of present-day Ecuador, extending southward to the port of Paita in the north of present-day Peru, northward to the port of Buenaventura and the city of Cali in the south of present-day Colombia, and well out into the Amazon River Basin in the east. Quito was also the site of the first (founded in 1547) and most important municipal council within the area comprising modern-day Ecuador. It consisted of several councilmen (*regidores*) whose extensive responsibilities included the maintenance of public order and the distribution of land in the vicinity of the local community.

The borders of the *audiencia* (or kingdom as it was also known) of Quito were poorly defined, and a great deal of its territory remained either unexplored or untamed throughout much of the colonial era. Only in the Sierra, and there only after a series of battles that raged throughout the mid-sixteenth century, was the native population fully subjugated by the Spanish. The jungle lowlands in both the Oriente and the coastal region of Esmeraldas were, in contrast, refuges for an estimated one-quarter of the total native population that remained recalcitrant and unconquered throughout most or all of the sixteenth and seventeenth centuries. Despite Orellana's harrowing journey of discovery, the Oriente remained terra incognita to the Spanish until its settlement by Jesuit missionaries beginning in the mid-seventeenth century, and it continued to be largely inaccessible throughout the remainder of the colonial period.

The coastal lowlands north of Manta were conquered, not by the Spanish, but by blacks from the Guinean coast who, as slaves, were shipwrecked en route from Panama to Peru in 1570. The blacks killed or enslaved the native males and married the females, and within a generation they constituted a population of *zambos* (mixed black and Indian) that resisted Spanish authority until the end of the century and afterwards managed to retain a great deal of political and cultural independence.

The relative autonomy of this coastal region nearest to Quito enhanced the effect of the Andes in isolating the Ecuadorian Sierra from the rest of the world during most of the nearly three centuries of colonial rule. Behind these barriers, a social system was established that was essentially a replica of the Spanish feudal system at the time of the conquest, with the *peninsulares* (Spanish-born persons residing in the New World) being the ruling, landed elite and the Indians being the subject people who worked the land. Although a few towns, particularly Quito, Riobamba, and Cuenca, grew along with the administrative and Roman Catholic bureaucracies and the local textile industries, colonial Ecuador was essentially a rural society.

The most common form in which the Spanish occupied the land was the *encomienda*. Settlers were granted land, along with its inhabitants and resources, in return for taking charge of defending the territory, spiritually indoctrinating the native population, and extracting the crown's annual tribute (payable half in gold, half in local products) from the *encomienda*'s Indian population. By the early seventeenth century, there were some 500 *encomiendas* in Ecuador. Although many consisted of quite sizable haciendas, they were generally much smaller than the estates commonly found elsewhere in South America. A multitude of reforms and regulations did not prevent the *encomienda* from becoming a system of virtual slavery of the Indians, estimated at about one-half the total Ecuadorian population, who lived on them. In 1589 the president of the *audiencia* recognized that many Spaniards were accepting grants only to sell them and undertake urban occupations, and he stopped distributing new lands to Spaniards; however, the institution of the *encomienda* persisted until nearly the end of the colonial period.

Land that was less desirable was never distributed, but rather was left to traditional Indian communities or simply remained open public land. In the late sixteenth century, the estimated one-quarter of the total native population on such public lands was resettled into Indian towns called *reducciones* in order to facilitate the collection of the Indians' tribute, their conversion to Christianity, and the exploitation of their labor.

Outside the *encomienda*, Indian labor was most commonly exploited through the *mita*, modeled after the Inca institution of the same name. All able bodied "free" Indians were required to devote one year of their labor to some public or private Spanish concern, be it constructing a church, road, or public building, or working in a textile mill. Although *mitayos* were paid for their labor, the amount was extremely meager, often less than debts accumulated through purchases from their employer, thus requiring them to continue working, sometimes indefinitely, after their assigned period of service. In this way, the *mita* system disintegrated into debt peonage. Debts were commonly passed on to ensuing generations, in which cases the *mita* was, in effect, slavery. Black slaves, in comparison, were extremely expensive and were thus used almost exclusively in the lowland plantation culture along the hot, humid coast, where the Sierra Indians proved unable to adapt. Black slaves numbered some 60,000 by the end of the colonial period.

The best estimates of the size of Ecuador's native population at the time of the conquest range between 750,000 and 1 million. Diseases imported by the Spanish, particularly smallpox and measles, virtually wiped out the indigenous coastal population during the sixteenth century and also decimated the Sierra population, although not as thoroughly as in the Costa or many other areas of Latin America. Despite a succession of deadly earthquakes and volcanic eruptions, the native population increased steadily during the seventeenth and eighteenth centuries except in the 1690s, when an epidemic of smallpox and diphtheria was reported to have killed one-third of Ecuador's population.

Ecuador's Indians probably owe their relative prosperity during the colonial period to the *audiencia*'s lack of mineral resources. The hardships of working in the silver and mercury mines of Peru cost the lives of millions of Indian *mitayos;* Ecuador, in contrast, had only small deposits of gold and silver in its southern provinces of Cuenca and Loja, and these deposits were depleted by the end of the sixteenth century. Its *serrano* economy was based, instead, on agriculture and textiles. Cotton, grown on the eastern slope of the Andes in Quijos Province, and wool, from imported merino sheep that thrived in the high Andean valleys, provided the raw materials for high-quality textiles that were manufactured in hundreds of sweatshops, called *obrajes,* and exported throughout Latin America. Indian *mitayos,* who commonly worked from dawn to dusk chained to their looms, provided the labor. As appalling as were the preindustrial working conditions in the *obrajes,* most historians agree that they were more bearable than those found in the Peruvian mines at the time.

The coastal economy revolved around shipping and trade. Guayaquil, despite being destroyed on several occasions by fire and incessantly plagued by either yellow fever or malaria, was a center of vigorous trade among the colonies, a trade that was technically illegal under the mercantilist philosophy of the contemporary Spanish rulers. The guiding principle of mercantilism in the New World was that the colonies existed to serve the commercial needs of Spain. Since trade among the colonies would not enrich Spain, it was banned. In addition to textiles and other light manufactures from the Sierra, hardwoods and cocoa from coastal plantations were exported from the port of Guayaquil to points all over Spanish America, while a wide variety of items were imported, including foods and wines from Peru. Guayaquil also became the largest shipbuilding center on the west coast of South America before the end of the colonial period.

The Ecuadorian economy, like that in the mother country, suffered a severe depression throughout most of the eighteenth century. Textile production dropped an estimated 50 to 75 percent between 1700 and 1800. Ecuador's cities gradually fell into ruins, and by 1790 the elite was reduced to poverty, selling haciendas

Aerial view of Cuenca
Courtesy Martie B. Lisowski Collection,
Library of Congress

and jewelry in order to subsist. The Indian population, in contrast, probably experienced an overall improvement in its situation, as the closing of the *obrajes* commonly led Indians to work under less arduous conditions on either haciendas or traditional communal lands. Ecuador's economic woes were, no doubt, compounded by the expulsion of the Jesuits in 1767 by King Charles III. Missions in the Oriente were abandoned, and many of the best schools and the most efficient haciendas and *obrajes* lost the key personnel that made them outstanding institutions in colonial Ecuador.

The Bourbon kings were best known for their economic and administrative reforms, which, like the expulsion of the Jesuits, were designed to enhance the flagging power of the crown in Spanish America. As a result of those reforms, the Quito *audiencia* was transferred in 1720 from the authority of the Peruvian viceroyalty to the newly created Viceroyalty of Nueva Granada, whose capital was in Bogotá. In the process, the *quiteño* authorities gained jurisdiction over their own political and military affairs, while the *audiencia*'s southern and eastern boundaries were delineated more specifically and retracted. A royal decree (*cédula*) in 1802 further shrank the area of the *audiencia* by transferring the provinces of Quijos and Mainas in the Oriente to Peru. Another decree by

15

Charles IV in 1803 transferred the port of Guayaquil to Peru, but resistance by port citizens led to its being returned to the jurisdiction of Quito in 1819.

Between 1736 and 1745, a French scientific mission with some of the best minds in Europe resided in Quito and contributed to the development of ideas in Ecuador. While carrying out their scientific mission—measuring the earth's circumference at the equator—the members of the mission disseminated the message of the Enlightenment, which stressed nationalism, individualism, and a questioning of authority and tradition. Works of Voltaire, Jean-Jacques Rousseau, and Thomas Paine, introducing such revolutionary concepts as equality and freedom, managed to elude the censors of both the Inquisition and a languishing political authority, and penetrated Ecuador's historical cultural isolation. The most famous Ecuadorian intellectual of the age, Eugenio de Santa Cruz y Espejo, was a physician and a writer who advocated emancipation from Spain and a republican, democratic system of government. Honored today as the precursor of Ecuadorian independence, Espejo was imprisoned for his ideas and died in jail in 1795.

The coming of independence was also foreshadowed by the numerous civil disturbances that rocked the Ecuadorian Sierra from the 1760s until the end of the colonial era. In 1765 the *quiteño* white and mestizo or *cholo* (a person of mixed white and Indian ancestry) population revolted against reforms in the colonial tax system. Potentially more serious was a subsequent series of Indian rebellions in Latacunga and Riobamba. Although clearly of a political nature, calling for the overthrow of the Spanish regime and the expulsion of all the whites from the land in addition to putting an end to the odious *mita* system, these uprisings never led to such large-scale insurrections as occurred in Peru at the same time. Ironically, the passing of the colonial era, according to most historians, occasioned a worsening of conditions for the indigenous population.

The Struggle for Independence

The struggle for independence in the Quito *audiencia* was part of a movement throughout Spanish America led by criollos (persons of pure Spanish descent born in the New World). The criollos' resentment of the privileges enjoyed by the *peninsulares* was the fuel of revolution against colonial rule. The spark was Napoleon's invasion of Spain, after which he deposed King Ferdinand VII and, in July 1808, placed his brother Joseph Bonaparte on the Spanish throne.

Shortly afterward, Spanish citizens, unhappy at the usurpation of the throne by the French, began organizing local juntas loyal to Ferdinand. A group of Quito's leading citizens followed suit, and on August 10, 1809, they seized power from the local representatives of Joseph Bonaparte in the name of Ferdinand. Thus, this early revolt against colonial rule (one of the first in Spanish America) was, paradoxically, an expression of loyalty to the Spanish king.

It quickly became apparent that Quito's criollo rebels lacked the anticipated popular support for their cause. As loyalist troops approached Quito, therefore, they peacefully turned power back to the crown authorities. Despite assurances against reprisals, the returning Spanish authorities (Bonaparte's men) proved to be merciless with the rebels and, in the process of ferreting out participants in the Quito revolt, jailed and abused many innocent citizens. Their actions, in turn, bred popular resentment among *quiteños,* who, after several days of street fighting in August 1810, won an agreement to be governed by a junta to be dominated by criollos, although with the president of the Audiencia of Quito acting as its figurehead leader.

In spite of widespread opposition within the rest of the Quito *audiencia,* the junta called for a congress in December 1811 in which it declared the entire area of the *audiencia* to be independent. Two months later, the junta approved a constitution for the state of Quito that provided for democratic governing institutions but also granted recognition to the authority of Ferdinand should he return to the Spanish throne. Shortly thereafter, the junta elected to launch a military offensive against the Spanish, but the poorly trained and badly equipped troops were no match for those of the viceroy of Peru, which finally crushed the *quiteño* rebellion in December 1812.

The second chapter in Ecuador's struggle for emancipation from Spanish colonial rule began in Guayaquil, where independence was proclaimed in October 1820 by a local patriotic junta under the leadership of the poet José Joaquín Olmedo. By this time, the forces of independence had grown continental in scope and were organized into two principal armies, one under the Venezuelan Simón Bolívar Palacios in the north and the other under the Argentine José de San Martín in the south. Unlike the hapless Quito junta, the Guayaquil patriots were able to appeal to foreign allies, Argentina and Venezuela, each of whom soon responded by sending sizable contingents to Ecuador. Antonio José de Sucre Alcalá, the brilliant young lieutenant of Bolívar who arrived in Guayaquil in May 1821, was to become the key figure in the ensuing military struggle against the royalist forces.

After a number of initial successes, Sucre's army was defeated at Ambato in the central Sierra, and he appealed for assistance from

San Martín, whose army was by now in Peru. With the arrival from the south of 1,400 fresh soldiers under the command of Andrés de Santa Cruz Calahumana, the fortunes of the patriotic army were again reversed. A string of victories culminated in the decisive Battle of Pichincha, on the slopes of the volcano of that name on the western outskirts of Quito, on May 24, 1822. A few hours after the victory by the patriots, the last president of the Audiencia of Quito signed a formal capitulation of his forces before Marshal Sucre. Ecuador was at last free of Spanish rule.

Two months later, Bolívar, the liberator of northern South America, entered Quito to a hero's welcome. Later that July, he met San Martín in Guayaquil and convinced the Argentine general, who wanted the port to return to Peruvian jurisdiction, and the local criollo elite in both major cities of the advantage of having the former Quito *audiencia* join with the liberated lands to the north. As a result, Ecuador became the District of the South within the Confederation of Gran Colombia, which also included present-day Venezuela and Colombia and had Bogotá as its capital. This status was maintained for eight tumultuous years.

They were years in which warfare dominated the affairs of Ecuador. First, the country found itself on the front lines of Bolívar's war to liberate Peru from Spanish rule between 1822 and 1825; afterward, in 1828 and 1829, Ecuador was in the middle of an armed struggle between Peru and Gran Colombia over the location of their common border. After a campaign that included the near destruction of Guayaquil, the forces of Gran Colombia, under the leadership of Sucre and Venezuelan General Juan José Flores, proved victorious. The Treaty of 1829 fixed the border on the line that had divided the Quito *audiencia* and the Viceroyalty of Peru before independence.

The population of Ecuador was divided during these years among three segments: those favoring the status quo, those supporting union with Peru, and those advocating autonomous independence for the former *audiencia*. The latter group was to prevail following Venezuela's withdrawal from the confederation during an 1830 constitutional congress that had been called in Bogotá in a futile effort to combat growing separatist tendencies throughout Gran Colombia. In May of that year, a group of Quito notables met to dissolve the union with Gran Colombia, and in August a constituent assembly drew up a constitution for the State of Ecuador, so named for its geographic proximity to the equator, and placed General Flores in charge of political and military affairs. He remained the dominant political figure during Ecuador's first fifteen years of independence.

The First Century of the Republic

Before the year 1830 drew to a close, both Marshal Sucre and Simón Bolívar would be dead; the former, murdered (on orders from a jealous General Flores, according to some historians), and the latter, from tuberculosis. Heartbroken at the dissolution of Gran Colombia, Bolívar is quoted as saying shortly before his death, "America is ungovernable. Those who have served the revolution have plowed the sea." These words would seem prophetic during the chaotic first thirty years in the life of the Republic of Ecuador.

Initial Confusion, 1830–60

Independence did not occasion a revolutionary liberation of the masses of Ecuadorian peasants. On the contrary, as bad as the peasants' situation was, it probably worsened with the loss of the Spanish royal officials who had protected the indigenous population against the abuses of the local criollos. This criollo elite, which had spearheaded the struggle for independence, was to be its principal beneficiary. The early battle to define the political parameters of the new state was fought, to a great extent, among the various sectors—Ecuadorians and foreigners, military personnel and civilians—of this elite.

Flores was of the foreign military variety. Born in Venezuela, he had fought in the wars for independence with Bolívar, who had appointed him governor of Ecuador during its association with Gran Colombia. Although of humble origins with little formal education, Flores married into the *quiteño* elite, gaining acceptance, initially at least, within the local criollo upper class. As a leader, however, he appeared primarily interested in maintaining his power. Military expenditures, from the independence wars and from an unsuccessful campaign to wrest Cauca Province from Colombia in 1832, kept the state treasury empty while other matters were left unattended.

In 1833 four intellectuals who had begun publishing *El Quiteño Libre* to denounce the "pillaging of the national treasury by foreigners" were killed by the authorities at a time when Flores was absent from Quito. Although not directly responsible for the killings, Flores inevitably became associated with them, and criticism of his regime grew. In 1834 opponents staged a rebellion in an effort to place José Vicente Rocafuerte y Rodríguez de Bejarano, a member of the Guayaquil aristocracy who had recently returned from fourteen years abroad, into the presidency. The rebels' effort failed; Flores then coopted his opponent and sponsored Rocafuerte as a presidential candidate. For four years following this Machiavellian political move—in effect the nation's first coup d'état—Flores continued to wield considerable power from behind the scenes as commander of the military.

President Rocafuerte's most lasting contribution was to begin development of a public school system. Although he had previously condemned Flores's violations of civil liberties, Rocafuerte argued that "the backwardness of Ecuador makes enlightened despotism necessary." At the end of his term in 1839, Rocafuerte returned to his native Guayaquil as provincial governor, while in Quito Flores was again inaugurated into the presidency. After four years in office, Flores summoned a constitutional convention that wrote a new constitution, dubbed "the Charter of Slavery" by his opponents, and elected him to a new eight-year term of office.

After 1843 the opposition to Flores often manifested itself in unpleasant ways: in reference to the dark skin of Flores and his fellow Venezuelan and Colombian soldiers, Rocafuerte (by now exiled in Lima) wrote that "the white oppressors of the peninsula were less oppressive than the Negro vandals who have replaced them." A young student named Gabriel García Moreno—later to become the most infamous of all of Ecuador's nineteenth-century dictators—tried unsuccessfully to assassinate Flores. Discontent had become nationwide by 1845, when an insurrection in Guayaquil forced Flores from the country. Because their movement triumphed in March (*marzo*), the anti-Flores coalition members became known as *marcistas*. They were an extremely heterogeneous lot that included liberal intellectuals, conservative clergymen, and representatives from Guayaquil's successful business community.

The next fifteen years constituted one of the most turbulent periods in Ecuador's century and a half as a nation. The *marcistas* fought among themselves almost ceaselessly and also had to struggle against Flores's repeated attempts from exile to overthrow the government. The first *marcista* president was a businessman, Vicente Ramón Roca, who served a full four-year term of office. The most significant figure of the era, however, was General José María Urbina, who first came to power in 1851 through a coup d'état, remained in the presidency until 1856, and then continued to dominate the political scene until 1860. During this decade and the one that followed, Urbina and his archrival, García Moreno, would define the dichotomy—between Liberals from Guayaquil and Conservatives from Quito—that remained the major sphere of political struggle in Ecuador in the 1980s (see Political Parties, ch. 4).

Liberalism under Urbina took on anticlerical, ethnic, and regional dimensions. In 1852 he accused a group of Jesuit priests—admitted by his predecessor, Diego Noboa, only a year earlier—

Juan José Flores
Courtesy Prints and
Photographs Division,
Library of Congress

Gabriel García Moreno
Courtesy Prints and
Photographs Division,
Library of Congress

of political meddling and expelled them. Urbina freed the nation's slaves exactly one week after his coup of 1851, and six years later, his successor and life-long friend, General Francisco Robles, finally put an end to three centuries of required annual payments of tribute by the Indian population. Henceforth, liberalism associated itself with bettering the position of Ecuador's non-white population. Urbina's and Robles's favoring of the Guayaquil business classes over the Quito landowners reinforced the regional aspect of the political dichotomy.

Opposition against Robles intensified after his signing, in 1857, of an unpopular contract aimed at alleviating the burdensome foreign debt. By 1859—known by Ecuadorian historians as the Terrible Year—the nation was on the brink of anarchy. Local caudillos had declared several regions autonomous of the central government. One of these caudillos, Guayaquil's Guillermo Franco, signed the Treaty of Mapasingue ceding the southern provinces of Ecuador to an occupying Peruvian army led by General Ramón Castilla. This action was outrageous enough to unite some previously disparate elements. García Moreno, putting aside both his project to place Ecuador under a French protectorate and his differences with General Flores, got together with the former dictator to put down the various local rebellions and force out the Peruvians. This effort opened the last chapter of Flores's long career and marked the entrance to power of García Moreno.

The Era of Conservatism, 1860–95

García Moreno is the father of Ecuadorian conservatism and no doubt the most controversial figure in the nation's history, condemned by Liberal historians as Ecuador's worst tyrant but exalted by Conservatives as the nation's greatest nation-builder. In the end, both appraisals may be accurate; the man who possibly saved Ecuador from disintegration in 1859 and then ruled the nation with an iron fist for the subsequent decade and a half was, in fact, an extremely complicated personality. Born and raised under modest circumstances in Guayaquil, he studied in Quito, where he married into the local aristocracy, then traveled to Europe in the aftermath of the 1848 revolutionary uprisings and studied under the eminent Catholic theologians of the day.

García Moreno's religious education had a profound impact on the future president. In the words of historian Frederick B. Pike:

> His personal experiences seem to have influenced his attitudes toward governing his country. In his own case, liberalism and religious indifference had gone hand-in-hand with personal debauchery and lack of self- control, while religious fervor had been intertwined with a life of rigorous self-control and spartan discipline. After coming to the presidency, García Moreno set out to rekindle religious fervor among Ecuadorians in the expectation that the entire country could be made to undergo a transformation paralleling his own.

President García Moreno saw Roman Catholicism as the ingredient of Ecuadorian culture that, through its emphasis on order, hierarchy, and discipline, could unite the nation and save it from the multiple crises and disorder of the 1850s. Catholicism thus held a prominent position in each of the two new constitutions that he introduced: the charter of 1861 named Catholicism as the exclusive religion, and its replacement in 1869, in addition to providing for a six-year presidential term and unlimited reelection, made citizenship dependent on one's adherence to the Roman Catholic religion. In 1863 García Moreno promulgated Ecuador's first concordat with the Vatican, bestowing vast powers on the Ecuadorian Roman Catholic Church, especially with respect to education. A decade later, the dictator's puppet congress dedicated the republic to the Sacred Heart of Jesus.

Despite such proclerical measures that have led many historians to dub his regime a theocracy, the local clergy believed García Moreno to be fanatical and criticized him for it. The president, in turn, replaced many local clergymen with foreign priests in an effort to revitalize the Roman Catholic Church in Ecuador, which he considered degenerate and dissolute.

The highly anticlerical Liberals were, of course, livid. Urbina organized an invasion in 1864, which was defeated with the help, once again, of General Flores. García Moreno was ruthless in his repression of the captured rebels, as he was commonly with less formidable opponents as well. Nor did he hesitate to manipulate the presidential succession. Finding his hand-picked successor deficient after two years in office, in 1867 García Moreno presided over the installation of a second puppet, whom he also overthrew in 1869, when it appeared that the Liberals might win scheduled elections. In 1869 García Moreno also formally established the Conservative Party (Partido Conservador—PC).

Shortly after the onset of his third presidential term in 1875, García Moreno was hacked to death with a machete on the steps of the presidential palace. The exact motives of the assassin, a Colombian, remain unknown, but the dictator's most outstanding critic, the liberal journalist Juan Montalvo, exclaimed, "My pen killed him!"

Although maligned for his highly proclerical and dictatorial ways, García Moreno made a number of vital contributions to the development of the nation. Perhaps the most important advances were in education. The establishment of many new schools at all levels, from primary to the polytechnical training school in Quito, elicited universal praise, despite the fact that the Jesuits were largely responsible for these accomplishments. Transportation links with Quito were also vastly improved with the building of roads to Esmeraldas and to Babahoyo, near Guayaquil, as well as the first portion of the railroad linking Quito with Riobamba and Guayaquil. These public works not only promoted national unity but also helped Quito begin a long-delayed effort to overcome the geographic barriers that had historically caused its isolation, an isolation that had hindered the nation's integration into the world economy.

Between 1852 and 1890, Ecuador's exports grew in value from slightly more than US$1 million to nearly US$10 million. Production of cocoa, the most important export product in the late nineteenth century, grew from 6.5 million kilograms to 18 million kilograms during the same period. The agricultural export interests, centered in the coastal region near Guayaquil, became closely associated with the Liberals, whose political power also grew steadily during the interval. After the death of García Moreno, it took the Liberals twenty years to consolidate their strength sufficiently to assume control of the government in Quito.

Five different presidents governed during the two decades of transition between Conservative and Liberal rule. The first, Antonio Borrero, tried valiantly to return the nation to the rule of law, but, after only ten months in office, he was overthrown by the only military dictator of the period, Ignacio de Veintemilla. Although he came to power with the help of the old Liberal General Urbina, Veintemilla later evolved into a populist military dictator rather than a politician with any party or ideological affiliation. He was extremely popular with his troops and able to woo the masses with employment on public works programs and large-scale public festivals and dances during holiday periods. In office until 1883, Veintemilla enjoyed a period of relative prosperity resulting primarily from increased maritime activity while Peru, Bolivia, and Chile were mired in the War of the Pacific.

José María Plácido Caamaño, a Conservative, then served as president until 1888, and he remained a powerful figure during the administrations of the duly elected Progressive Party (Partido Progresista) presidents who followed him, Antonio Flores Jijón and Luis Cordero Crespo. Flores, who was the son of President Juan José Flores, intended progressivism to represent a compromise position between liberalism and conservatism. The Progressive program called for support for the Roman Catholic Church, rule by law, and an end to dictatorship and military rule. Although neither Caamaño, Flores, nor Cordero was able to curtail the growing animosity between Conservatives and Liberals, their periods in office were, for the most part, characterized by relative political stability and prosperity. The latter resulted more from favorable international circumstances for cocoa exports than from astute government policy making.

In 1895, midway through his term in office, Cordero fell victim to scandal and charges of "selling the flag" over an agreement made with Chile. Cordero allowed the warship *Esmeralda,* which Chile was selling to Japan, to fly the Ecuadorian flag briefly in order to protect Chile's neutrality in the conflict between Japan and China. Bribes were apparently involved and, tremendously weakened by the scandal and also challenged by the outbreak of several military rebellions, the president resigned in April. In June the Liberals seized power in Guayaquil in the name of their most popular caudillo, General José Eloy Alfaro Delgado. Three months later,

Scenes of Quito and the gathering of cacao pods in 1907
Courtesy Prints and Photographs Division, Library of Congress

"the old battler" (a name Alfaro had earned during his armed struggle against García Moreno) returned after a decade of exile in Central America and marched triumphantly into Quito. It was the end
of Ecuador's brief experiment with progressivism and the beginning of three stormy decades of rule by the Radical Liberal Party
(Partido Liberal Radical—PLR), commonly referred to as the
Liberal Party (Partido Liberal).

The Rule of the Liberals, 1895–1925

Eloy Alfaro is the outstanding standard-bearer for Ecuador's
Liberals, much as García Moreno is for the Conservatives. Some
Marxist groups have also looked to Alfaro; although his political
program was in no way socialist, it did prove to be revolutionary
in the extent to which it stripped the Roman Catholic Church of
the power and privileges previously granted to it by García Moreno. Catholic officials and their Conservative allies did not give up
without a fight, however. During the first year of Alfaro's presidency, Ecuador was ravaged by a bloody civil war in which clergymen commonly incited the faithful masses to rise in rebellion against

25

the "atheistic *alfaristas*" and were, just as commonly, themselves victims of *alfarista* repression. The foreign-born Bishops Pedro Schumacher of Portoviejo and Arsenio Andrade of Riobamba led the early resistance to Alfaro. A full-fledged bloodbath may well have been averted only through the magnanimous efforts of the outstanding historian and Archbishop Federico González Suárez, who urged the clergy to abandon the pursuit of politics.

This final ecclesiastical struggle for control of Ecuador was in vain, however. By the end of the Liberals' rule in 1925, Roman Catholicism was no longer the constitutionally mandated state religion, official clerical censorship of reading material had been suppressed, many powerful foreign clergy had been expelled, education had been secularized, civil marriage as well as divorce had been instituted, the concordat with the Vatican had been broken, most of the church's rural properties had been seized by the state, and the republic was no longer dedicated to the Sacred Heart of Jesus. The Roman Catholic Church in Ecuador would never again hold prerogatives as extensive as those it enjoyed during the late nineteenth century.

The other accomplishment for which the three decades of PLR rule are remembered is the completion, in 1908, of the Guayaquil-Quito railroad. At the time, however, Alfaro was condemned by his critics for "delivering the republic to the Yankees" through a contract signed with North American entrepreneurs to complete the project begun by García Moreno. Although the criticism did not halt Alfaro on this project, a similar nationalistic outcry did force him to end negotiations with the United States, which wanted to protect the soon-to-be-completed Panama Canal, over military base rights in Ecuador's Galápagos Islands. Alfaro's affinity for the United States was also evident in 1910, when war between Peru and Ecuador over their perennial boundary dispute was narrowly averted through the mediation of the United States, together with Brazil and Argentina.

The Liberals can be credited with few further accomplishments of major proportions. The system of debt peonage that lingered in the Sierra came under government regulations, albeit weak ones, and imprisonment for debts was finally outlawed in 1918. These and other limited social benefits gained by the Indians and the mixed-blood *montuvio* (coastal mestizo) working class were overshadowed by the ruinous economic decline world wide and the severe repression of the nascent labor movement at the hands of the Liberals during the early 1920s. Furthermore, Liberal rule did little to foster the development of stable democracy. On the contrary, the first half of the period saw even more illegal seizures of power and military-led governments than in previous decades.

A major cause of the instability of the period was the lack of unity within the PLR itself. Alfaro and a second military strongman, General Leónidas Plaza Gutiérrez, maintained a bitter rivalry over party leadership for almost two decades. Following Alfaro's first period in the presidency, Plaza was elected to a constitutional term of office that lasted from 1901 until 1905. In 1906, shortly after a close associate of Plaza had been elected to succeed him, however, Alfaro launched a coup d'état and returned to the presidency. Alfaro, in turn, was overthrown in 1911 after refusing to hand power over to his own hand-picked successor, Emilio Estrada. Four months later, Estrada's death from a heart attack precipitated a brief civil war that climaxed the rivalry between Alfaro and Plaza. Alfaro returned from his exile in Panama to lead the Guayaquil garrison in its challenge to the Quito-based interim government, which was under the military authority of General Plaza. The rebellion was quickly defeated, however; Alfaro was captured and transported to Quito via the same railroad that he had done so much to complete. Once in the capital, Alfaro was publicly and unceremoniously murdered, along with several of his comrades, by a government-instigated mob.

Shortly thereafter, Plaza was inaugurated into his second presidential term in office. It was the first of four consecutive constitutional changes of government: following Plaza (1912–16) came Alfredo Baquerizo Moreno (1916–20), then José Luis Tamayo (1920–24), and Gonzalo S. Córdova (1924–25). Real power during this second half of the period of Liberal rule was held, not by the government, but by a plutocracy of coastal agricultural and banking interests, popularly known as *la argolla* (the ring), whose linchpin was the Commercial and Agricultural Bank of Guayaquil led by Francisco Urbina Jado. This bank gained influence by loaning vast quantities of money to the free-spending government as well as to private individuals. According to Ecuadorian historian Oscar Efrén Reyes, the bank was influential "to the point that candidates for president and his ministers, senators, and deputies had to have the prior approval of the bank." Many of the private loans were to members of the Association of Agriculturists of Ecuador, an organization that also received government funds intended to promote an international cartel of cocoa growers, but which instead were used to line members' pockets.

All parties involved in *la argolla,* from the government officials to the bankers and the growers, were professed militants of the Liberal cause. It was not only the political fortunes of the party that fell victim to their financial activities, however, but also the national economy, which experienced runaway inflation as a result of the printing of money by the private banks. The severe economic problems during the final years of Liberal rule were also partially caused by factors beyond the control of the politicians. A fungal disease that ravaged Ecuador's cacao trees and the growth of competition from British colonies in Africa abruptly ended conditions that had favored Ecuador's exportation of cocoa for over a century. What was left of the nation's cocoa industry fell victim to the sharp decline in world demand during the Great Depression.

Ecuador's economic crisis of the early 1920s was especially devastating to the working class and the poor. With real wages, for those lucky enough to have jobs, eaten away by inflation, workers responded with a general strike in Guayaquil in 1922 and a peasant rebellion in the central Sierra the following year. Both actions were aimed at improving wages and working conditions; both were put down only after massacres of major proportions.

President Córdova, closely tied to *la argolla,* had come to office in a fraudulent election. Popular unrest, together with the ongoing economic crisis and a sickly president, laid the background for a bloodless coup d'état in July 1925. Unlike all previous forays by the military into Ecuadorian politics, the coup of 1925 was made in the name of a collective grouping rather than a particular caudillo. The members of the League of Young Officers who overthrew Córdova came to power with an agenda, which included a wide variety of social reforms, the replacement of the increasingly sterile Liberal-Conservative debate, and the end of the rule of the Liberals, who had become decadent after three decades in power.

Reform, Chaos, and Debacle, 1925–44

The reformist officers initially named a governing junta consisting of prominent opponents of the Liberal plutocracy, but neither it nor a succeeding junta was able to consolidate the power necessary to govern effectively. In 1926 they named as provisional president Isidro Ayora, a dedicated reformer who, although married into one of the wealthiest coastal families, possessed a social conscience and the vision to see that reform would help preserve the status of the upper classes. Ayora quickly assumed dictatorial powers, with which he set out to institute reforms that were partly of his own making and partly the making of the League of Young Officers.

An advisory mission from Princeton University, headed by Edwin W. Kemmerer, was invited to propose measures to reorganize Ecuador's fiscal and monetary structures. Its major accomplishment was the creation of the Central Bank of Ecuador (Banco Central), which replaced the private banks' authority in the issuing of currency; in addition, the Kemmerer mission also reorganized the state budgeting and customs agencies. The appropriation of these functions, which were previously under the control of *la argolla,* brought a revenue windfall to the government during the next half-decade. In addition to building state fiscal and social agencies, the funds were used to initiate a number of programs, including pensions for state workers, that enhanced the security of the middle and lower economic sectors of the population. A range of social legislation—quite progressive for its day—intended to protect the working class from unscrupulous employers and to improve working conditions emerged from the enactment of the 1929 constitution.

The same constitution, Ecuador's thirteenth in just under a century as a republic, also provided for a powerful legislative body with authority to censure presidential ministers. This diminution of executive power, the appearance of a wide variety (socialist, communist, and populist) of new groupings in political competition with the traditional parties and with the military, and the devastating effects of the Great Depression combined to make Ecuador's political record especially unstable during subsequent years. Ayora was the first of fourteen chief executives during the 1930s.

World demand for cocoa and other Ecuadorian export crops dropped precipitously in the wake of the 1929 Wall Street crash: export crop value fell from US$15 million in 1928 to US$7 million in 1931 and US$5 million in 1932, causing widespread unemployment and misery. Few objections were voiced in 1931 when Ayora was the victim of a military coup. Neptalí Bonifaz Ascázubi was then elected with the help of a quasi-fascist grouping of the *serrano* lower classes called the Consolidation of National Workers (Compactación Obrera Nacional). In August 1932, after various Liberal and leftist elements in Congress blocked Bonifaz's assumption of power, the Compactación fought a bloody four-day civil war against other paramilitary forces amassed by opponents of the president-elect. The latter were victorious, largely because the great majority of the government military forces remained in their barracks rather than defend Bonifaz.

Another election two months later brought victory for the Liberal candidate, Juan de Dios Martínez Mera, but soon accusations arose that the election had been fraudulent. The congressional opposition censured virtually every minister as soon as he was named and also encouraged the Compactación to lead demonstrations against the president in the streets of Quito. The campaign against

Martínez was led by the charismatic president of the Chamber of Deputies, José María Velasco Ibarra, who at the time professed a "total lack of presidential ambitions." In September 1934, less than a year after Martínez was forced to resign, Velasco assumed the presidency after having won popular elections by an overwhelming margin.

The first of Velasco's five periods as president lasted only eleven months. He was overthrown by the military after attempting to assume dictatorial powers by dissolving Congress and jailing his congressional opponents. Shortly thereafter, the military placed Federico Páez in the presidential palace. An engineer and former senator, Páez ruled precariously for two years, first with the political support of the socialist left and then with that of the right, and he tried to advance the reforms undertaken by Ayora a decade earlier. Ongoing fiscal difficulties severely limited Páez's efforts, however, and in September 1937 he was overthrown by his minister of national defense, General Alberto Enríquez Gallo. Although he ruled for less than a year, Enríquez achieved note as a social reformer by his promulgation of the Labor Code of 1938.

Enríquez is also remembered for having initiated a protracted confrontation with the United States-based South American Development Company over the terms of its Ecuadorian concession and the wages it paid its Ecuadorian employees. The company refused to comply with Enríquez's entreaty that more of the profits from its mining operations stay in Ecuador, and it won the support of the United States Department of State. The Ecuadorian government continued its demands despite United States pressure. In 1940 the United States, hoping to obtain Ecuadorian cooperation in its anticipated war effort, ended its support for the mining firm. Ecuadorian president Carlos Alberto Arroyo del Río, in turn, proved generous in his cooperation with the Allies, allowing the United States to build a naval base on the Galápagos Islands and an air base at Salinas on the Ecuadorian mainland.

In addition to being a genuine friend and admirer of the United States, Arroyo del Río was the leader of the PLR and a representative of the Guayaquil-based "plutocracy." He came to power constitutionally in November 1939 upon the death of his predecessor, but he continued in office in January 1940 through fraudulent elections that were universally believed to have been won by Velasco, and continued in power later, through repression. Despite such antipopular methods of ruling, he managed to remain in office for almost four years, thanks to economic support by the United States and the recuperation of Ecuador's export markets as worldwide economic depression gave way to recovery during World War II.

Arroyo del Río's undoing was the disastrous 1941 war with Peru. Although the prior sequence of events—the breakdown of talks aimed at resolving the boundary issues in 1938, followed by repeated border skirmishes—had given ample warning of a possible outbreak of large-scale hostilities, Ecuador was unprepared to meet the July 5 Peruvian invasion. Furthermore, the president's fear of being left unprotected from his opponents led him to keep the nation's best fighting forces in Quito while Peruvian troops continuously attacked the nation's southern and eastern provinces until a cease-fire went into effect on July 31.

Peru's occupation ended only after January 1942, when the two nations signed the Protocol of Peace, Friendship, and Boundaries while attending the Third Conference of Foreign Ministers of the American Republics in Rio de Janeiro. Under the terms of the Rio Protocol, the informal name of the agreement, Ecuador renounced its claim to some 200,000 square kilometers of territory. Shortly afterward, the Rio Protocol was ratified by a bare plurality of the Ecuadorian legislature (see fig. 2).

The Ecuadorian government quickly regretted having become a party to the Rio Protocol. The protocol became the focus of a surge of Ecuadorian national pride and concomitant opposition to Arroyo in a new coalition—the Democratic Alliance. The coalition brought together a wide array of Ecuadorian politicians dedicated to replacing the "president who had been unable to defend the national honor." Arroyo's rejoinder that he would remain in office the full four years, "neither one day more nor one day less," and his being prominently hailed in Washington as "the Apostle of Pan-Americanism" only increased his political isolation. A persistent inflation that whittled away at the purchasing power of salaried workers was a further cause of popular resentment against Arroyo.

In May 1944, following an uprising in Guayaquil that pitted the military and civilian supporters of Velasco against Arroyo's police, the president finally resigned. The military handed power to the Democratic Alliance, which in turn named Velasco, whose electoral candidacy had recently been vetoed by Arroyo, as the popularly acclaimed president of the republic. The populist master returned triumphantly from exile in Colombia, greeted by throngs of enthusiasts during a three-day journey to Quito, to assume the presidency for the second time.

The Postwar Era, 1944–84

The *quiteño* multitudes standing in the pouring rain on May 31, 1944, to hear Velasco promise a "national resurrection," with social

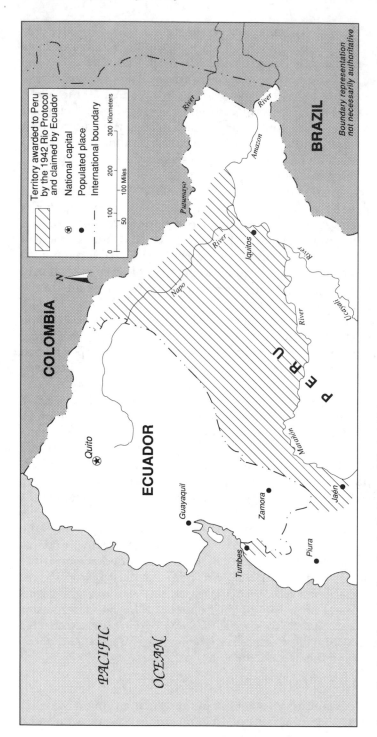

Source: Based on information from Keesing's, *Border and Territorial Disputes*, London, 1982, 368.

Figure 2. Territory Disputed by Ecuador and Peru

justice and due punishment for the ''corrupt Liberal oligarchy'' that had been responsible for ''staining the national honor,'' believed that they were witnessing the birth of a popular revolution. Arroyo partisans were promptly jailed or sent into exile, while Velasco verbally baited the business community and the rest of the political right. The leftist elements within Velasco's Democratic Alliance, which dominated the constituent assembly that was convened to write a new constitution, were nonetheless destined to be disappointed.

In May 1945, after a year of growing hostility between the president and the assembly, which was vainly awaiting deeds to substantiate Velasco's rhetorical advocacy of social justice, the mercurial chief executive condemned and then repudiated the newly completed constitution. After dismissing the assembly, Velasco held elections for a new assembly, which in 1946 drafted a far more conservative constitution that met with the president's approval. For this brief period, Conservatives replaced the left as Velasco's base of support.

Rather than attending to the nation's economic problems, Velasco aggravated them by financing the dubious schemes of his associates. Inflation continued unabated, as did its negative impact on the national standard of living, and by 1947 foreign-exchange reserves had fallen to dangerously low levels. In August, when Velasco was ousted by his minister of defense, nobody rose to defend the man who, only three years earlier, had been hailed as the nation's savior. During the following year, three different men briefly held executive power before Galo Plaza Lasso, running under a coalition of independent Liberals and socialists, narrowly defeated his Conservative opponent in presidential elections. His inauguration in September 1948 initiated what was to become the longest period of constitutional rule since the 1912–24 heyday of the Liberal plutocracy.

Constitutional Rule, 1948–60

Galo Plaza differed from previous Ecuadorian presidents. The son of former President Plaza Gutiérrez, he had been born in the United States, where he also attended several universities. His ties to the United States grew even closer as a result of serving there as ambassador under President Arroyo del Río. These links, as Pike points out, ''rendered him vulnerable to charges by Velasco Ibarra and other demagogic opponents of being the lackey of U.S. imperialism.'' Galo Plaza was not a professional politician, but a gentleman farmer with a sizable cattle ranch near Quito, where he customarily spent weekends throughout his four years as president.

Galo Plaza brought a developmentalist and technocratic emphasis to Ecuadorian government. He invited a wide variety of foreign experts in economic development and in governmental administration to recommend and catalog reforms in both areas. In large part because of a lack of political will within either the executive or the legislature, however, virtually none of the recommended reforms was enacted. Nevertheless, the economy experienced a marked improvement, with inflation finally slowing down and both government budget and foreign currency accounts balancing for the first time in many years. This achievement was even more remarkable in light of the series of major earthquakes, landslides, and floods suffered by Ecuador in 1949 and 1950.

No doubt Galo Plaza's most important contribution to Ecuadorian political culture was his commitment to the principles and practices of democracy. Galo Plaza endorsed such democratic guarantees as freedom of the press and the freedom of opponents to voice their opinions, to assemble for political purposes without fear of being jailed or worse, and to be elected to the legislature without fear of being defrauded or arbitrarily dismissed. Galo Plaza was able to create a mystique around the idea of his completing his term in office, something no president had accomplished since 1924, and this mystique no doubt helped him achieve his goal.

As Galo Plaza readily admitted, however, his greatest asset, both politically and economically, was the onset of the nation's banana boom, as diseases plaguing plantations in Central America turned Ecuador into an alternative supplier to the huge United States market. Ecuador's banana exports grew from US$2 million to US$20 million between 1948 and 1952. During these years, Ecuador also benefited from sizable price increases—generated by the Korean War—for its commodity exports.

A proof of the politically stabilizing effect of the banana boom of the 1950s is that even Velasco, who in 1952 was elected president for the third time, managed to serve out a full four-year term. He continued to spend as before—building bridges, roads, and schools at will and rewarding his political supporters (including, this time, the military) with jobs, salary increases, and weapons—but, in contrast to his previous times in office, there were now sufficient funds to pay for everything.

Always the master populist, Velasco (who by now liked to be known as "the National Personification") again came to power with the support of the common man, this time through the vehicle of the Guayaquil-based Concentration of Popular Forces (Concentración de Fuerzas Populares—CFP). Once in office, however, he arrested and deported the CFP boss, Carlos Guevara Moreno, together with several other party leaders. Guevara Moreno re-assumed control of the CFP in 1955 following a three-year exile. Velasco's subsequent party support during the 1950s came from the Conservatives, the conservative Social Christian Movement (Movimiento Social Cristiano—MSC), and the highly nationalistic, anticommunist, quasi-fascist Ecuadorian Nationalist Revolutionary Action (Acción Revolucionaria Nacionalista Ecuatoriana—ARNE).

On repeated occasions, members of ARNE acted as thugs and shock troops, attacking students, labor unions, and the press. In 1955 Velasco also chose to pick a fight with the United States. In the opening round of what would later become known as the "tuna war," Ecuadorian officials seized two fishing boats carrying the United States flag, charging them with fishing inside the 200-nautical-mile limit claimed by Ecuador as territorial seas under its sovereignty (see The United States, ch. 4).

In 1956 Camilo Ponce Enríquez, the MSC founder who had served in Velasco's cabinet, assumed the presidency after a close election replete with allegations of fraud. Although late support from Velasco proved crucial to Ponce's victory, shortly afterward "the National Personification" became the principal opponent of the new chief executive. In a display of statesmanship and political acumen, Ponce co-opted the Liberal opposition by including it, along with Conservatives and the MSC, in his cabinet.

Although Ponce did not enact the Social Christian reforms of which he spoke vaguely during the campaign, the relative political calm that prevailed during his four years in office was, in itself, an accomplishment given the worsening economic situation. Ponce's term saw the end of the banana boom that had sustained more than a decade of constitutional rule. Falling export prices led to rising unemployment and a social malaise that briefly erupted into riots in 1959. By the following year, the effects of the discontent were ready to be exploited by the populist appeal of the irrepressible Velasco, who was elected with his widest margin of victory ever. Velasco's fourth turn in the presidency initiated a renewal of crisis, instability, and military domination and ended conjecture that the political system had matured or developed a democratic mold.

Instability and Military Dominance, 1960–72

The instability began immediately. Ponce was so angry over Velasco's vicious campaign attacks on his government that he resigned on his last day in office rather than preside over the inauguration of his successor. During his campaign, "the National

Personification'' had promised government support to the masses of urban poor, many of whom had recently migrated to Guayaquil and other major cities in search of a decent job and a place to live. Velasco's populism continued into his inaugural address, when he renounced the hated 1942 Rio Protocol. He thus came to power with the adoration of the masses, but he saddled himself with expensive commitments to the poor at a time when deficits in the state coffers were approaching a critical level. Additionally, Velasco threatened Ecuador's shaky economy with what amounted to a declaration of hostilities against Peru and the guarantors of the Rio Protocol, namely Argentina, Brazil, Chile, and the United States.

Sensing the direction of the political wind in the wake of the Cuban Revolution, Velasco magnified his anti-United States rhetoric and included leftists in his government. Meanwhile, the United States encouraged Latin American governments to break diplomatic relations with Cuba. Before long, Ecuador's widening political polarization became manifest in outbreaks of violence between leftist students and the anticommunist right.

The rapidly deteriorating economic situation soon brought about a split in the *velasquista* coalition, however, with the left, led by Vice President Carlos Julio Arosemena Monroy (who was also president of the Chamber of Deputies) openly opposing the government in July 1961. By October relations between Velasco's government and Congress had deteriorated to the point where legislators and progovernment spectators engaged in a gun battle. Although dozens of bullet holes were later found in the Chamber, no one was injured.

A series of new sales taxes imposed during the same month in order to raise desperately needed revenues then sparked a general strike and a series of demonstrations and riots in several major cities. Amid growing chaos, Velasco ordered the arrest of his vice president, a move that opened him to charges of violating the constitution. On November 8, after only fourteen months in office, Velasco was ousted by the military and replaced by Arosemena, who was his constitutional successor as well as his leading opponent.

Arosemena came from a well-known Guayaquil family; his father had briefly served as president following a previous anti-Velasco coup in 1947. In an attempt to allay concerns about his being a dangerous leftist (as Velasco's vice president he had expressed warm sympathy for Cuban leader Fidel Castro Ruz and made a much-criticized trip to the Soviet Union), Arosemena named a cabinet that included Liberals and even Conservatives and quickly sent former President Galo Plaza on a goodwill trip to Washington.

Arosemena's insistence on maintaining relations with Cuba, however, became a major domestic political issue in Ecuador. Political opponents labeled Arosemena a dangerous communist, and part of the military went into open rebellion in March 1962. The following month, Ecuador broke diplomatic relations with Cuba, Poland, and Czechoslovakia. The crisis over Cuba proved to be very costly for Arosemena, who lost not only much of his local political support, but also the self-confidence to pursue his own, independent course. Afterward, the government drifted with little leadership from the president, who allegedly indulged in frequent drinking bouts.

The brief appearance of a guerrilla movement in the coastal jungle and a rash of small-scale terrorist incidents (many of which later were found to have been staged by right-wing provocateurs) also left Arosemena open to accusations of being either unable or unwilling to stop communist subversion. By early 1963, military conspiracy was again afoot. On July 11, the high command of the armed forces decided, without dissent, to depose Arosemena.

The four-man military junta that seized power announced its intention not to return the nation to constitutional rule until the institution of basic socioeconomic reforms, which both Velasco and Arosemena had promised but never implemented. This failure by their two civilian predecessors, the junta believed, had become a source of growing frustration within the lower classes, thus making them more receptive to the lure of communism. The junta combined its reformist anticommunism with the more traditional hard-line variety. After jailing or exiling the entire leadership of the communist left, the new government reorganized the nation's two leading universities in an effort to eliminate them as sources of left-wing political activity.

In July 1964, the junta decreed the Agrarian Reform Law to commemorate the first anniversary of its assumption of power. The law abolished the *huasipungo* system, the feudalistic land tenure arrangement widely used in the Sierra (see Peasants, ch. 2). However, the law resulted in little real improvement in the lives of the long-suffering Sierra peasants and died from lack of funding under subsequent civilian governments.

Meaningful reform was precluded, in part at least, by the increasingly cumbersome process of decision making within the politically heterogeneous, plural executive. Insubordination by the air force representative on the junta led to his dismissal and arrest in November 1965; thereafter, the junta had only three members.

In 1965 Ecuador also saw a dramatic drop in its revenue from banana exports, and, despite generous development assistance from

37

Plowing a field
Courtesy World Bank

the United States government and the Inter-American Development Bank, the junta suddenly faced an economic crisis of major proportions. The announcement of increased taxes on imports sparked the opposition of the powerful Guayaquil Chamber of Commerce, which in March called for a general strike. Long-disgruntled student groups and labor unions were only too happy to join in the protest, which rapidly spread to other cities. On March 29, 1966, following a bloody and demoralizing attack on the Central University in Quito, the disillusioned military reformers stepped down.

The following day, a small group of civilian leaders named Clemente Yerovi Indaburu, a non-partisan banana grower who had served as minister of economy under Galo Plaza, to be provisional president. In October a popularly elected constituent assembly drafted a new constitution and elected Otto Arosemena Gómez, a cousin of Carlos Julio and a political centrist, to act as a second provisional president. During his twenty months in office, the new constitution went into effect in May 1967, and popular elections for president were held in June 1968. Incredibly, Velasco—now seventy-five years old—was voted into the presidency for the fifth time, a remarkable thirty-four years after his initial victory.

The weakness of Velasco's mandate—he managed only a plurality of barely one-third of the popular vote in a crowded field of five candidates—foreshadowed political difficulties that plagued him during his final term. His newly formed National Velasquista Federation (Federación Nacional Velasquista—FNV) was far short of a majority in either house of Congress, and a failure to build any working coalition made for a stalemate in the legislative process. Even Velasco's own vice president, a *guayaquileño* Liberal named Jorge Zavala Baquerizo, turned into a strident and vocal critic. Cabinet ministers came and went with astonishing frequency. This political impasse soon combined with the fiscal and balance-of-payments crises, which by now had become customary under the spendthrift habits and administrative mismanagement associated with each of Velasco's terms in office, to spawn a major political crisis. The turning point came on June 22, 1970, when Velasco, in an action known as an *autogolpe* (self-seizure of power), dismissed Congress and the Supreme Court and assumed dictatorial powers.

Velasco subsequently decreed a number of necessary, though extremely unpopular, economic measures. After devaluing the sucre (for value of the sucre—see Glossary) for the first time since 1961, he placed tight controls on foreign exchange transactions and then decreed a number of new tax measures, the most controversial of which raised import tariffs considerably. Velasco attempted to compensate for his lost prestige by baiting the United States, seizing and fining United States fishing boats found within 200 nautical miles of the Ecuadorian coast. The intensification of the "tuna war" inflamed tempers in both countries; Ecuador dismissed United States military advisers, and the United States withdrew almost all economic and military aid to Ecuador. Such nationalistic adventures were of only momentary value to Velasco, however. In 1971, amid mounting civic unrest that verified the extent of the opposition, he was forced to cancel a scheduled national plebiscite in which he hoped to replace the 1967 constitution, which had a charter written under his own auspices in 1946. The constitution, Velasco argued, made the president too weak to be effective.

The president's *autogolpe* and his continuance in power were possible because of support from the armed forces. Velasco's key ally was his nephew and minister of defense, General Jorge Acosta Velasco, who continually reshuffled the high command in order to retain *velasquistas* in key posts. In the wake of a failed attempt to oust the powerful commandant of the Quito military academy in April 1971, however, Acosta himself was forced to resign his ministerial portfolio and was summarily dispatched to Madrid as ambassador. Having lost the man who was his linchpin in the armed forces and the only apparent heir to the *velasquista* throne, Velasco was left to the mercy of the high command.

Two circumstances proved critical in persuading the military to overthrow Velasco before the scheduled completion of his term in 1972. On the one hand, the state was due very shortly to begin reaping vast revenues under a 1964 petroleum concession. On the other hand, the overwhelming favorite to win the presidency in 1972 was Asaad Bucaram Elmhalim, a former street peddler who in 1960 had seized the leadership of the CFP from Guevara Moreno and later had twice been an extremely popular mayor of Guayaquil (see Constitutional Rule, 1948–60, this ch.; Political Parties, ch. 4). Both the military and the business community regarded Bucaram as dangerous and unpredictable and unfit to be president, especially at a time when unprecedented income was expected to flow into the state coffers. On February 15, 1972, four months before the scheduled elections, the military once again overthrew Velasco, who was sent into his final period of exile. He was replaced by a three-man military junta headed by the Army chief of staff, General Guillermo Rodríguez Lara.

Direct Military Rule, 1972–79

The military regime called itself "nationalist and revolutionary," but the well-known connections of Rodríguez Lara to the Guayaquil business community signaled disappointment for those who anticipated that he would head a progressive military regime such as was ruling in Peru at the time. It shortly became apparent that, ideologically, the Rodríguez Lara regime was a hybrid, reflecting a tenuous equilibrium among the widely divergent political tendencies within the Ecuadorian armed forces. Nevertheless, like the contemporary Peruvian and Brazilian regimes, the regime of Rodríguez Lara, he promised, would not be an interim government, but rather a long-term venture dedicated to introducing structural changes thought necessary to unfreeze the development process.

Rodríguez Lara's regime gave early emphasis to a campaign designed in part to exert firm control over the nation's petroleum resources and in part to consolidate the government's political authority. Several former political leaders, including ex-President Otto Arosemena, were tried for corruption in connection with oil concessions granted during the 1960s. In addition, a large number of functionaries of the Velasco government, supporters of Bucaram, as well as drug traffickers, legitimate importers, and customs officials were charged with corruption and "illegal enrichment." Although it thus assailed its major opponents from the start, the military regime, however, failed to build its own civilian base of political support.

Promises of a "meaningful agrarian reform" under the auspices of Minister of Agriculture Guillermo Maldonado, a dedicated reformer, were frustrated by intense opposition from traditional elites. Maldonado was eventually forced out, and by the end of Rodríguez Lara's four years in office less than 1 percent of Ecuador's cultivable land had changed hands under the reform. More notable achievements came in the areas of building infrastructure projects, such as the major oil refinery and petrochemical complex in Esmeraldas; various highway and electrification projects; and state capitalist enterprises, particularly the Ecuadorian State Petroleum Corporation (Corporación Estatal Petrolera Ecuatoriana— CEPE). The latter corporation was founded in 1972 and grew to become the major actor in Ecuador's exploitation of its oil reserves (see Petroleum and Natural Gas, ch. 3).

Oil policy was the regime's vehicle for its most forceful expression of nationalism. Minister of Natural Resources Gustavo Jarrín Ampudia presided over Ecuador's 1973 entry into the Organization of Petroleum Exporting Countries (OPEC), with all its attendant prestige and economic benefits. He was also responsible for Ecuador's renegotiation of a number of oil concessions, including the key Texaco-Gulf concession in the Oriente, on terms much more favorable to the state, such as substantial increases in both the royalties paid by foreign firms and the tax rate they paid on petroleum exports. These efforts were initially successful in allowing the government to retain a larger share of Ecuador's petroleum earnings.

The oil companies became increasingly disconcerted, however, when Jarrín proposed in late 1974 that the share of stock in the Texaco-Gulf subsidiary held by CEPE be increased from 25 to 51 percent. Claiming that the terms of their concessions negotiated with Jarrín had priced Ecuadorian oil beyond the world market price, the oil companies cut back drastically on their exports, at a cost to the government of hundreds of millions of dollars over the following nine months. This intense financial pressure finally led to a July 1975 announcement that taxes on the oil companies' exports were being reduced. It was thus clear that the military regime had overplayed its nationalistic oil policy, having failed to keep in mind that Ecuador was, after all, a relatively small oil producer and thus not a powerful player within OPEC.

The moderation of the regime's oil policy, however, did not result in the anticipated resolution of mounting economic problems. Oil exports rose only slightly, while imports, particularly of luxury items, continued to soar, aided by a low-tariff policy that had been designed to soak up petroleum earnings, and thus control inflation. In excess of 22 percent during 1974, inflation was rapidly eroding the real value of wages within the middle class.

In August, in an effort to resolve its balance-of-payments difficulties, the regime decreed a 60 percent duty on imported luxury items. The measure was condemned by the Chambers of Commerce in Quito and Guayaquil, whose constituents had grown dependent on the sale of imports, and caused, a week later, a bloody attempt led by the chairman of the Joint Chiefs of Staff, General Raúl González Alvear, to overthrow Rodríguez Lara. Although this coup attempt failed, at a cost of twenty-two lives, on January 11, 1976, a second, bloodless coup was successful in removing Rodríguez Lara. He was replaced by a Supreme Council of Government consisting of the commanders of the three armed services.

Virtually the only item on the agenda of the new military triumvirate was to preside over a return of the government to constitutional, civilian rule. The bloody September 1975 coup attempt had revealed the depth of the breach in the institutional unity of the armed forces. Handing the government back to civilians, it was hoped, might remove the causes of divisions within the military, or at least make it easier to hide them from public view.

The original timetable, announced in June 1976, called for a transition that was to culminate in presidential elections in February

1978. First, new government charters and electoral laws were to be drafted by appointed commissions, and then a public referendum would choose between two proposed constitutions. The transition was repeatedly slowed down, however, and in the end, instead of the less than two years originally scheduled, three years and eight months elapsed between the 1976 coup and the inauguration of a civilian president.

Two reasons are commonly cited for the delay: the slowness of decision making within the Supreme Council of Government because of ongoing disagreement within the military high command and repeated maneuverings by the military government to manipulate the electoral process, thereby controlling its outcome. Like the Rodríguez Lara government, the Council was particularly interested in seeing a poor electoral performance by the CFP and, especially, preventing Bucaram from winning the presidency.

The national referendum to choose the constitution was finally held on January 15, 1978. The results saw 23 percent of the voting population nullify their ballots, an action that had been advocated by the traditional right; 31 percent of the population voted in favor of a revised version of the 1945 constitution, and a plurality of 44 percent voted in favor of the newly drafted national charter. The charter was the more progressive of the two constitutions, its major reforms being the acknowledgement of a role for the state in socioeconomic development, the legalization of a worker self-managed (*autogestional*) sector in the economy, a unicameral legislature, no presidential reelection, and, for the first time in Ecuador, electoral suffrage for illiterates (see Constitutional Background, ch. 4).

Five candidates then campaigned for the presidency. The consistent favorite in polls was Rodrigo Borja of the social democratic Democratic Left (Izquierda Democrática—ID). Because the Supreme Council of Government made sure that Bucaram was barred from running, the CFP strongman named his second in command, Jaime Roldós, to be the party's candidate. In order to broaden the appeal of the ticket, Osvaldo Hurtado, the leader of the Christian Democratic Party (Partido Demócrata Cristiano—PDC), was tapped to be Roldós's vice presidential running mate. The traditional rightist vote was split between two candidates, and the various parties of the Marxist left coalesced to name one candidate. After a lengthy recount, the final results of the July 16 election confirmed the initial tally of a surprise victory by Roldós, with 27 percent of the national vote. Sixto Durán Ballén, candidate of a coalition of rightist parties, finished second with 24 percent. The electoral law mandated that when no candidate achieved a majority vote, a run-off election between the two top finishers be held.

It was more than nine months before the second-round election took place, however. They were months of considerable political tension and doubt as to whether the transition would proceed as planned. First, widespread problems in organizing the election and in the vote count during the first round left serious doubts as to the competence and honesty of the electoral authorities. The Supreme Electoral Tribunal (Tribunal Superior Electoral—TSE) was, as a result, completely reorganized. Second, the government—remembering a campaign slogan calling "Roldós to the government, Bucaram to power"—was understandably dismayed with results of the first-round election. By delaying the second round, the government sought to give rightists the time to build an anti-Roldós coalition under which Durán could emerge as the second-round victor. To complicate matters further, Abdón Calderón Múñoz, a populist candidate who had won 9 percent of the vote in the first round, was murdered under circumstances implicating the government. Finally, as a further distraction during this difficult period, Velasco returned from exile to bury his wife and died in March 1979 at age eighty-six.

The second round was finally held on April 29, 1979, with the Roldós-Hurtado ticket sweeping to an overwhelming 68.5 percent victory against a weak performance by Durán. Doubts persisted, however, up to the moment that the winners took office three months later, that the military would allow them to assume their duly elected offices. The size of their popular mandate and, according to political scientist John D. Martz, pressure from the administration of President Jimmy Carter in Washington made it difficult for the military to stop the "democratization" process at this late date. The military did extract as a price, in any case, unprecedented powers to name representatives to the boards of directors of major state corporations and to participate directly in the naming of the minister of defense. The outgoing government also made it clear to Roldós (who had an early campaign slogan of "we will not forgive, we will not forget") that it would not tolerate any investigation into the behavior of the military with respect to human rights. With his autonomy thus diminished, Roldós finally assumed the presidency on August 10, and thus Ecuador returned to constitutional, civilian rule after almost a decade of dictatorship.

Return to Democratic Rule, 1979–84

Roldós presided over a nation that had undergone profound changes during the seven years of military rule. During the ceremony to pass the mantle of power to Roldós, Admiral Alfredo Poveda Burbano pointed proudly to impressive indicators of economic growth between 1972 and 1979: the government budget expanded some 540 percent, whereas exports as well as per capita income increased a full 500 percent. Industrial development had also progressed, stimulated by the new oil wealth as well as Ecuador's preferential treatment under the provisions of the Andean Common Market (Ancom, also known as the Andean Pact) (see Growth and Structure of the Economy, ch. 3).

Past export "booms" in cocoa and bananas were managed by and for private coastal interests, but the state controlled the petroleum bonanza and thereby transformed the social landscape. Quito—the seat of the bureaucracy and the closest major city to the oil fields—reaped the benefits of the economic growth. The capital city lost much of its sleepy Sierra character and in the 1980s competed with Guayaquil as a center of modern economic endeavor. Employment in the public sector grew in excess of 10 percent annually throughout the late 1970s, creating a new consumption-oriented middle class in Quito. But such change highlighted the persistence of the traditional rural campesino and the unskilled urban subproletariat; petroleum revenues thus widened Ecuador's habitual inequality in income distribution (see Social Classes, ch. 2).

Expectations that the economic and social changes would transform the traditional political culture were unfulfilled. Customary aspects of civilian politics, such as regionalism and personalism, were reflected in the proliferation of political parties; and rivalry between the executive and legislature persisted during the five years that Roldós and his vice president, Osvaldo Hurtado, were in power.

The most destructive of these traditions was evident in the intense rivalry that developed between Roldós and Bucaram, the strongman of the president's own CFP, who, having twice been prevented from running for the presidency, was now determined to run the country from his power base in the unicameral legislature, the National Congress (Congreso Nacional—hereafter, Congress). Bucaram's coalition building secured him the presidency of the legislature during the first year of the new government. The president, for his part, was determined to retain his independence from the autocratic and increasingly conservative party boss. Bucaram had no apparent agenda other than blocking the reformist agenda of the president, who was thus forced to spend most of his first year in office scratching together his own political base, independent of the CFP, in order to achieve a legislative majority.

Roldós proved successful in this effort; in August 1980, his candidate for the congressional presidency narrowly defeated the

*Women and children in
a village near Riobamba
Courtesy Inter-American
Foundation (Miguel Sayago)*

bucaramista candidate, and the CFP also suffered major losses in the municipal and provincial elections in December. The president was not able to enjoy the fruits of his success, however; on May 24, 1981, he was killed, along with his wife and the minister of defense, in an airplane crash in the southern province of Loja.

The death of Roldós generated intense popular speculation. Some Ecuadorian nationalists attributed it to the Peruvian government because the crash took place near the border where, four months previously, the two nations had participated in a bloody flare-up in their perpetual border dispute. Many of the nation's leftists, pointing to a similar crash that had killed Panamanian president Omar Torrijos Herrera less than three months later, blamed the United States government.

Roldós's constitutional successor, Hurtado, immediately faced an economic crisis brought on by the sudden end of the petroleum boom. Massive foreign borrowing, initiated during the years of the second military regime and continued under Roldós, resulted in a foreign debt that by 1983 was nearly US$7 billion. The nation's petroleum reserves declined sharply during the early 1980s because of exploration failures and rapidly increasing domestic consumption.

The economic crisis was aggravated in 1982 and 1983 by drastic climatic changes, bringing severe drought as well as flooding, precipitated by the appearance of the unusually warm ocean current

47

known as "El Niño" (see Climate, ch. 2). Analysts estimated damage to the nation's infrastructure at US$640 million, with balance-of-payments losses of some US$300 million. The real gross domestic product (GDP—see Glossary) fell to 2 percent in 1982 and to -3.3 percent in 1983. The rate of inflation in 1983, 52.5 percent, was the highest ever recorded in the nation's history.

Although widely considered a center-leftist, Hurtado confronted the economic crisis by instituting highly unpopular austerity measures aimed at gaining the approval of the International Monetary Fund (IMF—see Glossary) and the international financial community at large. Hurtado eliminated government subsidies for basic foodstuffs—thus contributing to both inflation and the impoverishment of the masses—and substantially devalued the sucre. With unemployment increasing to as high as 13.5 percent, the United Workers Front (Frente Unitario de Trabajadores—FUT) launched four general strikes during Hurtado's period in office. The most militant of these nationwide strikes, in October 1982, was called off after forty-eight hours because of union leaders' fears of provoking a coup d'état.

Outside observers noted that, however unpopular, Hurtado deserved credit for keeping Ecuador in good standing with the international financial community and for consolidating Ecuador's democratic political system under extremely difficult conditions. The political right, nevertheless, believing that the economic crisis was caused by presidential policies that were inimical to free-enterprise capitalism, bitterly criticized Hurtado. The right united for the 1984 elections in order to back León Febres Cordero Ribadeneyra, a businessman from Guayaquil, with Borja running a close second. As Febres Cordero entered office on August 10, there was no end in sight to the economic crisis nor to the intense struggle that characterized the political process in Ecuador.

* * *

Beginning in the 1960s, Ecuadorian historiography benefited from publication of a handful of excellent studies. Nicolas P. Cushner's *Farm and Factory* and John Leddy Phelan's *The Kingdom of Quito in the Seventeenth Century* offer some of the best research ever conducted on colonial Spanish America. On the postindependence period, Osvaldo Hurtado's *Political Power in Ecuador* and Agustín Cueva's *The Process of Political Domination in Ecuador* are both excellent general studies by Ecuadorian scholars and have been translated into English. Frederick B. Pike's *The United States and the Andean*

Republics is also extremely valuable, although the reader interested in Ecuador might jump over extensive analyses of Peru and Bolivia.

A number of political analyses are also useful to the historian of the modern period. John Samuel Fitch's *The Military Coup d'Etat as a Political Process: Ecuador, 1948–1966* is a pioneering, in-depth study of the political mindset of the Latin American armed forces. John D. Martz's *Ecuador: Conflicting Political Culture and the Quest for Progress* is a more general study that concentrates on the 1960s. Literature on the military government of the 1970s remains scarce; David W. Schodt's ''State Structure and Reformist Politics'' provides useful information on the public sector during that period, however. *Crisis, Conflicto y Consenso: Ecuador, 1979–84* by Nick D. Mills, Jr. is a valuable study of the turbulent Roldós-Hurtado period. (For further information and complete citations, see Bibliography.)

Chapter 2. The Society and Its Environment

Ceramic curandero *(shaman)* *(Jama-Coaque culture)*

PROFOUND REGIONAL, ETHNIC, AND social divisions continued to characterize Ecuadorian society in the 1980s. The country's three main geographic regions, differing in their histories and economies, provided one of these divisions, and there were also ethnic and social cleavages within the regions. The Oriente (eastern region) traditionally was a neglected backwater, isolated geographically and culturally from the rest of the nation. Its population was limited to dispersed groups of indigenous tropical-forest Indians who lived by slash-and-burn agriculture or hunting and gathering. European intrusion was limited to the occasional missionary or trader. Beginning in the 1960s, however, the Oriente experienced colonization by land-poor peasants from the Sierra (Andean highlands) and exploration by oil companies. Both colonization and exploration had a devastating impact on the indigenous population.

The Sierra, the region of earliest European settlement, was ruled for most of its history by a narrow rural oligarchy whose power base lay in the sizeable haciendas they controlled. The haciendas dominated both social and economic relations. Most of the population depended to a greater or lesser extent on the largess of the white elite who controlled land. This elite ruled virtually without challenge until the mid-twentieth century. Between this white elite and the mass of Sierra Indians were the mestizos or *cholos*—persons of mixed Spanish and Indian ancestry. In values and identity, they were closer to the dominant whites. The Sierra Indians, who stood at the bottom of the social pyramid, had very limited opportunities for economic security or social advancement. Both mestizos and whites regarded Indians as immutably inferior. The latter's only hope for improvement lay in assimilating the norms and values of the dominant ethnic groups, thereby changing ethnic affiliation.

Like the hacendados of the Sierra, the elite of the Costa (coastal region) also had its roots in agriculture and the control of land, but its attention focused primarily on export crop production and commerce. Ethnically more diverse than the Hispanic elite of the Sierra, the Costa upper class included successful immigrant families drawn over the years by the region's expanding economy. Most of Ecuador's blacks, the descendants of the small numbers of African slaves who came to work on the region's plantations, were also *costeños* (residents of the Costa).

The twentieth century saw the rise of an Ecuadorian middle class whose interests were genuinely distinct from the narrowly based rural oligarchy, and the demise of the self-contained, autonomous

53

hacienda. Changes in the hacienda economy created a mobile, rural-based labor force, and by the end of the 1980s, society consisted of a small, privileged elite; a more numerous, diverse, and politically active middle class; and the mass of impoverished small-scale peasants, artisans, and wage earners. The middle class transformed Ecuadorian politics.

Like many other Latin American nations, Ecuador had enacted agrarian reform legislation in the 1960s and 1970s. These laws brought little substantive improvement in the lives of most peasants, but rather afforded Costa and Sierra landlords an impetus and an opportunity to replace their resident and permanent laborers with temporary workers. In the Sierra this trend, coupled with increased population pressure on land, continued a pattern of migration to the Costa and the Oriente that had begun in the 1950s. The volume of rural-urban migration grew in both the Costa and Sierra until, in the early 1980s, nearly half of all Ecuadorians lived in cities.

Geography

Ecuador is one of the smaller countries in South America. Located on the west coast and straddling the equator, Ecuador has a total area of about 280,000 square kilometers, which includes the Galápagos Islands. Roughly the size of the state of Colorado, Ecuador encompasses a wide range of natural formations and climates, from the desertlike southern coast to the snowcapped peaks of the Andes Mountains to the plains of the Amazon River Basin (see fig. 3).

Ecuador is bounded on the west by the Pacific Ocean, on the north by Colombia, and on the east and south by Peru. Ecuador continues to contest the boundary with Peru, which was established by the Protocol of Peace, Friendship, and Boundaries (Rio Protocol) of 1942 and ceded to Peru a large portion of territory east of the Andes (see Reform, Chaos, and Debacle, 1925–44, ch. 1).

Natural Regions

Ecuador is divided into three continental regions—the Costa, Sierra, and Oriente—and one insular region—the Galápagos Islands. The continental regions extend the length of the country from north to south and are separated by the Andes Mountains. The Galápagos Islands, officially called the Archipiélago de Colón, are located 1,000 kilometers west of the Ecuadorian coast within 1° south of the equator.

The Costa, located between the Pacific Ocean and the Andes Mountains, consists of coastal lowlands, coastal mountains, and rolling hills that separate river valleys. The widest part of the region stretches 150 kilometers from Cabo San Lorenzo in Manabí Province

to the foothills of the Andes Mountains. In the southern part of Guayas Province, east of the Gulf of Guayaquil, the narrow coastal plain is only fifteen to twenty kilometers wide. The lowlands of the Costa do not exceed 200 meters in elevation, whereas the coastal mountains extend no higher than 1,000 meters. The coastal mountain chain, known as the Cordillera Costañera, divides the region into the Costa Externa, next to the coast, and the Costa Interna, next to the Andes. The Cordillera Costañera reaches from Esmeraldas in the north to Guayaquil in the south. North of Portoviejo in Manabí Province, the Cordillera Costañera loses its character as a mountain chain and becomes a series of hills and small mountains.

The Sierra consists of two major chains of the Andes mountains, known as the Cordillera Occidental (Western Chain) and Cordillera Oriental (Eastern Chain), and the intermontane basin or plateau between the two chains. Several transversal mountain spurs, known as *nudos,* cut across the plateau. The Nudo del Azuay, at 4,500 meters the highest of these transversal spurs, divides the Sierra into two subregions—the area of modern volcanism to the north and the area of ancient volcanism to the south. The former area consists of newer, higher mountains than those in the ancient volcanism section, which with time have eroded to lower levels.

The Sierra has at least twenty-two peaks over 4,200 meters in height. Of the two cordilleras, the Cordillera Oriental is wider and generally higher, with peaks averaging over 4,000 meters. The Cordillera Occidental, however, contains the highest point in Ecuador, which is Mount Chimborazo at 6,267 meters. The Sierra also contains the highest point on the equator, Mount Cayambe at 5,790 meters.

The Sierra has at least thirty peaks of volcanic origin, including six still active. These peaks, which vary in width from 80 to 130 kilometers, are located in the area of modern volcanism known as the Avenue of the Volcanos. The most active volcano is Mount Sangay, 5,230 meters high. Although its last major outpouring of lava occurred in 1946, specialists consider Mount Sangay to be in a constant state of eruption because of fires and bubbling lava at its crater. Mount Cotopaxi, at 5,897 meters the highest active volcano in the world, last erupted in 1877 and is now listed as "steaming." Its crater is 800 meters in diameter. In addition to the other damage caused by eruptions, volcanos in the Sierra have melted snowcaps, which in turn generate massive mudslides and avalanches. Earthquakes and tremors also are common in the region.

The intermontane plateau between the two cordilleras is divided by the *nudos* into roughly 10 basins, or *hoyas,* that range from 2,000 to 3,000 meters in altitude. The average altitude of the plateau is 2,650 meters.

The Oriente to the east of the Cordillera Oriental consists of two subregions: the Andean piedmont and the Eastern lowlands. The piedmont drops from a height of 3,000 meters to the featureless lowlands, which spread out at an altitude of 150 to 300 meters.

The Galápagos Islands consist of a chain of large, medium, and small islands that have a combined area of roughly 8,000 square kilometers. The largest island is Isabela Island, also known as Albemarle Island, which is 120 kilometers long with an area of 4,275 square kilometers. All of the islands are of volcanic origin, and some have active cones. Santo Tomás, located on Isabela Island, is the highest peak of the Galápagos at 1,490 meters. Its crater is ten kilometers in diameter.

Drainage

Almost all of the rivers in Ecuador rise in the Sierra region and flow east toward the Amazon River or west toward the Pacific Ocean. The rivers rise from snowmelt at the edges of the snow-capped peaks or from the abundant precipitation that falls at higher elevations. In the Sierra region, the streams and rivers are narrow and flow rapidly over precipitous slopes. Rivers may slow and widen as they cross the *hoyas* yet become rapid again as they flow from the heights of the Andes to the lower elevations of the other regions. The highland rivers broaden as they enter the more level areas of the Costa and the Oriente.

In the Costa region, the Costa Externa has mostly intermittent rivers that are fed by constant rains from December through May and become empty riverbeds during the dry season. The few exceptions are the longer, perennial rivers that flow throughout the Costa Externa from the Costa Interna and the Sierra on their way to the Pacific Ocean. The Costa Interna, by contrast, is crossed by perennial rivers that may flood during the rainy season, sometimes forming swamps.

The Guayas River system, which flows southward to the Gulf of Guayaquil, constitutes the most important of the drainage systems in the Costa Interna. The Guayas River Basin, including land drained by its tributaries, is 40,000 square kilometers in area. The sixty-kilometer-long Guayas River forms just north of Guayaquil out of the confluence of the Babahoyo and Daule rivers. Briefly constricted at Guayaquil by hills, the Guayas widens south of the city and flows through a deltaic network of small islands and channels. At its mouth, the river forms a broad estuary with two channels around Puná Island, the deeper of which is used for navigation.

The second major Costa river system—the Esmeraldas—rises in the Hoya de Quito in the Sierra as the Guayllabamba River and flows westward to empty into the Pacific Ocean near the city

of Esmeraldas. The Esmeraldas River is 320 kilometers long and has a 20,000-square-kilometer drainage basin.

Major rivers in the Oriente include the Pastaza, Napo, and Putumayo. The Pastaza is formed by the confluence of the Chambo and the Patate rivers, both of which rise in the Sierra. The Pastaza includes the Agoyán waterfall, which at sixty-one meters is the highest waterfall in Ecuador. The Napo rises near Mount Cotopaxi and is the major river used for transport in the Eastern lowlands. The Napo ranges in width from 500 to 1,800 meters. In its upper reaches, the Napo flows rapidly until the confluence with one of its major tributaries, the Coca River, where it slows and levels off. The Putumayo forms part of the border with Colombia. All of these rivers flow into the Amazon River.

The Galápagos Islands have no significant rivers. Several of the larger islands, however, have freshwater springs.

Climate

Each region has different factors that affect its climate. The Costa is influenced primarily by proximity to warm or cool ocean currents. By contrast, climate in the Sierra varies more as a function of altitude. The Oriente has a fairly uniform climate that varies only slightly between the two subregions. Climate in the Galápagos Islands is both moderated by the ocean currents and affected by altitude. Throughout Ecuador variation in rainfall primarily determines seasons. Temperature is determined by altitude. With each ascent of 200 meters in altitude, temperature drops 1°C. This phenomenon is particularly significant in the Sierra.

The Costa has a tropical climate. Temperatures for the region as a whole remain fairly constant, ranging from 23°C in the south to 26°C in the north. Although seasonal changes in temperature are not pronounced, the hottest period occurs during the rainy season, especially from February to April. Near Guayaquil, the coolest months are August and September. Rainfall in the Costa decreases from north to south, with vegetation changing from tropical rainforest in the north to tropical savannah to desert in the south.

Differences in temperature and rainfall in the Costa are caused by the Peruvian Current and periodic appearances of El Niño. The Peruvian Current, also formerly known as the Humboldt, is a cold ocean current that flows north along the coasts of Chile and Peru. At Cabo Blanco, where the Gulf of Guayaquil begins, the main current veers to the west; a branch continues northward to Cabo Pasado, in Manabí Province, where it also turns westward to merge with the main current near the Galápagos Islands. The cold water and air temperatures associated with the Peruvian Current inhibit rainfall along the coast, creating dry to arid conditions. This effect is greatest along the southern coast of Ecuador.

El Niño occurs periodically every six or seven years. Starting in late December, a change in atmospheric pressure shifts ocean currents so that warm waters come closer to shore and displace the cold waters. During this time, air and water temperatures, tides, sea levels and wave heights, and relative humidity all are higher than usual. These conditions produce heavy rainfall that generally lasts until May in an area that normally experiences nothing more than a drizzle. The resulting flooding and landslides can be devastating.

When the Peruvian Current is dominant, the amount of precipitation along the coast varies from north to south, with levels ranging from 300 centimeters to 30 centimeters, respectively. Two rainy seasons in the northernmost part of the coast become a single season (December through June) not far south. Near Esmeraldas, average annual rainfall is 250 centimeters. The rainy season shortens farther south, lasting only from January to May at Guayaquil. Very little rainfall occurs on the end of the Santa Elena Peninsula west of Guayaquil. Arid conditions prevail on the border with Peru south of the Gulf of Guayaquil.

Separated from the effects of ocean currents by the Cordillera Costañera, the Costa Interna has a hot and humid climate.

Temperatures can surpass 26°C, and the vegetation and cloud cover tend to retain and augment the heat. Rain is constant during the winter months of December through May, with the heaviest rainfall occurring in February and March.

Temperatures in the Sierra do not vary greatly on a seasonal basis; the hottest month averages 16°C and the coolest month, 13°C in the upper elevations. Diurnal temperatures, however, vary dramatically, from cold mornings to hot afternoons. The almost vertical sun and the rarified air in the higher Sierra region allow the land to warm quickly during the day and lose heat quickly at night. Mornings typically are bright and sunny, whereas afternoons often are cloudy and rainy. In general, rainfall amounts are highest on exposed locations at lower altitudes. Rain also can vary on a local basis. Sheltered valleys normally receive 50 centimeters per year, whereas annual rainfall is 150 centimeters in Quito and can reach 250 centimeters on exposed slopes that catch rain-bearing winds. On a seasonal basis, the driest months are June through September.

Climate in the Sierra is divided into levels based on altitude. The tropical level—400 to 1,800 meters—has temperatures ranging from 20°C to 25°C and heavy precipitation. The subtropical level—1,800 to 2,500 meters—has temperatures from 15°C to 20°C and moderate precipitation. The temperate level—2,500 to 3,200 meters—has a year-round temperature in the range of 10°C to 15°C and an annual rainfall of 100 centimeters. The temperate level experiences rainstorms, hailstorms, and fog. Winter, or the rainy season, lasts from January through June, and the dry season, or summer, from July through December. Most rain falls in April. There also is a short rainy period in early October caused by moisture penetrating the Sierra from the Oriente. Quito and most other populated areas in the Sierra are located at this temperate level. The cold level extends from the temperate zone to 4,650 meters. Here, average temperatures are 3°C to 9°C, and the precipitation often appears in the form of rain, hail, and thick fog. Above 4,650 meters is the frozen level, where peaks are constantly capped with snow and ice, and temperatures range from below zero to 3°C. Precipitation frequently is in the form of snow, fog, and rain.

The Eastern lowlands in the Oriente experience an equatorial climate. Rainfall is abundant, especially in the Andean piedmont, sometimes exceeding 500 centimeters per year. Temperatures average 25°C in the western parts of this region. The jungle-covered plains of the Eastern lowlands register high levels of rainfall and temperatures surpassing 28°C.

Being located on the equator, the Galápagos Islands would have an equatorial climate were it not for the modifying effects of the Peruvian Current. Instead, climate on the islands follows a pattern

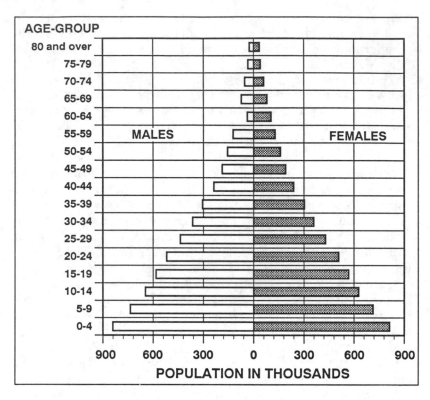

Source: Based on information from Centro Latinoamericano de Demografía, *Ecuador: Estimaciones y Proyecciones de Población, 1950–2000,* Quito, 1984, 78–83.

Figure 4. Projected Population by Age and Sex, 1990

more like that of the Sierra than the Costa. At sea level, the land is desertlike with temperatures of 21°C. The eight summer months experience no precipitation, whereas the winter months of January through April have some fog and drizzle. Above sea level to an altitude of 450 meters, the islands have a mixture of tropical, subtropical, and temperate climates. In general, temperatures are around 17°C. There is constant fog and drizzle in the summer and rain in the winter. The cold level above 450 meters has temperatures below 14°C.

Population

The government conducted national censuses in 1950, 1962, 1974, and 1982 and scheduled another for 1990. In the late 1980s, estimates of total population by 1990 ranged from 10.8 to 11 million (see fig. 4). The annual growth rate was an estimated 2.3 to

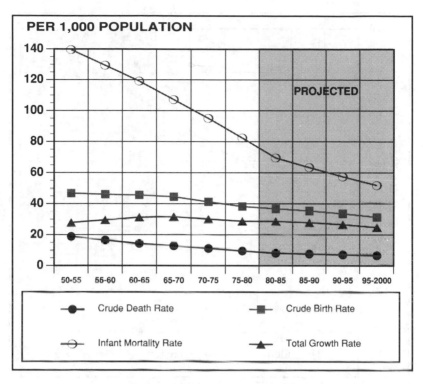

PER 1,000 POPULATION

PROJECTED

| 50-55 | 55-60 | 60-65 | 65-70 | 70-75 | 75-80 | 80-85 | 85-90 | 90-95 | 95-2000 |

Legend:
- ●— Crude Death Rate
- ■— Crude Birth Rate
- ⊖— Infant Mortality Rate
- ▲— Total Growth Rate

Source: Based on information from Centro Latinoamericano de Demografía, *Ecuador: Estimaciones y Proyecciones de Población, 1950-2000,* Quito, 1984, 48, 62.

Figure 5. Selected Demographic Indicators, at Five-Year Intervals, 1950-2000

2.8 percent. Population growth rates had been high since the onset of modern census-taking, with an increase of 3.2 percent annually in the 1960s and 3.0 percent in the 1970s. Demographers expected the rate to decline to approximately 2.4 percent by the end of the century. Their estimates of total population in 2000 ranged from 13.6 to 14.2 million, with the lower figure more commonly accepted.

Despite the declining growth rate, a variety of indicators from the 1980s showed the country to be in the midst of a population explosion that was likely to continue beyond the year 2000 (see fig. 5). Between the early 1950s and the mid-1980s, the crude death rate fell by nearly 60 percent. The infant mortality rate, which dropped by nearly half to approximately 63 per 1,000 live births in 1985, accounted for most of the decline. The crude birth rate dropped from 47 to 37 per 1,000 population during the same time;

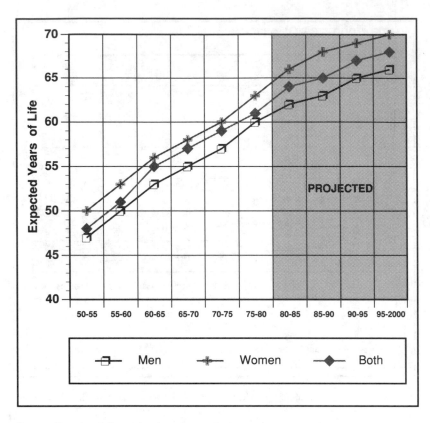

Source: Based on information from Centro Latinoamericano de Demografía, *Ecuador: Estimaciones y Proyecciones de Población, 1950–2000,* Quito, 1984, 48, 62.

Figure 6. Life Expectancy at Birth, by Five-Year Intervals, 1950–2000

given the relative youthfulness of the population, however, growth rates could be expected to remain high for decades. Only Bolivia had a higher population birth rate among South American countries. Life expectancy increased by more than 25 percent between the 1950s and the mid-1980s (see fig. 6).

The total fertility rate (the number of children a woman could expect to bear during her life) dropped by an estimated one-third between 1950 and 1990 (see fig. 7). Socioeconomic background had a significant impact on the rate; the mean by region or ethnic group varied by as much as 3.5 children per woman. Estimates of the rate by the year 2000 ranged from 3.6 to 4.3 children per woman.

The high rate of population growth generated pressure on the country's limited resources. Even assuming only moderate growth

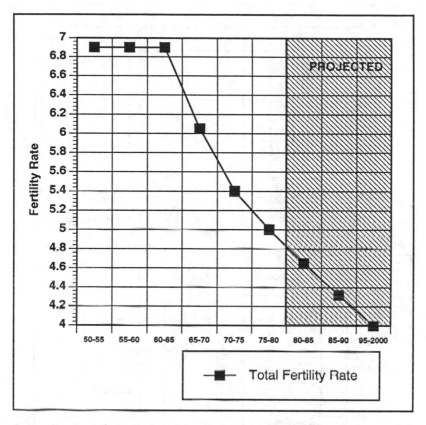

Source: Based on information from Centro Latinoamericano de Demografía, *Ecuador: Estimaciones y Proyecciones de Población, 1950–2000,* Quito, 1984, 48, 62.

Figure 7. Total Fertility Rate, at Five-Year Intervals, 1950–2000

to the end of the century, the primary and secondary schools' budget would have to rise to 70 percent over that of 1980 to keep pace with population. Moreover, more than 120,000 new jobs would be required each year to maintain employment levels of the early 1980s.

Increasingly aware of the high costs of continued population growth, the government in the 1970s accepted in principle the need for family planning and control of child spacing and attempted to incorporate demographic variables into national economic planning. Nonetheless, maternal and child health programs were often ineffective. A contraceptive practices survey in 1982 found that 65 percent of the women not using contraceptives nevertheless wanted to participate in some form of family planning and would have

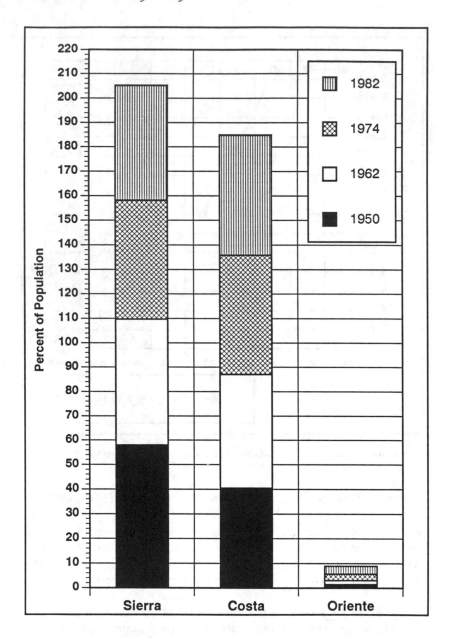

Source: Based on information from Ecuador, Instituto Nacional de Estadística y Censos,
IV Censo Nacional de Población y III de Vivienda, 1982—Resumen Nacional: Breve Análi-
sis de los Resultados Definitivos, Quito, 1985, 31.

Figure 8. Population Distribution by Region, Census Years, 1950–82

participated in family planning if a program were available. Given continued high birth rates, many demographers doubted government estimates that 40 percent of women of childbearing age were using contraceptives in the mid-1980s.

Migration and Urbanization

For most of Ecuador's history, the majority of the population lived in the Sierra. Most of the Sierra population was clustered in the more habitable *hoyas*. For example, the capital city, Quito, is located in a *hoya* at the foot of Mount Pichincha (see Geography, this ch.).

From 1950 to 1974, however, large numbers of land-poor Sierra peasants migrated to the Costa; as a result, the Costa grew substantially faster than the nation as a whole (see table 2, Appendix). By the mid-1970s, population figures for the Sierra and the Costa were roughly similar. The Costa expanded only at roughly the national average during the 1974–82 intercensal period. Nonetheless, by 1982 the Costa had become the most populated region in the country (see fig. 8).

Migration (coupled with the high birth rate) transformed the country in the twentieth century. *Costeños* from the central region often migrated to Guayaquil and its hinterland following declines in export crop production. *Serranos* (residents of the Sierra) were often first "pulled" by the expanding coastal economy and then "pushed" by population pressure, agrarian reform, and modernization. The cocoa-producing areas of Guayas and El Oro provinces—strategically located for those escaping the 1960s drought in Loja Province—became the most common destinations for *serranos* (see fig. 9).

The cocoa boom of the late nineteenth and early twentieth centuries also had initiated a limited pattern of immigration to the Costa. Immigrants from Europe and Latin America generally arrived with capital to exploit the lucrative Costa commercial opportunities. Significant numbers of Lebanese, referred to locally as *turcos* or *arabes*, also moved to Guayaquil and gained considerable influence in coastal commerce and local politics. The Lebanese retained their ethnic identity and married within their own community, and both their distinctiveness and their level of prosperity set them apart and made them the target of prejudice.

Two distinct migration waves to the Oriente occurred in the twentieth century. In the early 1900s, some *serranos* trekked to the Oriente to pan gold and stayed to settle on the east slopes of the Andes. These migrants acquired land from the indigenous population and

67

Source: Based on information from Federal Republic of Germany, Statistisches Bundesamt, *Länderbericht Ecuador, 1988*, Wiesbaden, 1988, 8.

Figure 9. Population Density, 1986

set up small, largely subsistence-oriented farming communities. Beginning in the 1950s, large numbers of *serranos* arrived in search of available land; most simply went to the Oriente province most accessible to their place of origin. Between 1950 and 1982, the Oriente experienced a more than fivefold population increase. The growth rate averaged approximately 5.6 percent annually, nearly double that of the nation as a whole. By the mid-1970s, migrants constituted nearly half the region's residents.

Beginning in the 1950s, large numbers of Ecuadorians also migrated from the countryside to the cities—a trend apparent in both the Costa and the Sierra. This migration changed life not only in the nation's two largest cities, Guayaquil and Quito, but also in intermediate-sized cities.

Both Guayaquil and Quito reflected their different histories, their distinctive regional settings, and their roles in contemporary national politics and economic development. Guayaquil was founded as a commercial link to Spain (see Spanish Colonial Era, ch. 1). The city's contemporary configuration began to take form with the beginning of cocoa production in the eighteenth century. Always tied to international markets, Guayaquil's development reflected the perturbations of whatever export crop was currently profitable. From the colonial era onward, Quito developed principally as an administrative center. As the capital city, Quito represented the epitome of the *serrano* elite's Hispanic values.

From 1950 to 1982, the population of Guayaquil and Quito expanded at rates substantially above the national average. Guayaquil's rate of growth was highest in the 1950s—a response to the rise in banana cultivation on the coast. Ecuador's oil boom of the 1970s generated rapid population growth in Quito during that decade, a trend that continued into the early 1980s. By 1982 Guayaquil's population stood at approximately 1.2 million residents and Quito's at roughly 870,000 (see table 3, Appendix). Together, they represented 60 percent of the urban population.

Both cities faced a number of common problems resulting from the tremendous influx of migrants. The numbers of the poor employed in marginal sectors and occupations increased to the point that they defeated the ability of Guayaquil and Quito governments to provide basic services and employment. Each city had a central core that was ringed with densely populated tenement slums. Much of the population of these slums consisted of relatively recent migrants.

Another phenomenon affecting Guayaquil and Quito was the emergence of large squatter settlements on previously unoccupied marginal lands. The establishment of *suburbio* (the collective name for squatter settlements) in the marshy areas southwest of Guayaquil proper began in the 1960s; by the early 1980s, *suburbio* had pushed into the Guayas River estuary and encompassed half of the metropolitan population. Although the older sections of *suburbio* had reasonably well-provisioned water lines, sewage disposal, and streets, newer communities lacked basic services. Those who had settled in the estuary system faced the added problem of persuading municipal authorities to provide landfill and to deal with periodic flooding. Quito municipal authorities tried to prevent the spread of squatter settlements up the mountainsides to the west of the city by strictly limiting the provision of water above certain altitudes. In addition, the government squelched numerous attempts by squatters to take over private or public lands. Despite these actions, however, settlements expanded throughout the 1970s and represented between 10 and 15 percent of Quito's population by the mid-1980s.

In contrast to much of Latin America, Ecuador's intermediate-sized cities experienced very high rates of growth after 1950. This was especially the case in the Costa, where the annual growth rate of intermediate-sized cities dwarfed even that of Guayaquil (see table 4, Appendix). Expansion of second-tier cities in the Costa resulted in part from export growth. In the 1950s and early 1960s, for example, the spread of banana cultivation and the increasing need for port facilities spurred the growth of cities like Santo Domingo, Quevedo, Esmeraldas, and Machala. In the 1970s and early 1980s, Santo Domingo continued to grow as African palm plantations spread throughout its hinterland. Other coastal cities expanded in response to shrimp raising, fishing (and related industries), or tourism.

In general, mid-sized cities in the Sierra were less dynamic than their Costa counterparts. From the mid-1950s to the early 1980s, only Cuenca—Ecuador's third largest city—achieved growth rates roughly comparable to that of Quito (see fig. 1). Agrarian reform and the reduction of the resident labor force on haciendas fostered expansion primarily of intermediate-sized cities in the Sierra. When employment opportunities existed, mid-sized cities drew migrants because they were closer to home, less disruptive to ties with the countryside, and less threatening than Guayaquil or Quito.

Social Classes
Elite

Ecuador's elite, in the late 1980s, included Sierra *latifundistas* (large landowners), Costa agro-exporters, financiers, and industrialists. Commercial and industrial interests overlapped with those of agriculture, as families in finance and industry often maintained at least a token interest in agriculture. Indeed, the purchase of land with the profits of commerce had long been considered a critical step in improving a family's standing. In addition to this overlap, there were strong intragroup ties among the elite; kinship and marriage contributed to cohesion. Newly rich families tried to turn their economic success into social capital by marrying into older, established families.

Historically, the basis of class in Ecuador lay in the control of land and the labor of those who lived on it. The Spanish conquistadors had found the region devoid of valuable minerals and the ready wealth mining provided, so the combination of land and Indians welded together in vast haciendas formed the basis of the colonial economy. The few who held land constituted a rural oligarchy. The rest of society depended on this pivotal group, in varying degrees, for livelihood, political participation, and social identity. Hacienda owners spent much of their time in their urban residences; cities existed principally to serve their wants. The small, ill-defined middle levels of urban professionals found employment serving the commercial and administrative needs of the hacienda. Artisans likewise produced mainly for hacendados.

The hacienda with its resident labor force was the center of the Sierra elite family's influence. The landowner's power within his domain was nearly absolute. Ideally, the hacendado exercised this power beneficently, to protect his followers and dependents. Whatever his inclination, everything from private morality to public religious observances fell within his purview. He settled land disputes among his resident peons, arranged marriages, and dispensed favors.

The Costa elite's lifestyle, values, and economic interests differed from its Sierra counterpart. Trade grew on the coast in response to the impetus of export agriculture. As a result, the elite on the coast had ties to other Latin American seaports and links with world commerce.

The cleavage between the two elite groups, in evidence at independence, continued to play a pivotal role in Ecuadorian politics in the 1980s (see Return to Democratic Rule, 1979–84, ch. 1; Political Dynamics, ch. 4). Governments parceled out political offices between the two groups, and region of origin was a critical factor in an individual's political career. Economic developments since the 1950s reinforced the dichotomies between the Costa and Sierra. The banana boom of the 1950s and 1960s revived the Costa cocoa elite and funneled money to Guayaquil; in contrast, the oil boom of the 1970s benefited Quito.

Agrarian organization provided the model for other social institutions and the exercise of authority in general. Social rank and power, in the elite view, were a natural part of the social order. Individuals were ranked on the basis of birth, race, wealth, breeding, and education. The elite (and middle class) often described itself as *la gente buena* (the good people) or *la gente decente* (the respectable people), contending that it had sufficient breeding, intelligence, and culture to rule others. The subordination of workers, peasants, servants, and all Indians was an essential part of this scheme. In the elite view, gains achieved by subordinates came not as their natural right but through the beneficence of their betters.

Land reform legislation in the 1960s and 1970s left elite hegemony in agriculture and landholding largely unscathed. For one thing, Costa and Sierra landholders mounted an intense effort to oppose those elements of agricultural reform that threatened their diverse interests. For another, the laws were designed to benefit resident agricultural laborers, but on most of the coast and on the more advanced haciendas of the northern and central Sierra, landowners had already begun switching to wage labor, so there were few peons and sharecroppers to receive expropriated land. Instead, the legislation merely freed the owners from their customary obligations to resident laborers. Land reform eliminated the paternal obligations landowners had previously assigned toward their workers.

The landed elite benefited in a number of others ways as well. The price paid in compensation for expropriated private land was often inflated well above market value. Well-connected landlords usually fared better in the courts than their less-privileged tenants. Those peasants who received land rarely became self-supporting and had to supplement their subsistence plots with seasonal wage labor elsewhere. Large landowners gained a supply of temporary wage laborers with limited political ability to make demands beyond a single season's work.

Middle Class

Ecuador's diverse middle class was concentrated in cities and larger towns. A minute, ill-defined group during most of the country's history, its numbers grew in the twentieth century. In the late 1970s, estimates based on income indicated that roughly 20 percent of the population was middle class. Economic expansion increased the opportunities available to the able and ambitious. The rapid increase in government employment contributed both to the size of the middle class in absolute numbers and to the group's political awareness. The rise of a middle class whose interests were not those of the rural oligarchy transformed national politics.

Businessmen, professionals, clerical employees, mid-level bureaucrats and managers, army officers, and teachers comprised the middle levels of society. They constituted a diverse group, often poorly defined in terms of both self-identity and criteria for membership. At a minimum, an individual had attained a certain level of education (at least a secondary school degree), practiced an occupation that did not require manual labor, and manifested proper manners and dress to be considered middle class.

The upper echelons frequently identified with and emulated the elite. By contrast, the lower levels of the middle class often made common cause with the more prosperous segments of the working class. The cleavage between these two groups—a prosperous, upper-middle class oriented toward the elite and a less economically secure lower group often allied with the more privileged sectors of the working class—was reflected in lifestyle, patterns of association, and political loyalties.

In addition to the economic division, an ethnic component emerged in the ranking of the various levels of the middle class. In general, individuals became more "white" and less obviously mestizo farther up the social ladder. In addition, the middle class was ethnically more diverse than other groups. Over the years, immigrants from southern Europe, the Middle East, and elsewhere in Latin America arrived to take advantage of expanding economic opportunities on the Costa. These immigrants formed the core of Ecuador's commercial interests.

Peasants

Until the early 1950s, peasant families formed the vast majority of the populace. Historically, these families were isolated from national society, a pattern reinforced by the nature of traditional rural social life. Social arrangements aimed at self-defense limited the intrusions of outsiders. The individual "nested" within the protective layers of family, kin, neighborhood, and village.

Peasant links to city, region, and nation were mediated through powerful outsiders, such as foremen, landowners, merchants, priests, or law enforcement officials. Such relations were typically exploitative to the peasant, but they were also multistranded. However uneven the exchange, the two parties were linked by more than just the naked self-interest of the powerful.

At the center of the peasant family's life and livelihood stood access to land. Landholding not only assured the family subsistence, but also defined its status within the community. Adult participation in village social life demanded land; nonholders remained peripheral to the most significant aspects of the community's social life, such as participation in justice.

Elite control over most land, however, left those at the bottom of the social pyramid with limited options and created the classic latifundio-*minifundio* (small landholding) complex. Large landholders monopolized the most desirable holdings and left marginal lands to peasants. Sierra haciendas extended from valley floor to mountain crest. The fertile valley bottoms were assigned to hacienda production whereas the steeper lands went to peons. Costa plantation owners reached the same end by controlling riverine land with ready access to markets.

Historically, the traditional Sierra hacienda engaged in mixed livestock and crop production and relied on a "captive" labor force. On the eve of land reform in the 1960s, about two-thirds of all farmers owned some land, but still remained dependent to varying degrees on haciendas. Haciendas regulated access to land mainly through the *huasipungo* system. The *huasipunguero* or *concierto* peon was a resident laborer who received a plot of land in return for labor on the hacienda and domestic service in the landlord's household. Although precise terms of tenure varied from valley to valley and from time to time, they were typically disadvantageous to the peon. The *huasipunguero* usually had to provide four days of work per week to the hacienda as well as domestic service—an especially onerous obligation that required both husband and wife to work full time at hacienda maintenance for a specified period. Finally, peons had to participate in collective work parties during planting and harvesting.

A variety of subsidiary arrangements provided an auxiliary supply of laborers. Peasants from neighboring free communities often negotiated for the use of hacienda firewood, water, and pastures. These peasants, known as *yanaperos,* typically worked one or two days per month and helped out at planting and harvest times. Other peasants worked hacienda lands through some type of sharecropping arrangement. Some casual wage laborers or skilled specialists were employed as production dictated, but these constituted a very minor part of the hacienda's total labor force.

The classic *huasipungo* system continued in use in the 1960s in relatively remote but well-populated valleys. Near towns, where other employment was available, smaller holdings and more diverse tenure arrangements typically prevailed. Merchants and other townsmen frequently owned small parcels of land, which peasants worked through sharecropping agreements. Typically, the sharecropper had lands of his own nearby; he provided labor, draft animals, tools, seed, and fertilizer. The landowner and sharecropper split the harvest.

Landowners who wished to exploit the growing urban market (especially for dairy products) found it more profitable to consolidate their holdings and sell the less desirable plots to their peons. This process of transferring marginal hacienda land to peasants was most evident in Pichincha, Imbabura, and Carchi provinces. Elsewhere (in Chimborazo, for example) landlords simply evicted peons and refused to compensate them, treatment that fueled peasant unionization drives.

A man in Esmeraldas Province
Courtesy Inter-American
Foundation (Juan García)

A hostel for migrant
workers in Guayaquil
Courtesy Inter-American
Foundation (Miguel Sayago)

Sharecropping and wage labor arrangements historically prevailed on the export-oriented Costa plantations. In the late nineteenth and early twentieth centuries, a cocoa boom occurred in the Costa. Sharecroppers on cocoa plantations cultivated the crop in exchange for advances on the harvest. Plantation owners controlled most marketing channels; their economic clout came not merely from landholding, but because rental agreements typically obliged the sharecropper to sell at terms set by the landlord.

Landlords' effective control over sharecroppers declined following the 1922 blight of the cocoa crop. Sharecroppers either purchased their plots, simply assumed control of them, changed the terms of their rental agreements, or they moved onto unoccupied land. As cocoa prices rose in the 1950s, however, landowners attempted to reinstate their control. Tenants responded with efforts to unionize and, by the early 1960s, with land invasions and rent strikes. Workers on banana plantations, which developed in the 1950s employing wage labor, also tried to unionize.

Land reform legislation in the 1960s and the 1970s aimed at eliminating *minifundio* plots under 4.8 hectares and subjected absentee landholders to the threat of expropriation. The threat prompted some landlords to sell off at least a portion of their holdings; the main beneficiaries were peasants who could muster sufficient resources to purchase land. Land reform also eliminated the various demands for time that landlords had placed on peasants. By 1979, however, when most expropriations were completed, less than 20 percent of peasant families and 15 percent of agricultural land had been affected by agrarian reform. The legislation did little to change the structure of landholding, which remained roughly as concentrated in the mid-1970s as it had been in the mid-1950s (see table 5, Appendix). Nearly 350,000 farms contained less than five hectares—the minimum experts considered necessary to support a family. Almost 150,000 plots were less than one hectare.

The degree of land fragmentation in the Sierra added to the problems of poorer farmers. Andeans had long preferred some dispersion of their lands in order to take advantage of the diversity in microclimates in the region and to limit the risks to any given field. A family might have as many as twenty to thirty small fields scattered around a village. In addition to the poor farmers, there were more than 220,000 landless laborers whose situation was even more tenuous.

For the mass of small producers, agrarian reform simply increased the amount of time available to work on their own holdings. Most had so little land, however, that their own farms could hardly absorb the added labor. Some peasants, especially in the northern

Crowds line the street at the main market in Guayaquil
Courtesy World Bank

Sierra around Otavalo, supplemented their farming with profitable crafts production. Other families produced items such as bricks and tiles for which there was a local market. In these instances, then, additional time afforded a measure of prosperity. A survey of Sierra families in the early 1980s found, however, that fewer than 10 percent earned any of their income from traditional rural crafts. Instead, families with sufficient resources might purchase a small truck and market agricultural products.

The mass of small farmers were not so fortunate; those who did not have any plots to work or whose plots were too small to provide subsistence had to seek wage labor, since land reform regulations had deprived them of the option of working on haciendas as peons or sharecroppers. By the mid-1970s, wages, not agricultural products, had become the largest portion of small farmers' income. As nonagricultural employment expanded during the oil boom, peasant laborers increasingly chose urban employment over agricultural work. Fully one-third of all rural Sierra families surveyed in the early 1980s had at least one member working away from the family landholdings. Peasant laborers had enjoyed a measure of well-being during the economic growth of the 1970s. Both the construction and the service sectors expanded apace and cushioned land-poor peasants. The economic downturn that occurred in the 1980s, however, hit wage earners particularly hard and severely limited employment opportunities.

In the late 1970s, analysts estimated that between 370,000 and 570,000 rural Ecuadorian families lived in poverty. The worst levels of Sierra poverty were found in Chimborazo Province. Poverty in the Sierra correlated with altitude: the higher the family's holdings, the more limited its production options and the greater its poverty. Access to modern transportation was a main determinant of farm income in the Costa. The poorest coastal areas were found in isolated settlements, fishing towns, and villages in Esmeraldas Province.

The emergence of crafts as a major component in some peasant families' livelihood created the potential for intergenerational conflict. Children learned new production techniques in school that sometimes increased their own earning power beyond that of their parents. As some family members sought wage labor farther from home, those remaining relied more heavily on nonfamily wage laborers to assist with farming. Cooperative work exchanges declined in favor of hired casual labor.

The increased pressure on land also sharpened disputes about inheritance and divisions among siblings. Traditionally, inheritance provided the main means of access to land. Individuals began receiving parcels of land from their parents at marriage. Without sufficient land, a couple could not fulfill the wider obligations of sharing and reciprocity that were part of community-wide fiestas. With less land available, moreover, parents tended to favor the youngest son—the child who would stay at home and care for them in their old age. Older siblings increasingly fended for themselves or depended on the largess of the younger sibling.

The need for wage labor in the Sierra reinforced traditional patron-client ties. Former peons found themselves and their children dependent on powerful and influential outsiders as they had once been on landowners. Clientalistic bonds linked the powerless with those who could help them in finding work, emergency loans, and other forms of assistance (see Family and Kin, this ch.).

Throughout the 1970s and early 1980s, the government pinned most of its hopes for a relief of rural poverty not on land redistribution but on colonization of relatively underpopulated regions, especially the Oriente. By the late 1970s, the Ecuadorian Institute of Agrarian Reform and Settlement (Instituto Ecuatoriano de Reforma Agraria y Colonización—IERAC) had awarded 2.5 times more land in areas of new settlement than it had redistributed in agricultural reform zones. Further, colonists normally received a forty- to fifty-hectare parcel in contrast to the *minifundio* typically awarded former sharecroppers or *huasipungueros*. Land distribution in the Oriente was more equal than in either the Costa or the Sierra. The average Oriente holding in the mid-1970s was thirty hectares. Farms from 10 to 100 hectares—65 percent of all holdings—accounted for 83 percent of the agricultural land.

Migrants to the Oriente were typically males between the ages of twenty-five and forty with little land in their home communities. They began homesteading with a small amount of savings accumulated through agricultural wage labor. Migrants cleared as much land as they could on their parcel and brought their families to join them as soon as possible. As savings were exhausted, migrants had frequent recourse to wage labor either for oil companies or for more established settlers.

The Oriente's poorly developed transport and marketing infrastructure severely constrained Sierra migrants (see Transportation, ch. 3). Settlements typically consisted of a series of long, narrow parcels of land strung along both sides of a road. Roadside land was at a premium; as it was claimed, subsequent settlers repeated the same pattern of narrow rectangular holdings behind those already established. In the more heavily settled areas, homesteads stood four to six properties deep by the late 1970s. Colonists at farthest remove were six to ten kilometers from an all-weather road—a significant impediment in marketing their crops and increasing family income.

Workers

The urban lower class had its roots, as a distinct social group, in the artisans of colonial society. Artisans were ethnically and socially separate from the mass of Indian laborers employed in the textile factories. Typically lower-class Spaniards or mestizos, artisans provided the urban elite with finished goods, especially luxury items. They were politically powerless. The local municipal council (*cabildo*) controlled the movement of artisans from their city of residence and regulated the details of workshop organization, labor practices, prices, and production.

The urban working class took on its contemporary configuration with the onset of industrialization in the twentieth century. Manufacturing remained heavily in the hands of artisans, but large-scale industries such as food processing, textiles, and the railroads began to employ significant numbers of workers.

A renewed industrialization drive beginning in the 1950s, increased levels of rural to urban migration, and the oil development of the 1970s all contributed to the growth and diversity of the contemporary urban working class. Workers in stable, well-established enterprises represented the most heavily unionized portion of the lower class and counted as an articulate, well-organized voice in political affairs. These employees earned steady wages and received the benefits of social security and worker protection legislation (see Political Forces and Interest Groups, ch. 4).

Few workers enjoyed such benefits, however; the vast majority were classified as artisans or self-employed. Artisan firms ran the gamut from small, family-run businesses to middling manufacturing enterprises employing as many as thirteen workers. Self-employment typically offered little in the way of economic security. The mass of street vendors, carpenters, tailors, painters, and the like worked long hours for low earnings. In the mid-1970s, nearly one-quarter of peddlers were classified as living in poverty; more than 30 percent of craftsmen and artisans also fell below the poverty line.

In addition to economic differences, the various segments of the working class were divided in other ways. Clerical workers and most white-collar workers considered themselves as superior to the rest of the working class because of education and, frequently, ethnic affiliation. The needs of wage earners for benefits and a living wage often conflicted with the interests of the more prosperous artisans, who needed to hire cheap labor.

Selling roasted bananas in Guayaquil
Courtesy World Bank

The volume of permanent and temporary migration from the 1960s to the 1980s changed the configuration of the urban working class. Temporary was a relative concept for many migrants: for example, surveys of Quito temporary construction workers in the early 1980s found they had worked in the city for an average of six years. Migrants followed a well-trod path to urban employment, relying on fellow villagers and kin who had made the transition earlier.

The informal sector offered a haven of sorts to many unskilled and uneducated migrants and first-time job seekers. Although fiercely competitive and usually poorly remunerated, it fit with the limited capital commanded by most of these workers. It cost relatively little to build a kiosk and stock it with secondhand goods, clothes, newspapers, and the like. Some ambulatory vendors or kiosk sellers obtained higher-cost items on consignment. Only a minimal cash outlay was required to repair electrical appliances in a corner of one's home or to do laundry or cook and sell food. Such endeavors also permitted the use of unremunerated family labor and, for women, meshed well with the demands of child care. Migrants also gained an entry into the city by selling fruits and vegetables from their villages.

The construction boom fueled by oil development in the 1970s generated considerable employment for temporary migrants to Quito. Labor contractors congregated at certain well-known meeting places in the city to gather the workers they needed. Construction offered unskilled recent male migrants (and minimally educated first-time job seekers in general) positions that were poorly remunerated, insecure, nonunionized, and untouched by most worker protection legislation. Nonetheless, such work provided the beginning of an urban livelihood. A fortunate migrant might form *compadrazgo* (the set of relationships between a person or couple, their parents, and their godparents) ties with a labor contractor—thus obtaining a better chance at regular employment. Some seemingly menial jobs, depending on the individual's circumstances, offered significant advantages. To receive a hut on the job premises in order to guard the construction materials and tools at night, for example, solved the worker's housing dilemma and allowed him to bring his wife, who then could earn income by cooking and washing for other laborers. Migrants who stayed in the city usually became master craftsmen in a construction trade, but some, especially those who remained identifiably Indian, often remained in menial employment.

Both temporary and permanent migrants sought to maintain ties with families in the countryside. Temporary migrants' work schedules remained tied to the agricultural cycle. Those workers returned home for planting and harvest and, whenever possible, weekend visits. A migrant's involvement in farm work was a sensitive barometer of his or her ultimate intentions. An end to routine participation in the agricultural cycle marked completion of the gradual switch from temporary to permanent city dweller. Although most migrants did not send remittances home, those who did increased the earnings of a one- to five-hectare plot by an average of one-third. Even permanent migrants occasionally returned to the village for the local patron saint's feast. If a migrant had enough money, he or she bought land—typically leaving the holdings to be farmed by a relative.

Workers made some gains during the economic expansion of the 1970s. Employment was plentiful, and earnings generally kept pace with inflation. Even this prosperity was relative, however; in 1975, for example, 43 percent of the urban work force received less than the minimum wage. The economic crisis of the early and mid-1980s hit the working class particularly hard. The number of workers totally unemployed reached 10 percent in 1986. Those classified as "subemployed by income" rose from 29 percent of the work force in 1970 to 40 percent in 1980. By the end of 1986, the average worker's salary met roughly half of a family's basic needs.

Ethnic Groups

The country's ethnic groups descended from Spanish colonizers and South American Indians; indeed, the relationship between the two groups defined Ecuador's subsequent pattern of ethnicity. The mix of these groups created a third category, described variously as mestizos or *cholos*. The fourth element consisted of descendants of black slaves who arrived to work on coastal plantations in the sixteenth century. Censuses did not record ethnic affiliation, which in any event remained fluid; thus, estimates of the numbers of each group should be taken only as approximations. In the 1980s, Indians and mestizos represented the bulk of the population, with each group accounting for roughly 40 percent of total population. Whites represented 10 to 15 percent and blacks the remaining 5 percent.

The precise criteria for defining ethnic groups varied considerably. The vocabulary that more prosperous mestizos and whites used in describing ethnic groups mixed social and biological characteristics. Typically, higher-status whites considered their own positions as derived from a superior racial background. Nonetheless, ethnic affiliation remained dynamic; Indians often became mestizos, and prosperous mestizos sought to improve their status sufficiently to be considered whites. Ethnic identity reflected numerous characteristics, only one of which was physical appearance; others included dress, language, community membership, and self-identification.

No pretense to equality or egalitarianism existed in ethnic relations. From the perspective of those in the upper echelons, the ranking of ethnic groups was undisputed: whites, mestizos, blacks, and Indians. As the self-proclaimed standard bearers of civilization, whites contended that only they manifested proper behavior, an appropriate sense of duty to family and kin, and the values integral to the Christian, European culture.

As with much of social life, this particular view of ethnicity had strongly feudal overtones. The conquistadors accepted and lauded hierarchy and rank. Their success in subduing the Inca Empire made them lords of the land and justified holding Indians as serfs, to serve as a cheap source of labor. Although individuals might change their position in the hierarchy, social mobility itself was not positively viewed. The movement of individuals up and down the social scale was regrettable—ideally, a person should be content with, and maintain, his or her assigned role in the social order.

The geography of ethnicity remained well-defined until the surge in migration that began in the 1950s. Whites resided primarily in larger cities. Mestizos lived in small towns scattered throughout the countryside. Indians formed the bulk of the Sierra rural populace, although mestizos filled this role in the areas with few Indians. Most blacks lived in Esmeraldas Province, with small enclaves found in Carchi and Imbabura provinces. Pressure on Sierra land resources and the dissolution of the traditional hacienda, however, increased the numbers of Indians migrating to the Costa, the Oriente, and the cities. By the 1980s, Sierra Indians—or Indians in the process of switching their ethnic identity to that of mestizos—lived on Costa plantations, in Quito, Guayaquil, and other cities, and in colonization areas in the Oriente and the Costa. Indeed, Sierra Indians residing in the coastal region substantially outnumbered the remaining original Costa inhabitants, the Cayapa and Colorado Indians. In the late 1980s, analysts estimated that there were only about 4,000 Cayapas and Colorados. Some blacks had migrated from the remote region of the Ecuadorian-Colombian border to the towns and cities of Esmeraldas.

Whites and Mestizos

Whites constituted the most privileged ethnic group and occupied the top of Ecuador's social pyramid. Despite their own realization that there was an admixture of Indian genes in their heritage, whites placed considerable emphasis on their purported purity of blood and Spanish ancestry. Although whites shared a common cultural background, differences in class and regional loyalties—especially the split between Quito and Guayaquil—remained important.

In general, financially successful whites were employed as high-status professionals, government officials, prosperous merchants, and financiers. In the white ideal, manual labor was viewed as degrading and evidence of an inability to maintain a proper lifestyle. Accordingly, business interests were geared toward maintaining the family's social status rather than the pursuit of economic success for its own sake.

Below the white elite, but merging with it, were mestizos or *cholos*. Mestizos shared, to a large extent, a common set of values and a general cultural orientation with whites. Indeed, the boundary between the two groups remained fluid. Geography also played a role. In the smaller towns of the Sierra, those of mixed ancestry would call themselves whites, but they would be considered as mestizos by whites of larger cities or by those with more clearly superior social status. Income and lifestyle also constituted impor tant factors; a wealthy mestizo might be called a white, whereas a poorer one would be classified as a mestizo. Those in rural areas sometimes distinguished between "whites" and "legitimate whites." The latter could demonstrate to the satisfaction of the local community that their parents were considered white. Differing views of ethnicity partially reflected status differences between those involved in a given exchange. Hacienda foremen, for example, typically thought of themselves as whites. Although Indians would agree with that classification, hacendados regarded foremen as mestizos.

The terminology and categories themselves derived from colonial legal distinctions. *Peninsulares* (Spanish-born persons residing in the New World) ranked at the top of the social hierarchy. They enjoyed a range of legal privileges and status denied even wealthy criollos born of Spanish parents in the colonies. The pedigree of forebears defined status at every level. Individuals were ranked by the number of grandparents legally classified as white.

Common usage, however, modified the categories through the centuries. In the nineteenth century, for example, the term *mestizo* described a person whose parents were an Indian and a white. In contrast, a *cholo* was one whose parents were an Indian and a mestizo. By the twentieth century, the terms *mestizo* and *cholo* were frequently used interchangeably. On occasion, however, some people used *cholo* in a derogatory sense to describe an Indian trying to rise above his or her proper station. Other people might use *cholo* to designate an intermediate category between Indian and mestizo.

As with whites, facility in Spanish, urban orientation, livelihood, manners, and fineness of clothing defined mestizo identity. Traditionally, mestizos filled the intermediate occupations, serving as clerks, small merchants, hacienda foremen, and low-ranking bureaucrats. Although mestizos were assumed to be of mixed Indian-white ancestry, an Indian might gradually become mestizo by abandoning his or her previous lifestyle.

Usually, individuals desiring to switch ethnic affiliation had to leave their villages, learn Spanish well enough to mask their origin, and acquire a mestizo occupation. They also had to acquire sufficient finesse and confidence in dealing with whites and mestizos not to be marked as Indians. It was virtually impossible for an Indian to change ethnic identity in his or her home community. No improvement in expertise, level of education, or facility in Spanish would cause locals to treat one born an Indian as a mestizo.

In special circumstances, individuals could move from one group to the other without leaving their communities. For example, the Saraguro Indians of southern Ecuador were generally more prosperous than local whites. Indeed, the latter either depended on the Saraguros for their livelihood or lived in communities where typically most of the populace was Indian. As a result, a distinctive pattern of ethnic change prevailed. Some whites opted to become Indians, usually improving their economic options in the process. A few Indians decided to improve their ethnic status and became white. The switch was made, however, without resort to subterfuge. Indians did not hide their origins or leave their home communities.

Blacks

Approximately one-half million blacks lived on the north coast and its riparian hinterlands. They were the descendants of African slaves who worked on coastal sugar plantations in the sixteenth century. Blacks held a slightly higher position in the ethnic hierarchy than Indians, manifesting little of the subservience that characterized Indians in dealing with whites and mestizos. Few readily identifiable elements of African heritage remained, although observers noted aspects of dance, music, and magical belief that represented purported vestiges of African influence. Some linguists saw evidence of an ''Africanized'' Spanish in the dialects spoken by those blacks living in the more remote areas.

Most blacks earned their livelihood in subsistence agriculture supplemented by wage labor, fishing, and work on cargo boats. Women on the coast earned income through shellfish gathering. Before the onslaught of Sierra to Costa migration in the 1960s and

1970s, some black males earned their living running small stores and cantinas, and others served as intermediaries between black laborers and white and mestizo employers. White and mestizo migrants, however, took over virtually all small-scale commerce and marketing efforts and increasingly served as employment brokers. The switch made skin color more important as an ethnic marker, with light-skinned blacks enjoying greater opportunities for mobility than those with darker skin.

Sierra Indians

Sierra Indians had an estimated population of 1.5 to 2 million in the early 1980s and lived in the intermontane valleys of the Andes. Prolonged contact with Hispanic culture, which dated back to the conquest, had a homogenizing effect, reducing the variation among the indigenous Sierra tribes.

The Indians of the Sierra were separated from whites and mestizos by a castelike gulf. They were marked as a disadvantaged group; to be an Indian, or *indígena,* in Ecuador was to be stigmatized. Indians were usually poor and frequently illiterate, they enjoyed limited participation in national institutions, and they commanded access to few of the social and economic opportunities available to more privileged groups.

Visible markers of ethnic affiliation, especially hairstyle, dress, and language, separated Indians from the rest of the populace. Indians wore more manufactured items by the late 1970s than previously; their clothing, nonetheless, was distinct from that of other rural inhabitants. Indians in communities relying extensively on wage labor sometimes assumed Western-style dress while still maintaining their Indian identity. Indians spoke Quichua—a Quechua dialect—although most were bilingual, speaking Spanish as a second language with varying degrees of facility. By the late 1980s, some younger Indians no longer learned Quichua.

Most whites and mestizos viewed Indians as inherently inferior. Some regarded *indígenas* as little better than a subspecies. A more benign perspective condescendingly considered the Indian as an intellectual inferior, an emotional child in need of direction. Such views underlay the elaborate public etiquette required in Indian-white/mestizo interactions. Common practice allowed whites and mestizos to use first names and familiar verb and pronoun forms in addressing Indians.

Although public deference to other ethnic groups supported stereotypes of Indians as intellectually inferior, Indians viewed deference as a survival strategy. Deference established that an individual Indian was properly humble and deserving of the white's or mestizo's aid and intercession. Given the relative powerlessness of Indians, such an approach softened the rules governing interethnic exchanges.

The tenor of such exchanges differed in cases of limited hacienda dominance. The Otavalos of northern Ecuador, the Saraguros, and the Salaacas in the central Sierra resisted hacienda intrusion and domination by whites and mestizos. These Indians were thus less inclined to be subservient and adopted instead an attitude of aloofness or distance in dealing with whites and mestizos.

Most Indians, however, could improve their situation only by changing their ethnic affiliation. Such a switch in allegiances was fraught with risk, since individuals thereby lost the security offered by their small community of family and neighbors. Many rejected such an extreme move and instead made a series of accommodations such as changing their dress and hairstyle while working for brief periods away from home and gradually increasing the length of their absences.

By the early 1980s, changes in Indian ethnic consciousness could be identified in some communities. An increasing number of educated Indians returned to work in their native communities instead of assuming a mestizo identity and moving away. They remained Indian in their loyalty and their ethnic allegiance. The numbers of Indian primary school teachers of Quichua increased, and literacy programs expanded; both trends reinforced Indian identity.

Although these developments were most prominent among prosperous groups such as the Otavalos and the Saraguros, the number of Indians in general moving into "mestizo jobs" increased during the oil expansion. New opportunities gave Indians the option of improving their economic status without sacrificing their ethnic identity. Observers also noted a general growth in ethnic pride coupled with negative reactions toward those Indians who chose to abandon their roots and become mestizos.

Oriente Indians

Although the Indians of the Oriente first came into contact with whites in the sixteenth century, the encounters were more sporadic than those of most of the country's indigenous population. Until the nineteenth century, most non-Indians entering the region were either traders or missionaries. Beginning in the 1950s, however, the government built roads and encouraged settlers from the Sierra to colonize the Amazon River Basin. Virtually all remaining Indians were brought into increasing contact with national society. The interaction between Indians and outsiders had a profound impact on the indigenous way of life.

In the late 1970s, roughly 30,000 Quichua speakers and 15,000 Jívaros lived in Oriente Indian communities. Quichua speakers (sometimes referred to as the Yumbos) grew out of the detribalization of members of many different groups after the Spanish conquest. Subject to the influence of Quichua-speaking missionaries and traders, various elements of the Yumbos adopted the tongue as a lingua franca and gradually lost their previous languages and tribal origins. Yumbos were scattered throughout the Oriente, whereas the Jívaros—subdivided into the Shuar and the Achuar— were concentrated in southeastern Ecuador. Some also lived in northeastern Peru. Traditionally, both groups relied on migration to resolve intracommunity conflict and to limit the ecological damage to the tropical forest caused by slash-and-burn agriculture.

Both the Yumbos and the Jívaros depended on agriculture as their primary means of subsistence. Manioc, the main staple, was grown in conjunction with a wide variety of other fruits and vegetables. Yumbo men also resorted to wage labor to obtain cash for the few purchases deemed necessary. By the mid-1970s, increasing numbers of Quichua speakers settled around some of the towns and missions of the Oriente. Indians themselves had begun to make a distinction between Christian and jungle Indians. The former engaged in trade with townspeople. The Jívaros, in contrast to the Christian Quichua speakers, lived in more remote areas. Their mode of horticulture was similar to that of the non-Christian Yumbos, although they supplemented crop production with hunting and some livestock raising.

Shamans (*curanderos*) played a pivotal role in social relations in both groups. As the main leaders and the focus of local conflicts, shamans were believed to both cure and kill through magical means. In the 1980s, group conflicts between rival shamans still erupted into full-scale feuds with loss of life.

The Oriente Indian population dropped precipitously during the initial period of intensive contact with outsiders. The destruction of their crops by mestizos laying claim to indigenous lands, the rapid exposure to diseases to which Indians lacked immunity, and the extreme social disorganization all contributed to increased mortality and decreased birth rates. One study of the Shuar in the 1950s found that the group between ten and nineteen years of age was smaller than expected. This was the group that had been youngest and most vulnerable during the initial contact with national society. Normal population growth rates began to reestablish themselves after approximately the first decade of such contact.

Increased colonization and oil exploration also displaced the indigenous population, hurt the nutritional status of Indians, and damaged tribal social relations. The Indians' first strategy was to retreat to more remote areas—an option that became less available with increased settlement of the tropical forest. Land pressures also produced a decline in the game available and, hence, in Indian protein levels. Even livestock raising did little to improve Indian diets, since this was done primarily for sale rather than consumption. In addition, the decline in migration opportunities increased tribal hostility and competition between rival shamans.

Critics contended that the government took little effective action to protect Indians. Although the government had designated some land as "indigenous communes" and missionaries had organized some Indians into cooperatives, Indians remained disadvantaged in conflicts with settlers, who had greater familiarity with the national bureaucracy.

Family and Kin

Family and kin constituted the most enduring and esteemed institutions in the country's social fabric. Both Indian and Hispanic traditions emphasized the family; indeed, few alternative institutions competed for an individual's loyalty. The family buffered Indians from the vagaries of a hostile world. For the landed gentry, a distinguished family name played a major role in the assignment of status.

As circumstances dictated, a household commonly consisted of a nuclear family—husband and wife with their unmarried children—and one or more members of the wider circle of kin. Couples often resided with the parents of one of the spouses for a period after marriage. Parents typically spent their declining years with the youngest son and his spouse, who remained at home to care for them. Although individuals owed their primary allegiance and responsibility to their families, ties extended outward from this group. The wider circle of kin offered the individual a potential source of assistance and support. Trust and responsibility flowed along the lines of kinship at each level of the social scale.

The Hispanic man served as the unquestioned head of the household and the model of manhood to his sons. Although he might also be a kindly and affectionate parent, he was unlikely to take an active role in the day-to-day functioning of the family. Social tradition granted men the right of independence in their leisure time; many took full advantage of their freedom, spending much time in clubs, coffeehouses, and bars or simply on the street, depending upon the social stratum to which they belonged.

A woman's range of activity, by tradition, rested within the home and that remained true into the 1980s. She managed the household and the day-to-day upbringing of children. Provided she ran the

*Young boy carrying water
to his home in Guayaquil
Courtesy World Bank*

family in a way her husband deemed appropriate, a woman could normally expect considerable autonomy. Even in the more cosmopolitan sectors of the larger cities, the traditional role of the wife and mother remained largely unchanged. Even young women who had high levels of education and a professional career were subordinate to their husbands in a wide variety of matters.

Less stress on the contrasting roles of men and women existed among Sierra Indians. Women's economic role in the household economy demanded that they take the initiative in many matters. Women bore primary responsibility for the health and welfare of the family's members. In addition, the double standard for marital fidelity—tacitly accepted or even lauded in Hispanic culture—was replaced among Indians by a moral code demanding faithfulness on the part of both members.

Family and kin served as a bulwark against the *indígena*'s frequently precarious circumstances. The married couple was the center of a social system extending outward in concentric circles. The couple's parents and their siblings (and the siblings' spouses) formed the primary extended kin group and were bound by strong ties of trust and cooperation. Most marriages took place within the small village or community; generations of intermarriage created a web of reticulate kin ties within the community. The bonds of kinship reinforced cohesion and a sense of shared identity among kin and community members alike.

For all ethnic groups, the range of recognized kin beyond the nuclear family and close relatives varied depending on their economic and social circumstances. Large landowning families of the Sierra derived part of their status and power from their far-reaching kinship ties. Families of lower status typically chose which of their kin to recognize and cultivate. Beyond a fairly narrow circle, an individual had an element of choice and activated the relationship through mutual gift giving, shared meals, and reciprocal participation at family and community fiestas.

The strength of kin ties at every level of society often allowed unrelated persons to establish bonds of fictive kinship through the institution of *compadrazgo*. In Hispanic and Indian traditions alike, *compadres* (people related through *compadrazgo*) should manifest the highest regard and loyalty toward one another. Although individuals might criticize and argue with relatives, such actions with *compadres* would be unthinkable.

The occasions for selecting godparents varied from group to group; Christian Indians and Hispanics commonly chose them at baptism, confirmation, and marriage. In each instance, the godparents assumed ritual and financial obligations to the child (or couple) and the parents involved. In the case of baptism, the tie between the child's godparents and parents persisted even if the child died. Marriage *compadres* were part of a four-way relationship linking the couple, the *compadres,* and each spouse's parents. Beyond their immediate responsibilities in the marriage ceremonies, *compadres* had a duty to take an ongoing interest in the marriage. Great care went into the choice of godparents for every occasion.

Compadrazgo ties cut across class and ethnic boundaries. Indians and mestizos often asked wealthy and influential whites to serve as godparents. In so doing, they established a patron-client relationship with the higher status person. The lower status person expected to receive various forms of assistance; in return, the higher status person gained a loyal follower. For Indians the link with white or mestizo *compadres* represented one of the few relationships of trust with members of the dominant ethnic group.

People also chose *compadres* of equal status, selecting distant kin, close friends, business associates, or neighbors to serve as godparents. The advantage in asking neighbors and kin was that the parents knew their reputation and standing in the community more thoroughly than they knew this about the others. Among *compadres* of equal status, people tried to match the economic resources of the couples involved, so that the reciprocal obligations and gifts between the two families balanced evenly.

Religion

The Roman Catholic Church assumed a pivotal role in Ecuador virtually at the onset of the Spanish conquest. Catholicism was a central part of Hispanic culture, defining the ethos and worldview of the time. Through the Office of the Inquisition, the church examined the "purity" of possible officeholders. The church was virtually the only colonial institution dealing with education or the care of the needy. It amassed great wealth through donations, dowries, and outright purchases. Virtually every segment of the organization—the hierarchy, individual clerics, and religious orders—owned some form of assets.

The liberals' ascendancy in 1905 brought a series of drastic limitations to the Roman Catholic Church's privileges (see The Rule of the Liberals, 1895–1925, ch. 1). The state admitted representatives of other religions into the country, established a system of public education, and seized most of the church's rural properties. In addition, legislation formally abolished tithes (although many hacienda owners continued to collect them). The 1945 constitution (and the Constitution of 1979) firmly established freedom of religion and the separation of church and state.

Beginning in the 1960s, the country's Catholic bishops became increasingly active in supporting social change. Church leaders organized literacy campaigns among the Indians, distributed the institution's remaining lands, assisted peasants in acquiring land titles, and helped communities form cooperatives. In the 1970s and 1980s, the bishops espoused a centrist position on social and political issues. The episcopate contended that the unjust organization of Ecuadorian society caused many to live in misery. The bishops also claimed that the economic development of the 1970s and early 1980s had merely widened the gap between rich and poor. At the same time, however, Catholics were warned against employing Marxian analyses of society or endorsing violence or class conflict.

Church support for social reform occasionally brought it into conflict with government authorities. In 1976, for example, police arrested Riobamba bishop Leónidas Proaño Villalba—the espiscopate's most outspoken critic of Ecuadorian society and politics—and sixteen other Latin American bishops who were attending a church conference in Chimborazo Province. After accusing the prelates of interfering in Ecuador's internal politics and discussing subversive subjects, the minister of interior released Proaño and expelled the foreign bishops from the country. Some Catholics formed groups to support conservative causes. The Committee of Young Christians for Christian Civilization, for example,

93

advocated scuttling the "confiscatory and anti-Christian" agrarian reform laws.

In 1986 the Roman Catholic Church was organized into three archdioceses, ten dioceses, one territorial prelature, seven apostolic vicariates, and one apostolic prefecture (see table 6, Appendix). The church had only 1,505 priests to minister to a Catholic population of slightly more than 8 million, a ratio of 1 priest for every 5,320 Catholics.

Although approximately 94 percent of Ecuadorians were Roman Catholic, most either did not practice their religion or pursued a syncretistic version. Most Sierra Indians, for example, followed a type of folk Catholicism in which doctrinal orthodoxy played only a small part. Indigenous beliefs combined with elements of Catholic worship. Much of community life focused on elaborate fiestas that marked both public and family events. Although the precise configuration of fiestas varied from community to community, in general public fiestas involved an individual in a series of increasingly demanding and expensive sponsorships (*cargos*) of specific religious celebrations. By the time individuals had completed all the expected *cargos,* they were recognized community leaders.

The Roman Catholic Church's relatively weak presence in the countryside and in squatter settlements, coupled with the nominal, syncretistic practice of most Catholics, created a fertile ground for Protestant evangelical and Pentecostal missionary activity. Although multidenominational groups such as the Gospel Missionary Union (GMU) had been active in Ecuador since the beginning of the twentieth century, significant levels of conversion did not occur until the late 1960s. By the late 1970s, the GMU reported that it had converted 20,000 Sierra Indians in Chimborazo Province alone. The Christian and Missionary Alliance indicated that conversions among Indians in Otavolo climbed from 28 in 1969 to 900 in 1979. By the mid-1980s, an estimated 50,000 Ecuadorians had converted to the Church of Jesus Christ of Latter-Day Saints (the Mormon Church). Other significant forces in the Protestant camp included World Vision, an evangelical development group based in California, and the Summer Institute of Linguistics (SIL). The Texas-based SIL dispatched linguists to remote areas of Ecuador to study and codify tribal languages. The eventual goal of such efforts was to translate the Bible.

The phenomenal pace of conversion—some observers estimated that evangelicals and Pentecostals totaled 40 percent of the population in Chimborazo Province in the late 1980s—had an impact on social relations in rural areas. Change in religious affiliation was a major rupture with an individual's past traditions and social

All Saints Cathedral, Cuenca
Courtesy Martie B. Lisowski Collection,
Library of Congress

ties, effectively removing him or her from participation in fiestas—a major focus of much of community life. Families and extended families found the break with the rest of the community easier in the company of fellow converts. Protestantism replaced the patterns of mutual reciprocity characteristic of peasant social relations with a network of sharing and support among fellow believers. This support system extended to migrants; converts who left for the city or the coast sought out their coreligionists for assistance in finding lodging and employment even as Catholics looked to their *compadres*.

Social Welfare

Education

In the late 1980s, formal education was divided into four cycles: a preprimary two-year cycle; six years of primary school; secondary school, which was divided into two three-year cycles; and higher education. Children could begin attending preprimary school at four; primary school began at age six. Attendance theoretically was compulsory for children from six to fourteen years of age. The first three-year cycle of secondary school was a general curriculum that elaborated on that of primary school. In the second cycle, students could specialize in one of several different curriculums. An academic, liberal arts course led to university admission; other specialized courses prepared students for technical schools or teachers' training.

Roughly 20 percent of primary and secondary schools were privately run. The role of private schools increased with grade level; slightly less than 20 percent of primary students and more than 40 percent of secondary students attended private schools. Private education was a predominantly urban phenomena. Approximately one-third of city primary and secondary schools were private.

The country had twelve state universities, equally divided between the Costa and the Sierra, and an additional five private universities—three in the Sierra and two in the Costa. A number of polytechnic schools and teachers' colleges offered specialized postsecondary studies. The number of university students per 100,000 population grew fivefold from 1960 to 1980; the number of professors grew ten times. About two-thirds of those enrolled in higher education attended public institutions, especially the Central University in Quito.

The 1960s and 1970s saw a major expansion in educational opportunities at every level. Spending increased until by 1980 education represented one-third of total government outlays. Enrollments, which had begun to climb in the 1950s, continued their increase (see table 7, Appendix). Retention rates at the primary and secondary level also improved.

Expansion created its own set of problems, however. Construction failed to keep up with the increase in students. A significant proportion of teachers lacked full accreditation, especially at the levels of secondary and higher education. These deficiencies were most evident in the countryside, where the percentage of uncertified primary teachers was estimated to be double that of the cities. Finally, despite enrollment increases, by the 1980s the percentage of school-aged children attending school lagged (see fig. 10). Rates were particularly low for rural primary-school-aged children. Relatively few children continued beyond the first cycle of secondary school.

Illiteracy rates, especially those in the countryside, also remained elevated (see table 8, Appendix). The Ministry of Education and Culture, municipal governments, and the military all offered literacy classes (see Recruitment and Conditions of Service, ch. 5). Overall, the programs had limited impact, however; most of the decline in illiteracy came through increased school enrollments. In the 1980s, there were efforts to target literacy programs to the needs of the rural populace and non-Spanish speakers.

Health and Social Security

Both the public and the private sectors provided health services. Most public health care came under the aegis of the Ministry of Public Health, although the armed forces, the Ecuadorian Social Security Institute (Instituto Ecuatoriano de Seguridad Social— IESS), and a number of other autonomous agencies also contributed. The Ministry of Health covered about 80 percent of the population and IESS another 10 percent.

The Ministry of Public Health organized a four-tiered system of health care. Auxiliary health-care personnel staffed posts that served small rural settlements of fewer than 1,500 inhabitants. Health centers staffed with health-care professionals serviced communities of 1,500 to 5,000 inhabitants. Urban centers took care of the larger provincial capitals. Provincial and national hospitals were located in the largest cities. In the early 1980s, there were approximately 2,100 health establishments nationwide; the Ministry of Public Health ran more than half. Both the limited numbers of health-care professionals and their lack of training hampered public health care. These deficiencies were most apparent in regard to medical specialists, technicians, and nurses.

Infant mortality-rate estimates in the early 1980s ranged from 70 to 76 per 1,000 live births, with government projections of 63

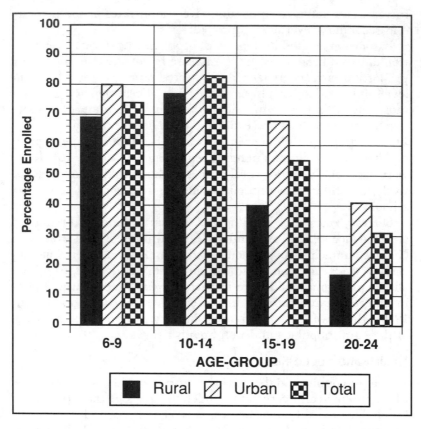

Source: Based on information from Ecuador, Instituto Nacional de Estadística y Censos, *IV Censo Nacional de Población y III de Vivienda, 1982—Resumen Nacional: Breve Análisis de los Resultados Definitivos,* Quito, 1985, 49.

Figure 10. Percentage of School-Aged Population Enrolled in School, Divided by Urban-Rural Residence, 1982

per 1,000 live births for the period 1985 to 1990. Although these rates were a significant improvement from the death figure of 140 recorded in 1950, they remained a serious concern. Infant mortality varied significantly by region and socioeconomic status. Surveys in urban areas showed a range of 5 to 108 infant deaths per 1,000 live births, whereas those in rural areas varied from 90 to 200. Intestinal ailments and respiratory diseases (including bronchitis, emphysema, asthma, and pneumonia) caused roughly three-fourths of all infant deaths.

Childhood mortality (deaths among one- to four-year-olds) dropped to 9 per 1,000 in the mid-1980s following immunization campaigns and some attempts to control diarrheal diseases. Acute respiratory infections represented one-third of all deaths in this age group. Further improvement in the childhood mortality rate demanded extending the immunization program, increasing the availability of oral rehydration therapy, improving nutrition, and controlling respiratory ailments.

Precise, detailed evidence about children's nutritional status remained limited and contradictory. The government conducted a national survey in 1959 and followed this with more limited studies in the late 1960s and 1970s. In the late 1960s, 40 percent of preschool children showed some degree of malnutrition. Among children under twelve years of age, 30 percent were malnourished and 15 percent anemic.

The main causes of death among adults in the mid-1980s were motor vehicle accidents, coronary heart disease, cerebrovascular disease, cancer, and tuberculosis. Maternal mortality remained high—1.8 per 100,000 live births in the mid-1980s. As with the case of infant mortality, maternal mortality national averages masked considerable regional variation, with the rate nearly three times higher in some areas. These higher percentages reflected the limited access many rural women had to health care. In the early 1980s, more than 40 percent of all pregnancies were not monitored; the majority of births were unattended by modern medical personnel.

A number of tropical diseases concerned health officials. Onchocerciasis (river blindness) was found in a number of small areas; its range was expanding in the mid-1980s. Although Chagas' disease (a parasitic infection) was not prevalent, environmental factors favored its spread. Leishmaniasis (also a parasitic infection) was expanding in the deforested areas of the coast and coastal tropical forest. Malaria was found in 60 percent of the country and became a major focus of public health efforts in the late 1980s. A drop in mosquito control programs coupled with severe flooding in 1981 and 1982 led to an increase in the prevalence of malaria in the mid-1980s. Between 1980 and 1984, the number of reported cases increased ten times. As of 1988, Ecuador also reported forty-five cases of, and twenty-six deaths from, acquired immune deficiency syndrome (AIDS).

The Ecuadorian Social Security Institute, an autonomous agency operating under the Ministry of Social Welfare, offered its members old-age, survivor, and invalidism benefits, sickness and maternity coverage, and work injury and unemployment benefits. In 1982, however, the system covered only approximately 23 percent of the economically active population (21 percent of men and 33 percent of women). Coverage varied widely according to urban or rural residence as well as sex. Urban women had the highest rates of coverage (42 percent), whereas rural men had the lowest (9 percent) (see table 9, Appendix). Employees in banking, industry, commerce, and government, and self-employed professionals had coverage for most benefits. Agricultural workers were covered for work injury and unemployment benefits and were gradually being included in pension funds and survivors' and death benefits.

*   *   *

Osvaldo Hurtado's *Political Power in Ecuador* describes the dynamics of Ecuadorian society from the colonial to the modern era. Norman E. Whitten, Jr.'s numerous studies offer a wealth of data concerning Costa blacks and Oriente Indians. Simon Commander and Peter Peek's "Oil, Exports, Agrarian Change, and the Rural Labor Process: The Ecuador Sierra in the 1970s" is an insightful analysis of social change in the Sierra. Frank Salomon, Peter C. Meier, Joseph B. Casagrande, and Wendy A. Weiss all describe the dynamics of ethnic relations. DeWight R. Middleton and Marilyn Silverman examine coastal society, especially the changes resulting from migration. Axel Kroeger and Françoise Varobora-Freedman, Mario Hiraoka, Shozo Yamamoto, and Michael J. Harner examine the indigenous peoples of the Oriente or the impact of colonization on that region. (For further information and complete citations, see Bibliography.)

Chapter 3. The Economy

Terra-cotta hunter (Jama-Coaque culture)

As THE 1980S DREW TO A CLOSE, Ecuador remained a lower middle-income nation with a gross domestic product (GDP—see Glossary) of US$9.4 billion, or US$940 per capita. In South America, only Peru, Bolivia, and Guyana had a lower per capita GDP. Agriculture (primarily bananas, coffee, and cocoa) and fishing were still important sectors of the economy, together providing 40 percent of export earnings in 1989. Petroleum, the other major export commodity, produced 50 percent of export earnings in the same year. Nevertheless, services, especially trade and financial services, constituted the fastest-growing economic sector and by the end of the 1980s employed almost half of the work force. Manufacturing also played a small but growing role in the economy.

Historically, Ecuador's economy has been characterized by the dichotomy, and sometimes bitter rivalry, between the large-scale, export-oriented agricultural enterprises of the Costa (coastal region) and the smaller farms and businesses of the Sierra (Andean highlands). Unlike many developing countries that have highly centralized infrastructures, Ecuador had two banking, communications, transportation, and trade centers—one in Guayaquil to handle the country's export trade and the other in Quito to serve the populace in the Sierra. Manufacturing was divided also, with Guayaquil leading Quito in output.

The discovery of substantial new petroleum deposits in 1967 spurred economic growth and a shift away from traditional agriculture to manufacturing and services. The government invested much of its petroleum revenue in domestic development programs. The rapid growth years in the 1970s were followed by hardship in the 1980s, however, as petroleum prices fell and the entire economy slumped.

Two administrations in the 1980s tried different approaches to restoring the economy. President León Febres Cordero Ribadeneyra (1984–88) applied free-market principles and deregulation, policies that initially promoted growth. Wage increases and high inflation, however, ultimately erased most gains. President Rodrigo Borja Cevallos (1988–) replaced the free-market approach with state intervention and imposed an austerity program. His policies resulted in new economic growth, but inflation and unemployment remained at record high levels.

Ecuador's chronically large foreign debt continued to stifle economic growth. Having borrowed heavily during the boom years of the 1970s, the government found itself unable to meet its foreign debt obligations at the end of the 1980s. An earthquake in 1987, which damaged the country's crude petroleum pipeline, further curtailed import earnings. Although by 1989 Ecuador had resumed its foreign debt payments and was again exporting oil, the nation's economic future remained uncertain.

Growth and Structure of the Economy

Colonial Ecuador was governed first by the Viceroyalty of Peru and then by the Viceroyalty of Nueva Granada (see Spanish Colonial Era, ch. 1). Ecuador differed significantly from the viceroyalty centers (Lima and Bogotá), however, in that mining never became a vital part of the economy. Instead, crop cultivation and livestock raising dominated the economy, especially in the Sierra. The Sierra's temperate climate was ideal for producing barley, wheat, and corn. The Costa became one of the world's leading producers of cocoa. Sugarcane, bananas, coconuts, tobacco, and cotton also were grown in the Costa for export purposes. Foreign commerce expanded gradually during the eighteenth century, but agricultural exports remained paramount. Manufacturing never became a significant economic activity in colonial Ecuador, but busy sweatshops, called *obrajes,* in Riobamba and Latacunga made Ecuador an exporter of woolen and cotton fabrics; a shipyard in Guayaquil was one of the largest and best in Spanish America; and sugar mills manufactured sugar, molasses, and rum made from molasses.

When Ecuador gained complete independence in 1830, it had a largely rural population of about one-half million. The rural economy came to rely on a system of peonage, in which Sierra and Costa Indians were allowed to settle on the lands belonging to the hacendado, to whom they paid rent in the form of labor and a share of their crop. The economy of the new republic, based on the cultivation of cash crops and inexpensive raw materials for the world market and dependent on peonage labor, changed little during the remainder of the nineteenth and first half of the twentieth century. Vulnerable to changing international market demands and price fluctuations, Ecuador's economy was often characterized by instability and malaise.

During the second half of the nineteenth century, cocoa production nearly tripled, and total exports increased tenfold (see The Era of Conservatism, 1860–95, ch. 1). As a result, the Costa became the country's center of economic activity. Guayaquil dominated banking, commercial, and export-import affairs. During the first two decades of the twentieth century, cocoa exports continued to be the mainstay of the economy and the principal source of foreign exchange, but other agricultural products like coffee and sugar and fish products were also important exports. The decline of the cocoa industry in the 1930s and 1940s, brought about by chronic pestilence and the loss of foreign markets to competitors, had debilitating repercussions for the entire economy. During the 1950s, government-sponsored replanting efforts contributed to a partial revival of the cocoa industry, so that by 1958 Ecuador was the world's sixth leading exporter of cocoa. Nonetheless, by the early 1950s bananas had replaced cocoa as the country's primary export crop.

The Ecuadorian economy made great strides after 1950, when annual exports, 90 percent of which were agricultural, were valued at less than US$30 million, and foreign-exchange reserves stood at about US$15 million. Between 1950 and 1970, a slow, steady expansion of nonagricultural activities took place, especially in the construction, utilities, and services sectors. Construction, for example, made up only 3 percent of the GDP in 1950, but it contributed 7.6 percent to the GDP in 1971. Agriculture's annual share of the GDP was 38.8 percent in 1950 compared with a 24.7 percent share in 1971 (see table 10, Appendix).

The 1960s saw an acceleration and diversification of the manufacturing sector to meet domestic demand, with an emphasis on intermediate inputs and consumer durable goods. By 1971 these accounted for about 50 percent of industrial output. Still, manufactured products—mainly processed agricultural goods—made up only about 10 percent of Ecuador's exports in 1971. Industry was still at an early stage of development, and about 50 percent of the labor force worked in agriculture, forestry, and fishing. Traditional industries, such as food processing, beverages, and textiles, were largely dependent on agriculture. The small size of the domestic market, the high production cost in relation to available external markets, and an undeveloped human, physical, and financial infrastructure all combined to limit the expansion of consumer durable goods in the Ecuadorian economy.

The discovery of new petroleum fields in the Oriente (eastern region) after 1967 transformed the country into a world producer of oil and brought large increases in government revenue beginning in 1972 (see Petroleum and Natural Gas, this ch.). That year saw the completion of the Trans-Ecuadorian Pipeline, a 503-kilometer-long oil pipeline leading from the Oriente to the port city of Esmeraldas (see fig. 11). A refinery also was constructed just south of Esmeraldas. In addition, in 1970 large quantities of natural gas deposits were discovered in the Gulf of Guayaquil.

105

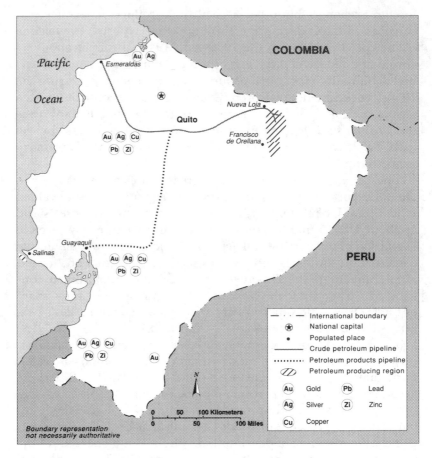

Source: Based on information from Orlando Martino, *Mineral Industries of Latin America,* Washington, 1988, 58.

Figure 11. Petroleum and Mineral Resources, 1988

Largely because of petroleum exports, Ecuador's net foreign-exchange earnings climbed from US$43 million in 1971 to over US$350 million in 1974.

The production and export of oil that began in the early 1970s, coupled with dramatic international price increases for petroleum, contributed significantly to unprecedented economic growth. Real GDP increased by an average of more than 9 percent per year during 1970 to 1977, as compared with only 5.9 percent from 1960 to 1970. The manufacturing sector alone experienced a 12.9 percent average annual GDP real growth rate during 1975–77. Ecuador became a lower middle-income country, although it remained one of the poorer countries of South America. Economic growth had negative side effects, however. Real imports increased by an annual average of 7 percent between 1974 and 1979; this spawned an inflationary pattern that eroded income. During the same period, the country's external debt grew from US$324 million to about US$4.5 billion.

Recent Economic Performance

In the early 1980s, the economy faltered as the international price of petroleum began a gradual decline and the country lost some foreign markets for its traditional agricultural products. Dramatic climatic changes caused by El Niño during 1982–83 produced coastal floods, torrential rains, and severe drought, which were highly damaging to crops and to the transportation and marketing infrastructures (see Return to Democratic Rule, 1979–84, ch. 1; Climate, ch. 2). The economy also began to feel the pinch of the country's growing external debt, which amounted to US$8.4 billion in 1984. Debt servicing in that year absorbed approximately 60 percent of the country's export earnings. Foreign sources of credit began to dry up as early as 1982, leaving the national government and hundreds of state-owned companies short of capital. Inflationary pressures mounted during the early 1980s; consumer prices, which rose 14 percent in 1980, increased by 25 percent in 1982 and by 53 percent in 1983 (see fig. 12).

In March 1983, the government, with an eye toward rescheduling the external debt, introduced several austerity measures, including a second devaluation of the sucre (S/; for value of the sucre—see Glossary) in two years, this time a 21-percent devaluation of the sucre, a 16-percent rise in the commercial interest rate, and a deceleration of government spending. The government's stabilization program, which included new exchange controls and the reduction of fuel and export subsidies, was unpopular domestically, but it enabled Ecuador to successfully negotiate a new debt repayment schedule with the International Monetary Fund (IMF—see Glossary), which also proved willing to grant Ecuador an additional US$107 million in financial assistance. The government, after several months of negotiation, also concluded multiyear rescheduling agreements with foreign private banks in December 1984 and with the Paris Club (a financial consortium of Western banks and governments) in April 1985. By successfully refinancing nearly all of the public-sector debt, the government narrowly avoided defaulting on payments, and, for the period 1985–89, the external debt-service ratio was reduced from 60 percent of export

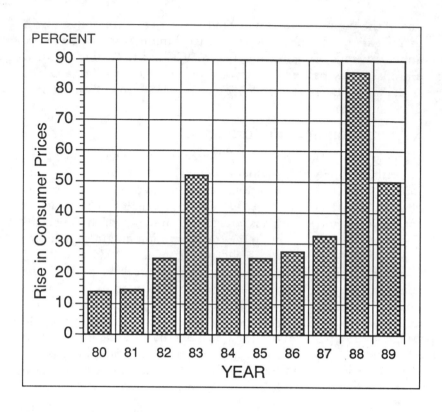

Figure 12. Rise in Consumer Prices, 1980–89

earnings to a manageable 30 percent. From 1985 until the beginning of 1987, Ecuador paid only the interest on its external debt (see External Debt, this ch.).

The Ecuadorian economy recovered during 1984, partly as a result of temporary stability in the international price of crude oil and partly because of a rebound in the agricultural sector. By late 1984, the balance-of-payments current account, which had reflected a US$58 million deficit in 1983, had a US$19 million credit, and the trade surplus reached US$1 billion. The real GDP growth rate was 4 percent, nearly a 7-percent increase over 1983. These improvements in the economy, combined with wage restraints and a tight national government budget, made it possible to reduce the inflation rate in 1984 to 25 percent; for the next two years, the inflation rate was contained at about 24 percent.

In 1985 Ecuador withdrew for one year from the Organization of Petroleum Exporting Countries (OPEC) in order to free itself

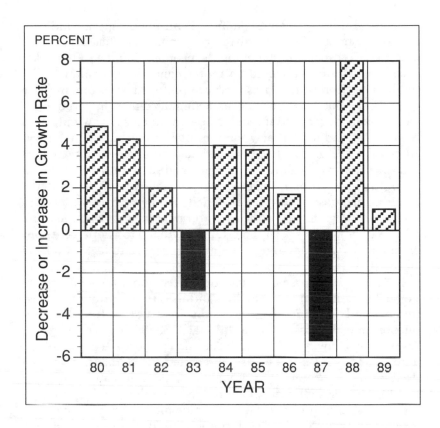

Figure 13. Real Gross Domestic Product (GDP) Growth Rate, 1980–89

from that organization's export quotas and thus increase oil export revenue. In 1984 petroleum had accounted for about 70 percent of all commodity exports and about 50 percent of the central government's revenues. In 1985 Ecuador earned over US$1.8 billion in revenue from petroleum exports, two-thirds of Ecuador's export revenue that year. But a sharp decline in international oil prices in 1986 resulted in a US$1.1-billion drop in petroleum export revenue. The balance-of-payments current account, which registered a surplus of US$149 million in 1985, showed a US$613-million deficit for 1986. Foreign-exchange reserves declined to US$145 million by mid-1986, and real GDP growth for 1986 came to only 1.7 percent, compared with 3.8 percent in 1985 (see fig. 13). To meet the economic crisis, in January 1987 the government suspended debt repayments to all private lending institutions and imposed a 25-percent surcharge on many imported items.

109

Febres Cordero had entered office promising prosperity and neo-liberal economic reforms featuring governmental efficiency, a free-enterprise approach in managing the economy, and a free-market exchange system that would promote economic deregulation. To fulfill these promises, Febres Cordero removed government price controls, devalued the currency, and eliminated most import quotas. In addition, he reduced import tariffs on industrial raw materials by one-half and invited new foreign investment into the country. Although GDP growth had bounced back from a negative 2.8 percent in 1983 to a healthy 4.0 percent in 1984 and 3.8 percent in 1985, the sharp drop in petroleum export revenue in 1986 and the resulting increase in the fiscal deficit, 81 percent of which was financed through foreign borrowing, brought the nation to the brink of an economic crisis. In 1986 GDP growth fell to 1.7 percent, unemployment went up, and per capita income fell to its lowest level since 1978.

In March 1987, an earthquake destroyed about forty kilometers of the Trans-Ecuadorian Pipeline and its pumping stations, causing a nearly six-month suspension in crude petroleum production and the loss of an additional US$700 million in export revenue. Meanwhile, revenue from other exports—cocoa, coffee, and shrimp—did not increase and failed to compensate for the decline in oil income. The Ecuadorian government acquired a World Bank (see Glossary) loan of US$80 million to help finance the reconstruction of the damaged pipeline, but repairs cost the government a total of US$150 million. GDP fell to –5.2 percent in 1987, inflation inched up to 32.5 percent, and the trade deficit stood at US$33 million. The government responded to its financial emergency by raising domestic gasoline prices by 80 percent and bus and taxi fares by 14 percent. To help make up for the oil revenue shortfall, a consortium of international banks loaned Ecuador an additional US$220 million, bringing public-sector external debt at the end of 1987 to about US$9.6 billion, one of the world's highest on a per-capita basis. (Ecuador's GDP for 1987 was US$10.6 billion.)

During Febres Cordero's last two years in office, his economic team concentrated on implementing monetary reforms, renegotiating the external debt, and encouraging foreign investment. Its efforts were only partially successful. The government failed to hold wages down, and, despite efforts to curtail government spending, public-sector expenditures increased dramatically in 1987 and in the first half of 1988. Ecuador's halting experiment with neoliberal economic measures unofficially came to a close on March 3, 1988, when Febres Cordero announced the end of the free-market foreign-exchange system (see Monetary and Exchange Rate Policies, this ch.). Two months later, on May 8, 1988, Febres Cordero's longtime rival, Rodrigo Borja of the Social Democratic party, the center-left Democratic Left (Izquierda Democrática—ID), was elected president with 46 percent of the vote (see Political Parties, ch. 4).

In contrast to Febres Cordero, Borja advocated an expanded state role in the national economy. During the campaign, he promised to promote industrialization and nontraditional exports and stressed the importance of agrarian reform. Borja, however, inherited a rapidly worsening economy as he assumed office on August 10, 1988; within a month he announced a national economic austerity program that included a sharp devaluation of the sucre, tax increases, new import restrictions, a reduction in public-sector spending, a 100-percent increase in fuel prices, and a 40-percent boost in electricity rates for private households. Borja also opened new negotiations with foreign creditors to whom Ecuador was in arrears for almost US$1 billion. The president, however, refused to lift the suspension of foreign debt payments, imposed by Febres Cordero in 1988, until April 1989 (see External Sector, this ch.).

Borja's austerity policies and the resulting climb in the unemployment rate to 13 percent by the end of 1988, the highest in ten years, spawned strikes by labor unions, public employees, and students. The government, however, continued its anti-inflationary program. Despite government cost-cutting efforts, inflation reached 86 percent in 1988, the highest in the country's history. On the positive side of the economic ledger, GDP expanded by 8 percent in 1988, as petroleum exports returned to pre earthquake levels.

In an attempt to blunt criticism of his policies, Borja introduced a new package of economic liberalization measures in 1989, including a relaxation of import restrictions, a further devaluation of the official exchange rate to prod exports, and a loosening of banking controls to stimulate the manufacturing sector. About 62 percent of the import items that had been barred since mid-1988 were to be allowed into the country beginning in 1990.

Role of Government

The Constitution reserves to the state the sole right to exploit natural resources and to create and maintain the basic national economic infrastructure. The central government traditionally handled this responsibility through a decentralized approach to economic development. Over the decades, the government formed numerous autonomous or independent agencies in an ad hoc fashion to perform public services or develop natural resources. Some of these independent enterprises became large and powerful and functioned largely beyond government control or monitoring.

Mismanagement and inefficiencies characterized many independent agencies. Petroecuador, for example, the largest and perhaps most important state-owned enterprise, which was responsible for much of Ecuador's petroleum production and refining, was not required to pay dividends or to meet established performance standards. Because it had no control over oil-generated income, Petroecuador lacked the incentive to keep production costs down or to improve efficiency. The Ecuadorian Institute of Electrification (Instituto Ecuatoriano de Electrificación—Inecel), which was founded in 1961 under the auspices of the Ministry of Energy and Mines, was unable to coordinate its major departments, or to set the rates charged to electricity consumers. As a result, Inecel relied on the government to meet operating costs. The Ecuadorian Institute of Telecommunications (Instituto Ecuatoriano de Telecomunicaciones—Ietel), established in 1972 and attached to the Ministry of Public Works and Communications, suffered from poor internal organization and weak financial management (see Natural Resources and Energy, this ch.).

The government's highly bureaucratic and decentralized approach to economic development thus served as a disincentive to entrepreneurs, who were forced to battle an array of regulations controlling business and commerce. Cumbersome administrative procedures often resulted in protracted and costly delays in such fundamental activities as procurement, business registration, and trade transactions.

Fiscal Policies

The Ecuadorian public sector, comprising the central government, state enterprises, and autonomous agencies operating on a national scale, expanded rapidly during 1972–77. Public-sector expenditures, adjusted for an average annual inflation rate of 14 percent, swelled about 65 percent during this period. Such increases were made possible because of the boost in revenue derived from a rise in international oil prices and the expansion of oil exports, especially during the 1972–74 period, when petroleum revenues rose as a proportion of GDP from 2 percent to 8.4 percent. Meanwhile, revenues from nonpetroleum commodity exports declined from 18.7 percent of GDP in 1972 to 13.8 percent in 1975. In effect, the government substituted the taxation of oil for the taxation of other traditional products.

This policy caused no harm until 1975, when the volume of petroleum exports began to moderate and oil revenues declined relative to GDP. As the gap between public revenues and expenditures widened, budget deficits became the norm, and the government resorted increasingly to foreign borrowing as a substitute for declining tax revenues from nonoil products. Between 1976 and 1979, the foreign debt more than quadrupled; after 1979 the rate of borrowing decelerated, but still the foreign debt had doubled by the end of 1986 (see fig. 14). In 1983, as foreign banks reduced the amount of credit available to the government, unpopular austerity measures were adopted to help reduce the public-sector deficit.

The oil bonanza encouraged the government to undertake two deficit-producing policies. First, the government used about 50 percent of total public revenues from oil exports to subsidize domestic consumption of such items as food products, electricity, and gasoline and other oil derivatives. Government subsidies to consumers reached a peak of 10 percent of GDP in 1981. Second, the government increased substantially its public-sector employment and public capital expenditures. Although the labor force increased at an average annual rate of only 2.8 percent between 1970 and 1984, public-service employment rose at an average annual rate of 7 percent during the same period. A moderate expansion in public capital expenditures during the 1974–82 period contributed to improvements in the transportation and utility infrastructure and also in water and sewerage systems. During this period, public capital spending increased from 7.3 percent of GDP to 10.1 percent of GDP. Overall government revenue, however, had declined by 1 percent of GDP between 1973 and 1982. The public-sector deficit in 1982 represented 7.5 percent of GDP, most of which was financed by foreign borrowing.

The sharp drop in the international price of petroleum in 1986, followed a year later by a US$700-million loss of oil revenue in the aftermath of the March 1987 earthquake, generated increased foreign borrowing by the government, reduced debt-service payments, and induced the government to print money to make up for revenue shortfalls. To help keep inflation down to 32.5 percent in 1987 (about a 5-percent increase over 1986), liquidity was restricted in the private sector by raising bank reserve requirements. This policy made it difficult to acquire a commercial loan during the second half of 1987.

Although oil production reached near-record levels of 310,000 barrels per day following the repair of the Trans-Ecuadorian Pipeline in August 1987, international crude oil prices remained low, averaging about US$17.70 for that year. The government's failure to raise domestic energy prices or reduce spending in other areas contributed to a fiscal deficit approaching 12 percent of GDP.

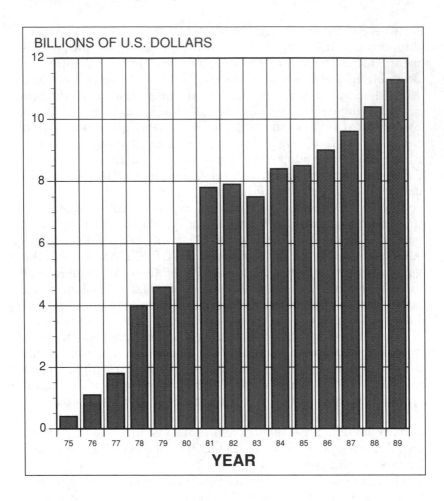

BILLIONS OF U.S. DOLLARS

Figure 14. Foreign Debt, 1975–89

Real GDP improved 8 percent in 1988, mainly as the result of increases in crude petroleum exports. The government's deficit reached about 12 percent of GDP. The government controlled the fiscal deficit by doubling domestic fuel prices, eliminating wheat import subsidies, and increasing electricity rates by 40 percent for household users and 60 percent for industrial users.

In 1989 the fiscal budget totalled US$1.4 billion, of which 49 percent was financed by oil export revenues and most of the remainder through taxes. About 38 percent of expenditures went to meet foreign debt payments after April, 10 percent for internal investment, and the balance to meet internal debt payments and current government expenditures. During 1989 the Borja administration accelerated efforts to curtail public spending, but the deficit, 10 percent of GDP, was still too high to be fiscally sound. The government continued its tight money policies, sustaining high interest rates and strict credit requirements, especially for noncorporate consumers.

Monetary and Exchange Rate Policies

The Monetary Board, created in 1948, formulated the government's monetary, credit, and public debt policies, including maintenance of a stable currency, management of the foreign-exchange reserves, control of import and export permits, and regulation of international transactions. The Central Bank of Ecuador was the official government bank, responsible for carrying out the policies of the Monetary Board and for supervising the activities of private banks (see Financial System, this ch.). The Central Bank also issued the sucre (S/), the Ecuadorian unit of currency. Notes were issued in denominations of 5, 10, 20, 50, 100, 500, and 1,000 sucres; copper-zinc coins in denominations of 5, 10, 20, and 50 centavos; and a pure nickel 1-sucre coin.

The official exchange rate was used for foreign debt repayment and import transactions. During the 1970s, the currency's exchange rate had remained fixed at S/25 = US$1. At the end of December 1983, after a series of currency adjustments, the rate stood at S/54 = US$1. The Febres Cordero administration quickened the pace of currency rate adjustments. In September 1984, Febres Cordero changed currency transactions from the official to the Central Bank intervention exchange rate. The official exchange rate was set at S/67 = US$1, or a 24-percent devaluation in comparison with the rate prevailing in December 1983. During 1985 the sucre depreciated a total of 19 percent. The shock of a US$15 per barrel drop in the value of Ecuadorian crude oil between December 1985 and April 1986 forced the government to devalue the currency another 14 percent in January; a rate of S/109 = US$1 held until July. This last devaluation was part of a reform package that included a 15-percent increase in prices paid to farmers and further reductions in import tariffs to discourage smuggling and thereby increase tariff revenues.

To help set the government's fiscal house in order and to help persuade foreign creditors to provide essential foreign exchange, in mid-1986 Febres Cordero ordered an across-the-board 5 percent spending cut. Febres Cordero, however, faced with a serious political setback to his party in midterm elections, lacked the will and support to fully implement planned austerity measures.

In August 1986, Febres Cordero decreed that all private-sector transactions would take place at the private free-market exchange rate used by the private sector for overseas trade. This action and the devaluation of the official sucre exchange rate produced a 35-percent decline in the value of the national currency. Monetary board officials took these measures to protect the country's diminishing dollar reserves and to boost nonoil exports by making them more competitive in price.

The lifting of foreign-exchange controls for private-sector imports in 1986 and the government's tightened monetary and credit policies resulted in a strong demand for dollars to finance imports. This pressure on the sucre led to an oscillating free-market exchange rate during 1987. By September 1987, the free-market rate had reached S/206 = US$1. Inflationary pressures also began to have a significant impact on the exchange rate. In 1987 the consumer price index showed a 32.5 percent inflation rate for that year, depreciating the value of the sucre by the end of the year to S/280 = US$1. Capital flight and inflationary pressures contributed significantly to the devaluation of the sucre by an additional 56 percent during the first half of 1988, from S/280 to S/550 = US$1.

In a last-ditch effort to improve his popularity and project a populist image, Febres Cordero increased government spending and allowed the Central Bank to loosen controls on public-sector financing during the final seven months of his administration. The monthly inflation rate averaged 7.16 percent in 1988, reflecting relaxed government credit policies as well as increased food prices brought on by a drought and by faulty agricultural policies during 1987. These policies included insufficient credit to farmers and price controls that dampened their incentive to plant.

As he prepared to assume the presidency in mid-1988, Borja unveiled an economic stabilization package of restrictive measures aimed at stimulating GDP growth, devaluing the sucre to control imports and save foreign-exchange earnings, and reducing the central government's fiscal deficit, which had reached 12 percent of GDP. Although the new president permitted price increases for some food items, he sought to keep monetary growth below the rate of inflation as a restraint on overall price increases. Interest rates were allowed to rise. In August the Central Bank initiated a gradual adjustment of the exchange rate, devaluing the currency by S/2.5 per week. In 1989 Borja's anti-inflationary policies had begun to pay off, even though the consumer price index increased from 58 percent in 1988 to 76 percent in 1989.

During 1988 the free-market value of the sucre fluctuated somewhat, ending the year at about S/500 = US$1. By year end 1989, however, the sucre traded at S/648 = US$1. Throughout 1989 the government maintained its contractive monetary policy to help control inflation and sought to narrow the gap between the official and free-market exchange rates. By December 1989, these policies had produced mixed results. The inflation rate dropped to an annual rate of 54 percent in December 1989, but real wages and salaries declined markedly, and the country's fiscal deficit climbed to 17 percent of GDP. Overall GDP growth in 1989 did not exceed 1 percent.

Government Budget Process

Ecuador had a complex and splintered budget process. Only about 65 percent of tax revenues were dedicated to financing the national budget. The remainder were earmarked for direct and automatic allocation to autonomous agencies, state enterprises, and local governments on a predetermined basis. Despite tax reform efforts in the 1980s, several funds continued outside the regular budget process. About 5 percent of income, for example, was designated for revenue sharing with 100 municipalities and 20 provincial governments. This system, which did not require recipients to justify their need for the automatically appropriated sums, reduced the amount of economic planning and fiscal control that could be exercised by policy makers. Not only did recipient agencies and local governments lack the incentive to be frugal, but the central government was left with inadequate funds to begin new programs or establish new agencies as needed.

With the national budget, preparations for current and for capital expenditures were each handled differently. The Ministry of Finance and Credit established current expenditures based on actual budgets from the previous year, allowing for increases needed to offset inflation. The National Development Council (Consejo Nacional de Desarrollo—Conade) formulated a budget proposal for all capital expenditures relying on project requests from public agencies, which was sent to the Ministry of Finance and Credit; a national budget plan was then drafted at the ministry and forwarded to the National Congress (Congreso Nacional—hereafter, Congress).

Authorization for both current and capital expenditures was complete when Congress passed the budget plan, but disbursements against authorizations were at the discretion of the Treasury. The Constitution requires each budget to be balanced, but throughout the 1980s deficits were the norm.

In 1987, of total government revenues, 65 percent was derived from taxes on income and capital gains, 13.7 percent from domestic taxes on goods and services, 17.3 percent from taxes on international trade and transactions, 2 percent from other taxes, and 2

117

percent from nontax revenues. Total revenues for that year represented about 18.5 percent of Ecuador's gross national product (GNP—see Glossary).

During the same year, of total government expenditures, 11.8 percent was earmarked for the military, 24.5 percent for education, 7.3 percent for health, 0.9 percent for housing and social security, 19.8 percent for economic services, and 35.7 percent for other purposes. Total expenditures represented 16.3 percent of GNP; the overall budget deficit represented 2.1 percent of GNP.

Human Resources and Income

Composition of Labor Force

In 1987 about 3.3 million people, or 33 percent of Ecuador's total population, were estimated to be economically active. The economically active population was almost evenly divided between the self-employed and wage earners. Agriculture remained the largest employer in 1987, but the previous fifteen years had seen the total percentage of the work force employed in this sector drop from almost half (46 percent) to just slightly over a third (35 percent) (see table 11, Appendix). The service sector experienced the largest growth, with the percentage of the work force employed in government and other services rising from 17 to 24 percent from 1974 to 1987. Manufacturing and commerce each employed about 10 percent of the economically active populace in 1987.

Although the percentage of the economically active population employed in manufacturing declined from 12 percent in 1974 to 11 percent in 1987, the percentage engaged in commerce rose from 10 percent to 12 percent over the same period. Artisan manufacturing, defined as firms employing up to thirteen workers, declined compared with larger-scale factory manufacturing. Employment in manufacturing also shifted to larger urban areas; in the late 1980s, over half of the labor force engaged in manufacturing was in the provinces that included Quito and Guayaquil.

In the late 1980s, analysts estimated the median age for the total labor force to be slightly under thirty. When broken down by sex, however, data showed that women in the work force tended to be younger. The median age for men alone was over thirty. Other employment statistics broken down by gender revealed a higher ratio of women employed in urban areas, whereas men had higher percentages of employment in rural districts.

Employment Indicators and Benefits

Figures for unemployment and underemployment varied and were considered unreliable, but analysts agreed that both problems increased during the 1980s. Unemployment in urban areas was officially estimated at 10.2 percent in 1987, up from about 6 percent in 1975. According to government statistics, underemployment climbed from 25 percent in 1975 to 40 to 50 percent in 1987. Underemployment in rural areas was particularly high and had proven an intractable problem.

The government set minimum wages and increased them frequently to keep abreast of inflation and devaluations of the currency. Minimum wages alone, however, did not accurately represent economic conditions of the average worker because Ecuadorian labor enjoyed an extensive system of mandatory fringe benefits. For example, the average wage earner was entitled to a yearly bonus equal to three months of his or her basic monthly wage and to a monthly cost-of-living and transportation allowance. Paid vacations, overtime pay, and severance pay were all obligatory. These and other supplements could raise a wage earner's average monthly income by as much as 70 percent over his or her basic wage. Workers also benefited from legislation making it difficult to fire employees.

Organized Labor

Because of the government's strong regulation of the economy and direct control over wages and prices, organized labor directed its challenges against the government rather than against the private sector. Even disputes between labor and government, however, lacked the acrimony or frequency found elsewhere in Latin America, largely because a succession of populist governments curried favor with low-income groups by conceding economic benefits and expanded worker rights. With little struggle, workers gained the right to organize, to strike and bargain collectively, to withhold union dues from paychecks, to work a forty-hour week, and to receive minimum wage and social security benefits. Thus, while the legal framework favored union development, government endorsement of benefits undercut the power of union leadership. High underemployment and rising unemployment in the 1980s also moderated aggressive bargaining (see Political Forces and Interest Groups, ch. 4).

Labor-government relations became more strained during the Febres Cordero presidency, however, because of that administration's free-market philosophy. Labor called two national strikes in 1987, a one-day stoppage on March 25 to protest rises in gasoline and transportation prices and a second strike on October 28 to demand the ouster of the minister of government and justice. The first stoppage was highly successful and showed an unprecedented degree of unity among Ecuador's divergent labor groups. The second, more political in nature instead of being focused on monetary issues, had much less impact on national activity.

In contrast to growing tension between organized labor and government, the number of conflicts and strikes centered on collective bargaining issues with the private sector declined during the 1980s. Analysts attributed the decline to the increasing reluctance of the average worker to risk his or her job in the face of rising unemployment and a deteriorating economy. The most serious strikes during this period involved work stoppages by public-sector employees, usually teachers or university personnel. Short strikes by petroleum workers and employees of the state electric utility also occurred.

Agriculture

Agriculture and fishing were the country's largest employers in the late 1980s, providing nearly half of all export earnings. Including livestock raising, forestry, and fishing, agriculture generated almost 16 percent of the GDP in 1986 and nearly 18 percent in 1987. The three principal export crops—bananas, coffee, and cocoa—alone accounted for 2.4 percent of the total GDP in 1986, while livestock raising contributed 5.3 percent of the GDP, and forestry and fishing contributed 1.1 and 1.9 percent, respectively.

Land Use and Tenure

Data on land use varied widely and were often considered by analysts as unreliable or at best an approximation of actual numbers. In the mid-1980s, for example, estimates of cropland ranged from 1.6 to 2.5 million hectares out of the total land area of 27.1 million hectares. Different sources put the amount of pastureland at 4.4 or 4.8 million hectares. Estimates for the total land area suitable for agriculture showed an even wider variation, from less than 50 percent to as high as 90 percent.

Over half of the cultivated land was in the Costa (coastal region), about a third in the Sierra, and the remainder dispersed throughout the Oriente region. The Costa, with the exception of the area near the Santa Elena Peninsula, had generally fertile land with a climate conducive to agriculture. Altitude, rainfall, and soil composition determined land use in the Sierra. The intermontane basins near Quito and farther south near Cuenca and Loja offered the most productive Sierra lands, whereas the basins surrounding Latacunga and Riobamba had dry and porous soil and the least fertile lands. Higher areas of the Sierra contained grasslands suitable only for grazing or cold-tolerant crops, such as potatoes.

A peasant family in the Sierra
Courtesy Inter-American Foundation (Miguel Sayago)

Modern land tenure patterns developed from Spanish colonial land systems. The Spanish encountered large native populations in the Sierra and established the *encomienda* system whereby the crown granted individual colonists rights to land and the Indians who lived there. This system gradually produced haciendas worked by a "captive" labor force composed of *huasipungueros* (see Spanish Colonial Era, ch. 1; Peasants, ch. 2). These *huasipungueros* worked without salary in return for the farming rights to *minifundios* (small plots) on the haciendas. In many cases, the *huasipungueros* were bought or sold with the hacienda. Large-scale agriculture developed later in the Costa, where farming for export used sharecroppers or paid labor to harvest crops. The monetary labor system that developed in the Costa began to compete with the feudal system of the Sierra for cheap labor.

Pressure to reform feudal agricultural practices came from abroad, from humanitarian and liberal elements within the country, and from large landowners in the Costa, who needed additional cheap labor. A land reform law enacted in 1964, the Land Reform, Idle Lands, and Settlement Act, outlawed the *huasipungo* system and also set up the Ecuadorian Institute of Agrarian Reform and Settlement (Instituto Ecuatoriano de Reforma Agraria y Colonización—IERAC) to administer the law and to expropriate idle arable land for redistribution to farmers. The law outlawed absentee ownership and limited the size of holdings to 800 hectares of arable land in the Sierra, 2,500 hectares of arable land in the Costa, and 1,000 hectares of pastureland in either region. The law also set the minimum amount of land to be granted in the redistribution at 4.8 hectares. Revisions of the law in the early 1970s required that all land with absentee landlords be sold to the tenants and that squatters be permitted to acquire title to land they had worked for three years.

Although IERAC made some progress initially, political opposition slowed implementation of the land reform act. IERAC received little government funding and was not permitted to actively encourage expropriation. Later amendments to the land reform act exempted all farms that were efficiently run. In addition, redistributed land was frequently poor or on mountainsides because the large landowners kept fertile valley lands for themselves. Except for a few showcase examples, farmers on *minifundios* received no government assistance or services to make the plots productive. In spite of these difficulties, however, by 1984 over 700,000 hectares had been distributed to 79,000 peasants.

Distribution of the land remained highly unequal. In 1982, 80 percent of the farms consisted of less than ten hectares; yet these small farms accounted for only 15 percent of the farmland. Five percent of the farms had more than fifty hectares, but these large farms represented over 55 percent of the land under cultivation. In addition, *minifundios* were more likely to be found in the Sierra in areas of poor soil or with poorer growing conditions than in other areas.

Agricultural censuses revealed that over three-quarters of the farms were worked by their owners. About 12 percent of the farms were occupied by families that did not hold title to the land but rented it, sometimes hiring additional laborers. Sharecroppers or communal farmers cultivated the remaining 7 percent.

Although intensely cultivated, *minifundios* in the Sierra could not sustain the region's occupants. Because of the higher wages for nonagricultural jobs, many farmers held unskilled jobs in the cities while family members stayed on the land to grow crops for home use or for sale (see Migration and Urbanization, ch. 2). A study in the late 1970s indicated that over half of small farm earnings came from off the farm.

Patterns of cultivation ranged from primitive to modern, with the more modern methods generally used in the Costa, where much of the production was geared for export. In 1982 Ecuador had fewer than 7,000 tractors in use. Ox-drawn plows were used on some farms, and digging sticks were used for cultivation on slopes. High prices limited the use of chemicals; manure was the common form of fertilizer in the Sierra, but farmers had increased the use of pesticides and fungicides.

Sizeable areas of land, estimated at over 320,000 hectares, were under irrigation using ditches dug by individual farmers, and about 40,000 hectares were irrigated under government-supported irrigation projects. State support for irrigation schemes began in 1944 with the creation of the Ecuadorian Institute of Hydraulic Resources (Instituto Ecuatoriano de Recursos Hidráulicos—Inerhi). Inerhi's largest project, inaugurated in 1970, brought water to 10,000 hectares of land in Pichincha Province.

Crops

A variety of temperature and rainfall patterns resulted in a diversity of tropical and temperate crops (see table 12, Appendix). Moderate or cool temperatures in highland areas allowed the cultivation of products usually associated with more northern latitudes. In the Costa, a warm climate, fertile soils, and proximity to ports led to large-scale production of such export crops as coffee, bananas, sugar, cocoa, palm oil, and rice. Smaller plots in the Sierra produced potatoes, corn, beans, wheat, barley, and tea. Larger farms practiced dairy farming as well as increasing production of nontraditional crops such as cut flowers, asparagus, and snow peas. Farmers planted some coffee and tea in transition areas between the Sierra and the Oriente, but in general the Oriente's poor soil made it badly suited to agriculture.

Ecuador began marketing bananas abroad after World War II. By 1947 bananas had become the country's leading export crop. Capitalizing on problems with hurricanes, disease, and labor unrest in the traditional banana-growing regions of Central America, Ecuador emerged as the world's largest exporter of bananas by the mid-1980s. The main banana-producing areas were the eastern parts of Los Ríos, Guayas, and especially El Oro provinces. Banana production involved few very large or very small plantations; most ranged from 80 to 120 hectares.

In 1969 the Ecuadorian National Board of Planning and Economic Coordination recommended that land devoted to banana cultivation be more than halved and that the higher yielding, disease-resistant Cavendish-type bananas replace the traditional Gros Michel variety. This latter change prompted modifications in production patterns. Cavendish bananas bruise easily and require more careful handling. In addition, they cannot tolerate

123

transport in open trucks, so boxing must take place at the plantation. Centralized, specialized packing meant the end of small-farm production. Since the new variety had triple the yield of the Gros Michel banana, the government realized that the hectares planted in bananas needed to be reduced to avoid a sharp drop in world prices. Statistics showed the change: land devoted to bananas dropped from 200,000 hectares in 1972 to about 110,000 in 1980, yet production remained fairly constant. In 1987, 2.4 million tons of bananas were produced on 120,000 hectares of land; 1.4 million tons were exported.

Coffee, introduced into the country early in the nineteenth century, was the second most valuable crop throughout the 1980s. Ecuador produced both arabica and robusta varieties, with over half of the plantings in the hilly areas of Manabí Province; most of the remaining plantings were found in the western foothills of the Andes south of Guayaquil. In 1987 over 380,000 hectares were devoted to coffee, and 373,000 tons were produced. Most of this coffee was exported. Coffee was generally grown on small landholdings with about half the land planted in coffee trees alone and the rest planted with coffee trees mixed with cacao, citrus fruits, bananas, or mangoes.

The small size of typical coffee farms usually resulted in poor production techniques, yields, and quality. Much of the coffee produced retained the pulp after processing and therefore brought a lower price on world markets. Other than establishing minimum prices for coffee, the government provided little technical assistance to coffee farmers.

Cocoa was the mainstay of the economy in colonial times. The Spanish found the Indians cultivating cocoa when they arrived in the sixteenth century, and it first became an export crop in 1740. Produced on large Costa plantations, the crop was nearly wiped out by a fungal disease in the 1920s. Low world prices during the Great Depression further discouraged production, and the plantations were broken up and diversified into rice, sugar, corn, and bananas. After World War II, increased prices and new disease-resistant strains revitalized the industry.

Most cocoa production took place on small farms, frequently only to provide supplemental income to the farmer. Most small producers preferred traditional cultivation techniques and did not harvest the beans in years when the price was low. In contrast, the few large plantation owners systematically replaced older trees with newer disease-resistant varieties and used fertilizer to increase yields. Most cocoa farmers grew an aromatic variety used for flavoring. In 1987, 311,000 hectares produced 57,000 tons of cocoa beans.

Cutting sugarcane
Courtesy World Bank

Field worker in
a banana orchard
Courtesy World Bank

125

Sugarcane was grown widely, both in the Sierra and in the Costa. Over 44,000 hectares were planted in 1987, producing 3 million tons of sugarcane. The sugar extraction rate from the cane was about 10 kilograms of sugar from 100 kilograms of cane. Sugar was an important export crop in the 1960s and 1970s, but production levels dropped in the 1980s, and the supply could not satisfy the domestic market, so that Ecuador had to import refined sugar.

Almost all of the sugarcane grown in the Costa was used to make centrifugal sugar, so called because of the means of extracting the sugar. Centrifugal sugar was the type most used in foreign trade. Sugarcane in the Costa was grown on large plantations and processed in one of the five mills located east of Guayaquil. Sierra peasants grew sugarcane on small landholdings and used much of the cane for noncentrifugal sugar, mainly in a form known as *panela* (a raw brown-sugar cake). Growers also marketed molasses, a sugarcane by-product, exporting some of it and using the rest for the domestic manufacture of alcohol or for livestock feed.

Farmers cultivated rice, a staple of the Ecuadorian diet, mainly on the flood plains of the Guayas River Basin in Guayas and Los Ríos provinces. Rice production fluctuated depending upon the weather, but during the 1980s the harvest increased by an annual average of 7 percent. In 1987, 780,000 tons were produced on 276,000 hectares of land. In years of good harvest, growers produced enough rice to meet domestic demand and to export a surplus. Because of low international market prices for rice, however, the government policy stabilized rice production at the level required to meet domestic needs.

Corn, another basic foodstuff, had been grown since precolonial times. Corn was widely grown throughout the country and could be planted from sea level to an altitude of 2,200 meters. Farmers used about half the crop for animal feed, particularly for poultry. In 1987 over 422,000 tons were produced on 460,000 hectares.

Barley, a crop introduced by the Spaniards, proved highly adaptable to the rigorous climate of the Sierra. Its tolerance for cold and severe weather allowed it to be grown at higher altitudes than corn. Widely planted on small landholdings in the central highlands areas, it was grown both for food and for malt for the beer industry. Figures for 1987 showed 43,000 tons produced on 61,000 hectares.

Wheat, almost all of which was used to make bread, was formerly widely grown in the Sierra. Ironically, however, as bread increased in popularity and replaced potatoes and corn as a dietary staple, domestic wheat production decreased. Perhaps the most significant reason was that the government introduced subsidies on wheat imports in order to ease the effects of the inflation that

*Irrigated fields in
Imbabura Province
Courtesy Patricia Mothes*

began in the oil-boom years of the 1970s. As a result, consumption of the more expensive domestic wheat declined from 46 percent in 1946 to 7 percent in 1980. The breakup of the large wheat-producing haciendas in the Sierra also contributed to lower levels of wheat production.

Cotton and hemp were the principal fiber crops. The government carried out a program in the 1980s to increase both the quality and quantity of cotton produced. Output increased, and by 1986 Ecuador was nearly self-sufficient in cotton. Hemp was turned into Manila hemp fiber used to produce tea bags. Lesser fiber crops included aloe, which was used to make cloth for sacks, and ramie, which was woven into a cloth resembling linen.

Tea was produced near Puyo on the eastern slopes of the Andes at elevations of about 1,000 meters. An even distribution of rainfall allowed for year-round harvests, a condition not usually found in tea-producing nations.

African palms were widely planted and were the main source of vegetable oil. The government promoted and financed large plantings to cut imports of expensive cooking oils. Although not as high in oil content as the nuts of the royal palm, previously the principal domestic source of vegetable oil, African palms bore more nuts and matured more quickly.

Cottonseed, sesame seed, peanuts, coconuts, and soybeans were other sources of vegetable oils. Cottonseed production fluctuated,

127

depending upon weather conditions. Sesame could be planted from two to three times a year on the warm coastal plains where it took only three months to mature. About 9,000 hectares of peanuts were planted, but most of the production was used for direct consumption as peanuts rather than for crushing into oil. Production of coconut oil varied because most coconuts were consumed directly and not processed. Soybean plantings had increased, and soybeans could be grown both in the Costa and lower reaches of the Sierra.

Ecuador was one of the world's major castor bean producers. Although the bean was inedible, its oil was used for medicinal purposes and as a lubricant in precision tools. The plant could be grown on dry lands where it was uneconomical to raise other crops, or planted along with corn, peanuts, or cotton.

Black tobacco, Ecuador's traditional type, made up the bulk of the 3,600 tons grown in 1987. Blond tobacco for cigarettes was introduced in the late 1960s and was produced mainly in Loja Province. The growth of a domestic cigarette industry was slowed, however, by the high volume of cigarettes smuggled into the country.

Farmers also grew numerous minor crops for domestic food consumption or for export in small quantities. Growers raised pears, peaches, apples, berries, grapes, and plums in the Sierra and citrus fruit, avocados, mangoes, and a wide variety of tropical fruits in the Costa. Important vegetable crops included garlic, onions, cabbage, lettuce, cucumbers, tomatoes, and various types of melons and peppers. Spices included annatto seed, anise, and cardamon. Rubber and *mocora* and *toquilla* grass, used to make Panama hats, were minor nonfood crops.

Livestock and Poultry

Livestock raising represented an important part of agricultural output and grew significantly throughout the 1980s. Livestock was produced primarily for domestic consumption and was one of the few agricultural products found throughout the country. Although animal husbandry was widespread, it was generally practiced on small plots of land.

The Costa and Oriente produced mainly beef cattle with dairy cattle found mostly in the Sierra. Cattle were grazed on Costa land otherwise unsuited for agriculture, such as the hilly terrain in Manabí Province, seasonally flooded river plains, or semiarid parts of the far south. Dairy production in the Sierra typically was carried on in fertile valleys, particularly between Riobamba and the Colombian border. Beef cattle were fairly new to the Oriente, although large parcels of land were suitable for grazing. The beef industry in the Oriente suffered a serious setback in 1987, however, when the earthquake damaged roads used to transport the beef to markets. Ecuador had about 3.7 million head of beef cattle in 1986.

The 1980s saw an improvement in stock with the introduction of European and Asian breeds. The native criollo breed represented about half of all cattle, with the rest a cross between criollo and Holstein, Brown Swiss, or Jersey for dairy, and criollo and Santa Gertrudis or Charolais for beef. The absence of veterinarians and medicines remained a problem, however, and diseases and parasites plagued many herds.

Besides cattle, livestock included pigs, sheep, and a small number of goats. The number of pigs increased dramatically in the 1980s to about 5 million in 1986; they were raised nationwide, but the greatest concentration was in coastal areas. Sheep numbered 2 million in 1986 and were generally found in pastureland higher than 3,000 meters in altitude. Analysts estimated that Ecuador had fewer than 300,000 goats in 1986.

Poultry raising was another rapid-growth area in the 1980s, although floods in 1983 from El Niño caused a sharp drop in production. Chickens were raised both for eggs and for meat, and in 1986 there were more than 45 million birds. Historically, peasant families raised chickens, but the 1980s saw the establishment of large-scale poultry enterprises near larger cities.

Fishing

The Pacific waters along the coast and as far west as the Galápagos Islands had abundant and varied fish resources. The importance of marine resources to the economy increased steadily, and fisheries were one of the faster-growing industries in the 1980s, as both export sales and domestic consumption increased.

Tuna represented the most important of the many varieties of saltwater fish. Most of the tuna caught was skipjack or albacore, although the yellowfin was the variety most often exported. Ecuador modernized its tuna fleet in the late 1980s with the addition of refrigerated vessels and the leasing of several large seiners (nets) from the United States.

Shrimp production was the strongest growth area in the fishing industry. Although ocean shrimping declined, Ecuador's warm climate and shallow coastal waters, especially in the Gulf of Guayaquil, provided ideal conditions for shrimp farming. In 1986 Ecuador overtook Mexico as the world's largest shrimp exporter.

Other important fish included sardines, anchovies, and mackerel. Most of the anchovies and sardines were canned for the export market, with the remainder ground into fishmeal for poultry feed. Except for a few trout hatcheries in the Sierra, the country gave little attention to freshwater fish.

Forestry

An estimated 50 percent of Ecuador (about 14 million hectares) was forested, about half of this in government-owned lands. Although officially contributing only 4 percent to Ecuador's GDP, the forest resources were important because of wood's wide use for fuel and rural construction. Erosion and deforestation from widespread cutting of timber for fuel had emerged as significant national problems in the 1980s.

The original forests in the Sierra had long ago been cleared to provide space for pastures and wood for fuel and construction. Eucalyptus trees introduced from Australia in the 1800s supplied the Sierra with fuel and construction material and helped prevent soil erosion. In the 1980s, the northern province of Esmeraldas contained most of the forests in the Costa and supplied the majority of the country's wood. The jungles of the Oriente contained several thousand known species of trees, the most valuable of which was the balsa. Isolation from population centers and lack of roads hampered exploitation of the Oriente's resources, however. Other forest products included cinchona bark for quinine, ivory palm nuts for buttons, and kapok from the ceiba tree for mattress stuffing.

Natural Resources and Energy

The natural resource sector of the Ecuadorian economy contributed almost 15 percent to the GDP in 1986, with the petroleum industry providing virtually all of that total. Although analysts believed that Ecuador had numerous mineral deposits, few metals had been exploited. Hydroelectric power from several large dams provided the primary source of energy.

Petroleum and Natural Gas

Petroleum was the single most important element in the Ecuadorian economy, accounting for over 14 percent of the GDP in 1986, two-thirds of all export revenues in that year, and much of the foreign investment. In 1987 petroleum and mining together accounted for only about 8 percent of GDP because of a significant drop in petroleum production, but estimates for 1988 indicated that petroleum production had risen, exceeding its 1986 level. Although Ecuador's level of production in the late 1980s ranked near the bottom of the thirteen members of OPEC, it exceeded all countries in Latin America except Mexico and Venezuela.

A fishing village in Esmeraldas Province
Courtesy Inter-American Foundation (Miguel Sayago)

Petroleum was first discovered in the early 1900s both on and offshore from Salinas on the Santa Elena Peninsula west of Guayaquil. More than 100 million barrels of crude petroleum were removed in six decades of exploitation; by the mid-1980s, however, Costa production had fallen to less than 1,000 barrels per day (bd). Old, expensive-to-maintain equipment produced high operating costs, making continued exploitation uncertain.

The Oriente, however, had long since eclipsed the Costa as the center of Ecuador's petroleum activity. In the late 1980s, the vast majority of Ecuador's 1.6 million barrels of proven reserves lay in the northern part of the Oriente, between the Napo River and the Colombian border (see fig. 11). This area formed part of a rich oil-bearing region extending from southern Colombia through Ecuador and northeastern Peru. Indeed, analysts believed that this region represented one of the richest oil-bearing areas of the Western Hemisphere.

Although exploration in the Oriente began in the 1920s, petroleum was not actually found until a consortium formed by the Texaco Petroleum and Gulf Oil companies discovered several rich fields near Lago Agrio (now Nueva Loja) in 1967. The success of the Texaco-Gulf exploration attracted other companies, and over

131

the next two decades more than fifty new wells began producing commercial quantities of crude petroleum. Production in 1989 had risen to over 1.1 billion barrels, over 99 percent from the Oriente fields (see table 13, Appendix).

Ecuador built the 503-kilometer Trans-Ecuadorian Pipeline to carry crude petroleum from the Oriente fields across the Andes to a new refinery just south of Esmeraldas. Although the pipeline was designed to carry as much as 400,000 bd, volume averaged just over 300,000 bd in the late 1980s. A landslide caused by a severe earthquake in March 1987 destroyed forty kilometers of an above-ground section east of Quito. To keep exports from stopping completely, Ecuador quickly constructed a thirty-eight-kilometer spur from the Oriente fields to Colombia's pipeline. Oil was then either exported directly as crude from Colombian ports or taken by tanker from Colombia to Ecuador's largest refinery at Esmeraldas. Although this stopgap measure allowed for some petroleum to be exported, production at the Oriente fields had to be trimmed by more than half for the five months it took to repair the Trans-Ecuadorian Pipeline.

Unlike many of the larger OPEC countries, Ecuador refined less than half of the petroleum it produced. Most of the country's 123,000 bd refining capacity was located at two refinery complexes, one at Esmeraldas and a complex of three refineries at the Santa Elena oil fields. The Esmeraldas refinery had a 90,000 bd capacity, whereas the three older Santa Elena refineries had a combined output of 32,000 bd. Ecuador's newest refinery, completed in 1987 near Nueva Loja in the Oriente fields, had a capacity of 1,000 bd.

Control and ownership of petroleum production and refining was held by foreign oil companies, the government-owned Petroecuador which replaced the former Ecuadorian State Petroleum Corporation (Corporación Estatal Petrolera Ecuatoriana—CEPE), or consortia composed of both. Petroecuador assumed complete control of the Trans-Ecuadorian Pipeline in 1989 and announced it would take over most other foreign interests in the petroleum industry in the early 1990s.

In addition to abundant supplies of petroleum, observers estimated that the country had natural gas reserves in the Oriente and offshore in the Gulf of Guayaquil totalling 400 billion cubic meters. Reserves in the Oriente were collocated with petroleum deposits. Producers flared most of the gas associated with petroleum drilling, using only small amounts as fuel. Distance from markets made exploitation of the gas uneconomical, although a small plant to harness the gas as a fuel was completed near Nueva Loja in the mid-1980s. Reserves in the Gulf of Guayaquil, thought to be among the largest in Latin America, remained unexploited because of an uncertain domestic market for natural gas and a legal dispute between the government and foreign companies over ownership.

Mining and Minerals

Mining played a small role in the economy in the 1980s, contributing only 0.7 percent to the GDP in 1986 and employing about 7,000 persons. Inaccessibility of the regions where minerals were located and the incomplete exploration of resources hampered mining activities. Although observers believed that Ecuador had reserves of gold, silver, copper, zinc, uranium, lead, sulfur, and kaolin, as well as limestone, the latter dominated the industry. Miners generally produced limestone in many small operations countrywide and used it in local cement plants.

Gold, largely forgotten since its early exploitation in the sixteenth century, grew in importance in the 1980s; by 1987 Ecuador was exporting 2.4 tons per year. The southern Sierra region held the country's largest deposits; the newest veins were discovered in the southeastern province of Zamora-Chinchipe.

In 1985 Congress passed a new law to encourage foreign exploration and investment in the mining industry. Designed to simplify regulation of the industry, this legislation also offered higher financial incentives for the investor and lower overall taxation and established the Ecuadorian Institute of Minerals (Instituto Ecuatoriano de Minería—Incmin) under the Ministry of Energy and Mines.

Electric Power

The period from 1976 to 1985 saw a rapid rise in the demand for electricity and in the construction of generating facilities. During the same period, the country switched from primarily oil-fired thermal plants to hydroelectric-power generation. In 1986 total generating capacity reached 1,802 megawatts, and the country produced 5,202 gigawatt-hours of electricity. Although Ecuador had a larger generating capacity from thermal plants than from hydroelectric facilities, 70 percent of the electricity produced in 1986 came from hydroelectric sources because many of the thermal plants sat idle or underutilized. Completion of three new hydroelectric complexes under construction in the late 1980s was expected to allow complete dependence on hydroelectric sources by 1992.

The Amaluza complex on the Paute River near Cuenca offered Ecuador's largest single source of power. Current from this complex was carried to Guayaquil and to Quito via a 230-kilovolt transmission line. Disruptions of these lines caused occasional blackouts, and to provide for alternate routing, a second 230-kilovolt line was completed in 1988. Expansion of the grid continued throughout the early 1980s, until by 1984 more than half the households nationwide had access to electricity. Access for urban households considerably exceeded that for rural dwellings, however.

A government agency, the Ecuadorian Institute of Electrification (Instituto Ecuatoriano de Electrificación—Inecel), functioned as the nation's generation and transmission company. Inecel in turn sold electricity to local distribution companies over which it exercised some control through majority ownership of their stock.

Manufacturing

Industrialization occurred later in Ecuador than in most other Latin American countries. As late as 1960, the small industrial sector consisted almost entirely of textile production, food processing, and artisan activity. Manufacturing began to develop in the mid-1960s, and during the 1970s, spurred by petroleum revenues and exports to other nations in the Andean Common Market (Ancom; also known as the Andean Pact), manufacturing became the most dynamic sector of the economy. Manufacturing stagnated in the 1980s, however, with an average annual growth of only 0.8 percent for the period 1981–87. In 1987 it accounted for over 17 percent of the GDP.

Food processing and textile manufacturing accounted for almost 60 percent of the total value of manufacturing in 1986. Nonmetallic minerals and metals comprised 12 percent of the total value; all other industries accounted for the balance (see table 14, Appendix).

Most industrial establishments were small and barely more than handicraft operations. A government industrial census in the early 1980s listed more than 35,000 firms, but only 28 of these had more than 500 employees; more than 31,000 had from 1 to 4 workers. Individual proprietors owned and managed most firms. Shoemaking shops, woodworkers, or furniture makers represented nearly half of the establishments listed in the census.

Guayaquil was the most important industrial center, followed by Quito. Together the two cities accounted for about two-thirds of total factory employment. Agricultural and beverage processing plants, sawmills, shipyards, iron foundries, and cement and chemical plants were Guayaquil's main industries. Textile production and food processing topped the list of industrial activities in Quito. The government had made an attempt in the early 1970s to disperse industrial activity by promoting industrial parks in other cities, with some success.

Workers in a cooperative in Chimborazo Province
Courtesy Inter-American Foundation (Miguel Sayago)
Sewing children's clothes in a small shop in Guayaquil
Courtesy Inter-American Foundation (Miguel Sayago)

Sugar refining, rice milling, and flour milling were among the largest sectors in the food-processing industry. Two sugar mills dominated the industry and processed most of the sugar used domestically. Rice milling was concentrated in the Costa and consisted of numerous publicly owned mills, as well as many smaller private ones. Most flour mills were located near larger cities in the Sierra and used locally grown wheat; the three large flour mills near Guayaquil used mainly imported wheat. Ecuador also had a large baking industry, and nearly all cities had commercial bakeries producing bread and cakes.

The textile industry, which ranked next to food processing in value of production, was concentrated in the Sierra, where it originated as an outgrowth of home weaving. Most textile plants remained small, although one Quito firm was among the largest employers in the country.

The construction industry showed a steady decline during the 1980s and accounted for only about 4 percent of the GDP in 1987. Because over 95 percent of the construction in Ecuador resulted from government-financed projects, the industry remained highly vulnerable to periods of austerity in government spending. Indeed, the sector's only growth year in the decade of the 1980s occurred in 1987, reflecting large-scale highway rebuilding after the earthquake. High interest rates and a shortage of cement also hampered construction projects.

Artisan activity constituted a large part of the manufacturing labor force. Although many of the artisans had considerable skills in such occupations as weaving, their wages were among the lowest in the labor force, and as machine-weaving became more widespread their skills were increasingly obsolete. In the 1980s, the government offered special credits and loans to encourage a transition from artisan workshops to small factories.

The largest number of artisans produced clothing and furniture. This group included dressmakers, tailors, shoemakers, cabinetmakers, and carpenters. Several thousand additional artisans were goldsmiths or silversmiths.

Services

The service sector constituted the largest component of the Ecuadorian economy, accounting for almost 50 percent of the GDP in 1987. The largest parts of the service sector were wholesale and retail trade at 29 percent, financial services at 23 percent, and transportation and communications at 15 percent of services. Although contributing half the nation's wealth, financial services were inadequate, and the communication and transportation networks remained underdeveloped.

Financial System

The country's modern finance and banking system began in 1948 with the establishment of the Central Bank. The Law of the Monetary System of 1961 defined the functions of the Central Bank, which included issuing and stabilizing the national currency, providing credit to the private sector, managing foreign-exchange reserves, controlling import-export permits, carrying out the Monetary Board's policies, supervising private banks, and regulating international financial transactions. The bank also maintained a check clearinghouse, rediscounted and made advances to commercial banks, and published economic data.

In 1989 the structure of the banking system resembled a three-tiered pyramid with the Monetary Board at the apex. The Bank Superintendency and the Central Bank occupied the next tier and lent funds to four state-owned financial institutions. At the bottom came the commercial banks, savings and loan associations, and finance companies, which operated at the local level.

The Monetary Board regulated the entire banking and credit system, including the Central Bank. In the 1980s, the board's eleven members included the chairman, appointed by the president of Ecuador, and the ministers of finance and credit; agriculture and livestock; energy and mines; and industry, commerce, integration, and fishing. Also included were the president of the National Planning Board, two representatives of national chamber of commerce organizations, a representative of the commercial banks, the general manager of the Central Bank, and the head of the Bank Superintendency. The Monetary Board's functions included formulating the country's economic policy; determining interest rates; and setting Central Bank credit levels, minimum reserve requirements, and exchange rates.

The Bank Superintendency supervised and controlled banks, finance companies, and insurance companies. The Congress appointed the head or superintendent from three candidates proposed by the president. Funded by compulsory contributions from the financial institutions under its control, the Bank Superintendency also collected and published banking statistics.

The national government and the private banks jointly owned the Central Bank and tasked it with carrying out the policies of the Monetary Board and for supervising the activities of private banks. All private banks in Ecuador were required to invest at least

5 percent of their capital and reserves in the Central Bank, and together they owned the majority of shares in the Central Bank. Headquartered in Quito, the Central Bank had sixteen branches in other cities and towns in the late 1980s.

The four major government-owned financial institutions were the National Development Bank (Banco Nacional de Fomento— BNF); the Securities Commission-National Financial Corporation (Comisión de Valores-Corporación Financiera Nacional—CV– CFN), more commonly known as the National Financial Corporation (Corporación Financiera Nacional—CFN); the Ecuadorian Housing Bank (Banco Ecuatoriano de la Vivienda—BEV); and the Development Bank of Ecuador (Banco de Desarrollo de Ecuador—Bede), formerly known as the Cooperatives Bank of Ecuador. Each institution had a specialized role: the BNF provided loans for agriculture and industry, the CFN lent capital to industries utilizing local raw materials or making handicrafts, the BEV promoted low-income housing, and the Bede lent funds to local credit cooperatives, especially those in rural areas.

The thirty-one commercial banks were the most important financial institutions in the country, attracting the major portion of deposits and making the largest percentage of total loans in the banking system. Only four of the commercial banks were foreign: the United Holland Bank from the Netherlands, Citibank and the Bank of America from the United States, and Lloyd's Bank from Britain, formerly known as the Bank of London and South America. In 1986 the Bank of Pichincha, Pacific Bank, Philanthropic Bank, People's Bank, and Continental were the five largest locally owned commercial banks.

Several other types of private financial institutions existed in 1988. Eleven savings and loan associations, 26 finance companies, 123 cooperative savings institutions, and 4 credit card companies provided various forms of financing or credit. The Ecuadorian Development Finance Company (Compañía Financiera Ecuatoriana de Desarrollo—Cofiec) was founded in 1966 by local and foreign commercial banks, local businessmen, several international finance firms, and the CFN. Cofiec was an important source of funds to private industry, both in the form of loans and in equity investment.

Two stock exchanges operated, one each in Quito and Guayaquil. Although the Quito exchange handled almost twice as many transactions as the Guayaquil exchange in 1986, neither was large. The great majority of trading occurred in government issues and mortgage bonds, with only a small amount of trading in common stocks or other securities. Most Ecuadorian businesses were owned by small numbers of individuals, and few resorted to public financing to raise capital.

Tourism

In contrast to many other Latin American countries, Ecuador had a small tourist industry, and it played only a minor role in the economy in the 1980s. In 1985 approximately 250,000 tourists visited Ecuador and contributed over US$200 million to the economy. Colombia was the source of 36 percent of the visitors, followed by the United States with 21 percent and Western Europe with 18 percent. Ecuador did not include brief cross-border visits in official tourist statistics, so these figures do not include the many Colombian visitors who were only on short shopping trips, taking advantage of the generally lower prices in Ecuador.

The government provided limited support of tourism, and many colonial towns, ancient ruins, and areas of natural beauty were undeveloped because of lack of promotion or inadequate infrastructure for visitors. The most popular tourist destination in the 1980s was the Galápagos Islands, but concerns over the delicate and unique environment limited large-scale tourism there. The National Directorate of Tourism was attempting to broaden the tourist destinations available.

Communications

Although the system underwent expansion and modernization in the 1970s and 1980s, telecommunications remained underdeveloped with most facilities located in Quito or Guayaquil. The media and broadcast facilities likewise remained concentrated in the country's two main urban areas and often displayed regional rivalries or biases in their coverage. Foreign television, motion pictures, and books dominated the entertainment and publishing arena.

Despite improvements beginning in 1970, the telephone system still failed to provide adequate service to most customers, and facilities remained concentrated in Quito and Guayaquil. In 1987 the country counted 343,000 telephone lines, 70 percent residential and 30 percent business, an average of only 3.5 lines per 100 inhabitants. This compared poorly with averages for other countries—5.8 lines per 100 inhabitants in Venezuela, 9.5 in Colombia, and 78.7 in the United States. Over three-quarters of the country's telephones were in the capital and in Guayaquil, with most of the remainder scattered throughout provincial capitals. In rural areas, with about 40 percent of the population, many towns had only one public telephone or were totally without telephone service. Customers in Quito and Guayaquil took advantage of a small telex network with more than 3,000 subscribers.

The quality of telephone service remained poor, with frequent breakdowns of the entire system and difficulties in completing calls. In the late 1980s, much of the equipment in the telephone switching centers was obsolete and overworked, and an average of only one-third of the telephone calls dialed could be completed. This completion rate dropped to nearly zero on calls between cities during business hours. Nearly all telephones were connected to automatic exchanges, and domestic long-distance calls could be dialed by customers without the assistance of an operator. International calls, however, had to be placed through an operator, with call completion waits ranging from several minutes to several hours.

Most long-distance calls within the country travelled on a 960-channel microwave trunk that linked Quito with Guayaquil. A lower-capacity microwave route extended out to smaller cities and also ran north from Quito into Colombia and south from Guayaquil into Peru. Most international calls were routed to the ground satellite station east of Quito. With a 30-meter antenna permanently pointed to the International Telecommunications Satellite Organization's Atlantic Ocean satellite, this ground station could handle more than 300 simultaneous telephone calls from Ecuador to locations in North America, South America, and Europe.

The Ecuadorian Institute of Telecommunications (Instituto Ecuatoriano de Telecomunicaciones—Ietel), a government-owned corporation, provided all international and domestic long-distance telephone services, the telex services, and 95 percent of local telephone service. The Public Municipal Enterprise for Telephones, Potable Water, and Sewers (Empresa Pública Municipal de Teléfonos, Agua Potable y Alcantarillado—Etapa) provided local service for the remaining 5 percent of the population with telephones in the city of Cuenca. The Ministry of Public Works and Communications controlled both Ietel and Etapa.

Radio broadcast facilities were numerous, and all areas of the country could receive at least one domestic station. As with other communication services, however, Quito and Guayaquil dominated mediumwave amplitude-modulation (AM) stations; of the more than 260 stations nationwide, more than 40 were in Guayaquil and three dozen in the capital. Most broadcasting was in Spanish, but a few rural stations had programming in Quichua and Shuar. Sixteen stations of the National Radio (Radio Nacional) were publicly owned; the remainder were in private hands and loosely organized into five networks. The country had an estimated 3 million radio receivers.

In addition to mediumwave broadcasts, in 1989 Ecuador boasted thirty-nine domestic shortwave stations, one international short-wave transmitter, and several frequency-modulation (FM) stations. Shortwave frequencies were used to transmit to isolated areas in the Oriente or to reach a broader audience nationwide. The country's sole shortwave station intended for an international audience, the Quito-based HCJB, the "Voice of the Andes," was missionary-run with primarily religious programming. FM service was found primarily in Quito and Guayaquil.

Ecuador had only ten television stations—four in Quito, three in Guayaquil, and one each in Esmeraldas, Portoviejo, and Cuenca. Channel 10 in Quito, however, maintained a network of small relay stations so that most of the country could receive its signal. Each station was required to broadcast a minimum of five minutes of literacy programming every day. Ecuador had the same television system as the United States, thus permitting the use of United States made television sets or the taping and viewing of United States programs on video recorders without modification or conversion. A 1989 estimate showed 600,000 television receivers including 250,000 color sets.

The National Postal Enterprise provided postal service and maintained more than 500 offices throughout the country. Service was slow and unreliable, however, with frequent reports of thefts or loss of mail.

The press was concentrated in Guayaquil and Quito, each city having four daily newspapers. *El Universo,* an independent paper published in Guayaquil, had the largest circulation in 1989, with 225,000 subscribers, followed by *El Comercio,* a conservative, business paper from Quito with a circulation of 130,000 (see The Media, ch. 4).

Ecuador had no national news agency. Foreign wire services with offices in Quito and Guayaquil included Associated Press and United Press International from the United States, Reuters from Britain, the West German Deutsche Press-Agentur, Agencia EFE from Spain, the Cuban Prensa Latina, TASS from the Soviet Union, and the New China (Xinhua) News Agency.

Motion pictures remained a popular source of entertainment and communication. Because Ecuador produced no films domestically, all movies were imported and either dubbed or subtitled in Spanish. Movie attendance was high, with an average of 5.5 visits to a theater annually. Increased sales of video cassette recorders made home viewing of movies as well as sports events and foreign television programs increasingly popular.

Transportation

Until the twentieth century, the transport pattern reflected and reinforced the historical division of the country into two antagonistic regions—the Costa and the Sierra (see Natural Regions, ch. 2). Transport routes on the Costa were laid out to move export crops from the production areas to the ports, and routes in the Sierra ran north-south through the inter-Andean valleys. Interregional movement was confined to a few crude pack trails that permitted only limited exchange of goods or people between the two regions.

Completion of the Guayaquil-Quito railroad in 1908 provided the first effective interregional link and cut the travel time between the two cities from twelve days to twelve hours. In 1989 the rail system totaled 965 kilometers, all owned and operated by the State Railways Company (Empresa Nacional de los Ferrocarriles del Estado—ENFE) (see fig. 15). The principal line in the late 1980s remained the 447-kilometer link between Quito and Guayaquil. Floods in 1982 and 1983 disrupted service on this line, with service only partially restored by early 1989.

In the 1950s, the rail system added two extensions: a spur south to Cuenca and, with French help, an outlet to the Pacific from Quito to the port of San Lorenzo. The Quito-San Lorenzo line suffered frequent suspensions of service, and in 1989 trains ran only on the portion from a point well north of Quito to the port. Several short lines, built in the late 1800s or early 1900s to transport agricultural products to ports, had all been abandoned by the 1980s.

Until the 1950s, the railroads were the prime mover of passengers and freight and had played an important role in integrating the economy. After World War II, the government began to stress investment in the highway system, and highways gradually became the principal means of transportation. A comparison of statistics from 1969 to 1989 illustrates the decline in the overall importance of the rail system: the amount of freight carried dropped from 260,000 to 37,000 tons, and passenger traffic declined from 4.6 million trips to slightly over 1.6 million.

Construction of highways began on a small scale in the 1920s and continued sporadically until after World War II, when a greatly expanded effort created the outlines of a network covering many parts of the country and opening up vast tracts of land to new settlement. By 1989 Ecuador had about 28,000 kilometers of roads, of which about 3,600 were paved, 17,400 were gravel and improved earth, and 7,000 kilometers were dirt roads.

The 1,148-kilometer Pan American Highway remained the oldest and most heavily traveled route in the road network, following the route of the Inca imperial highway through the Sierra and connecting all the towns along the inter-Andean corridor between the Colombian border and the southern border with Peru. Except for a twelve-kilometer segment, this highway was paved from the Colombian border south through the capital to Cuenca. From Cuenca south to the Peruvian border, however, most of the surface was gravel and in fair condition.

A paved north-south route through the Costa from Esmeraldas in the north through Quayaquil to the Peruvian border just south of Machala roughly parallelled the Pan American Highway. From Quevedo to Quayaquil, this route split into two branches with the eastern branch passing through Babahoyo and the western branch along the Daule River. This highway carried an important portion of the traffic in tropical produce of the Costa.

Four paved highways connected the Pan American Highway and the north-south Costa route. In addition, asphalt roads linked Guayaquil with the small port of Manta and the oil-producing area of Salinas on the Pacific. These east-west arteries served to integrate the regions, as evidenced by the growing volume of goods trucked between the Costa and the Sierra.

In the late 1980s, the Oriente continued to suffer from an almost total lack of all-weather highways. A few gravel or dirt roads extended east from the Pan American Highway, mostly to oil-producing areas in the northern part of this region. Although usually built by the petroleum companies for easier access to their fields, the roads served to increase colonization of the Oriente, and small population centers sprang up along their paths.

A large number of bus lines and trucking companies provided intercity motor transport. The majority of the trucking enterprises were small with no schedules and were operated by the owner-driver. Most bus owners and drivers, and a few of the truck drivers, belonged to cooperatives, which set uniform rates. Intercity bus service among towns was frequent and inexpensive but often crowded and plagued by frequent vehicle breakdowns. In 1986 there were an estimated 250,000 passenger cars, 14,000 buses, and 22,000 trucks.

Air transport was fairly well developed with 179 airports, of which 43 had permanent surface runways. Since the 1920s when commercial air service was first established, airlines held a secure, if limited, segment of the transport market. Because of the short distances between most population centers, particularly in the Sierra, and the steadily expanding road network, few air routes were heavily traveled. The largest volume of passenger and cargo traffic moved

Figure 15. Transportation System, 1989

between Quito and Guayaquil. Throughout most of the Oriente, air travel provided the only means of communication with the rest of the country.

Ecuador had four main airlines, one with both domestic and international routes and three smaller companies with mostly domestic service. Private interests originally established the largest company—the Ecuadorian Aviation Company (Compañía Ecuatoriana de Aviación—CEA, known as Ecuatoriana)—but sold it to the government in 1974. Designated the national airline of Ecuador, Ecuatoriana maintained service from both Quito and Guayaquil to more than a half dozen cities in Latin America and four in the United States.

Water transport was more important for foreign trade than for domestic commerce, although the country had well-developed coastal shipping and businesses extensively used some rivers, particularly the waterways of the Guayas Basin. Although ships with moderate draught could navigate the rivers of the Oriente, only small canoes and vessels were used there. Competition from highways had diminished waterborne traffic, but riverboats continued to ply traditional routes calling at towns and farming areas not reached by roads. Boats sailed frequently between coastal cities and between the mainland and the Galápagos Islands.

Ecuador's ports carried about 95 percent of all imports and exports. Guayaquil handled about 60 percent of all seaborne trade, including most of the agricultural exports. The Old Port (Puerto Viejo) was located on the banks of the Guayas River; in 1962 the New Port (Puerto Nuevo) was built ten kilometers south of Guayaquil on an estuary and connected to the Old Port by a canal. The New Port, Ecuador's largest, could berth up to five ships.

Three other small ports had limited trade. Puerto Bolívar, near Machala, handled most of the agricultural exports, especially bananas, from the southern part of the country. Coffee, castor beans, and frozen fish from the central provinces passed through Manta. Balao, sixteen kilometers south of Esmeraldas, was greatly expanded in the 1970s to accommodate petroleum exports.

As of 1983, the national merchant marine consisted of 130 vessels with 530,000 gross registered tons (GRT). Ecuador's national oil tanker fleet, the Ecuadorian Petroleum Fleet, accounted for 164,000 GRT. The principal maritime carrier, the Grancolombian Merchant Fleet, was jointly owned by Ecuador and Colombia, and its thirty-five ships accounted for a total of 250,000 GRT. The Banana Fleet was a subsidiary of the state general cargo line, the Ecuadorian Ship Transport.

External Sector

External Debt

Ecuador's growing external debt problem was linked to the country's heavy dependence on volatile petroleum export revenues. During the 1970s, the government made optimistic forecasts concerning potential future revenues accruing as a result of oil exports, and it borrowed heavily from foreign sources to help meet development goals and to finance large public-sector deficits. In real terms, government spending grew by 9.6 percent each year during 1973–82. Interest payments on the debt quintupled between 1978 and 1982. During 1983–85, while the government implemented austerity measures as it sought to meet international debt obligations, Ecuador successfully negotiated with about 300 foreign creditor banks a multiyear refinancing package on a US$5.2-billion portion of its external debt. Although the rescheduling agreement allowed Ecuador twelve years to repay 95 percent of its debt obligations, it eased the country's burden of debt repayments only temporarily. A US$13 per barrel drop in international oil prices in 1986 created a serious revenue shortfall, forcing the government to announce in January 1987 that it would impose a three-month moratorium on payment of its foreign debt obligations.

Ecuador was exporting about 220,000 barrels of petroleum per day in the first few months of 1987. The earthquake that hit the country in March destroyed forty kilometers of the vital Trans-Ecuadorian Pipeline that connected productive oil fields in the Oriente region with port facilities just south of Esmeraldas. Repairs to the pipeline were completed in mid-August 1987, and by September Ecuador once again was exporting about 220,000 to 230,000 barrels of oil per day. But the loss to the government of US$700 million in oil export revenue during this period was devastating and undercut the country's ability to meet its external debt obligations. Debt payments to foreign private lending institutions were not resumed until early 1988, and then only for two months.

During 1987 the country's external debt increased by about US$1 billion to US$9.6 billion. At the beginning of 1988, Ecuador faced a debt-servicing burden of US$1.45 billion, and foreign-exchange reserves were nearly exhausted. The international price of Oriente crude had improved slightly during 1987 but dropped to US$12.50 per barrel in 1988. Government officials, mindful that the country would not earn enough export revenue in 1988 to cover the expected balance-of-payments deficit or to meet the country's external debt-service obligations, suspended interest payments to private banks in April 1988.

When Borja assumed the presidency in 1988, Ecuador's interest arrearages to private commercial banks amounted to almost US$1 billion. In November 1988, Ecuadorian officials began a new round of negotiations to refinance US$6.5 billion of the country's growing external debt, which by then was approaching US$11 billion. At the end of these unsuccessful negotiations, Ecuador's Monetary Board chairman, citing low oil prices and damage from the 1987 earthquake, announced that service payments would be resumed only after the country's economic situation had improved. Foreign debt payments to commercial banks finally were resumed in April 1989, but creditor banks were doubtful that Ecuador could make payments sufficient to cover the accumulated arrears.

*A truck hauling bananas
in the Costa
Courtesy
Martie B. Lisowski Collection,
Library of Congress*

*Boarding a ferry
on the Coca River
Courtesy
Martie B. Lisowski Collection,
Library of Congress*

Meanwhile, Ecuador had not stopped making payments to multilateral lending organizations, and it secured new loans from the World Bank and the IMF. During the first half of 1989, more than US$600 million in loans, all of which was earmarked for development purposes, was received from the World Bank. The IMF provided Ecuador with US$254 million in credit during 1987–88, and an additional US$137 million standby credit agreement was reached in September 1989.

Trade and Balance of Payments

The health of the Ecuadorian economy was dependent on foreign trade. But this dependence left the country vulnerable to the vagaries of international commerce, especially the unpredictability of prices for Ecuadorian export goods.

The improved performance of the economy during the 1970s was the result mainly of the rapid acceleration of Ecuador's oil exports beginning in 1972 and a sharp increase in international petroleum prices starting in 1974. In 1971 crude petroleum exports made up less than 1 percent of total exports and were valued at US$1.2 million. The volume of petroleum exports expanded dramatically in 1972 and 1973; by 1974 petroleum made up almost 65 percent of the country's commodity exports and was valued at US$792 million. Although domestic consumption of petroleum derivatives rose steadily and the volume of Ecuadorian oil exports moderated during the remainder of the 1970s, the spectacular rise in the early 1980s of the crude oil price, which reached a peak of US$34.50 in 1981, resulted in sharp increases in petroleum export revenue. The rapid decline in international oil prices that began in 1986 and the 1987 suspension of crude petroleum production in the aftermath of a destructive earthquake produced a 50-percent drop in the value of Ecuadorian crude petroleum exports in 1986–87 (see table 15, Appendix).

Ecuador's substantial income from crude oil exports had positive and negative effects on the economy. During the 1960s, foreign-exchange reserves averaged about US$25 million. Because of the oil boom, the balance-of-payments situation improved during the mid- to late 1970s. Net foreign-exchange earnings, for example, had reached US$230 million by the end of 1973 and more than US$350 million in 1974. This improvement in foreign exchange had a positive impact on the economy, but that gain was partially wiped out by the relaxation of import restrictions, which allowed the import volume to go up almost 50 percent in 1974. Growing oil export revenue also encouraged the government to subsidize commodities such as gasoline and food items, expand public-sector employment, increase government-sponsored social benefits, and finance the growing budget deficit through foreign borrowing. Austerity measures were implemented in the mid-1980s to reduce the cost of subsidized goods, but by the end of the decade the government had failed to adequately tackle its growing budget deficits or its foreign debt payment problems.

In 1970 fish, timber, and other agricultural products, mainly bananas, coffee, cocoa, and sugar, had accounted for almost 90 percent of foreign-exchange earnings. But the dramatic increase in petroleum production that began in 1972 profoundly altered the country's long-term export structure. First, petroleum displaced agricultural products as the country's major export commodity, and, second, the overall value of exports grew tenfold between 1970 and 1980, from US$235 million in 1970 to US$2.52 billion in 1980. Between 1974 and 1981, gains in export earnings were mainly the result of favorable international prices for Ecuadorian commodities, including farm products. The value of commodity exports leveled off during the first half of the 1980s and then declined moderately to US$2.19 billion in 1986, reflecting the fall of international crude petroleum prices. The value of commodity exports remained stable during 1987, 1988, and 1989—US$2.0 billion, US$2.2 billion, and US$2.3 billion, respectively. In 1989 petroleum accounted for about 50 percent of export revenues. In the same year, the value of shrimp exports amounted to US$348 million; banana exports, US$316 million; coffee, US$191 million; and cocoa, US$73 million.

Also during the 1970s, imports rose by an average of 11 percent per annum, and the value of imports grew steadily between 1970, when it stood at US$249.6 million, and 1981, when it stood at US$2.36 billion. The value of imports declined after 1981, falling to US$1.6 billion in 1986. Although the value of imports had multiplied sixfold since 1970, the structure of imports changed only in minor details. Capital goods for industry, for example, represented 15.4 percent of total imports in 1970; by 1975 capital goods were averaging about 22 percent of total imports, and they would remain at that level until 1987. The growth in imports of capital goods was consistent with increases in manufacturing output. Imports of durable consumer goods averaged about 15 percent of total imports during the early 1980s, compared with an average of slightly less than 5 percent during the 1970s, when the process of import substitution (see Glossary) for consumer goods was moderately more successful than in the 1980s. In 1986, however, as the government's import restrictions and devaluations of the sucre took effect, only 7.7 percent of imports would come under the category of durable consumer goods (see table 16, Appendix).

In 1987, 61 percent of exports went to the United States, and 30 percent of imports came from the United States, making that country Ecuador's main trading partner. Wheat, assorted machinery, transport equipment, and chemicals were the principal United States exports to Ecuador in 1987. Shrimp, petroleum, bananas, coffee, and cocoa were the principal United States imports from Ecuador in the same year. Other major trading partners included the European Community, other Latin American and Caribbean countries, and Japan (see table 17, Appendix).

Ecuador's current-account balance varied, registering an average yearly deficit of US$100 million during the 1970s. Financing the current-account deficits was not difficult as long as Ecuador enjoyed continuing improvements in its terms of trade (see Glossary). By 1977 it was clear that the balance of payments was being supported by high oil receipts and external borrowing. The gradual decline of international crude petroleum prices beginning in 1982, coupled with a poor export performance during 1982–83, made it more difficult for the government to secure external financing from foreign commercial banks. Export earnings fell by about 8 percent in 1982, and despite a moderate reduction in the volume of imports, the current-account deficit passed the US$1 billion mark, which in 1982 represented 9 percent of GDP.

To deal with the balance-of-payments crisis, in 1982 the government, in cooperation with an IMF fiscal austerity program, devalued the sucre for the first time since 1971. Another sharp devaluation occurred in 1983, when the government also introduced new exchange controls, prohibited or limited the importation of some items, and reduced fuel and export subsidies. During late 1982 and early 1983, crop production and exports dropped sharply because of the devastating effects of El Niño, but they returned to 1980 levels by mid-1984. Meanwhile, the government began negotiations to reschedule the external debt. The austerity plan, although painful, helped Ecuador to virtually eliminate its current-account deficit by the end of 1983. Ecuador's current-account deficit was offset by a virtually identical surplus in 1985.

In 1986 the international price of crude petroleum dropped sharply to an average of US$15.35 from the previous year's average of US$27.16. The result was a decline in foreign-exchange earnings and a return to chronic current-account deficits during the 1986–89 period. In 1987, the year of the US$700 million oil revenue loss, the current-account deficit reached –US$1.13 billion. The current-account deficit improved in 1988 when it stood at –US$597 million; in 1989 the deficit decreased slightly to about –US$500 million (see table 18, Appendix). Nevertheless, despite these improvements, the prospects for Ecuador's balance of payments, as for its economy as a whole, were uncertain.

* * *

Relatively few book-length studies exist on the Ecuadorian economy. The most comprehensive introduction to the subject can be found in David W. Schodt's *Ecuador: An Andean Enigma.* Luis Mendoza's *Geo-Economía del Ecuador* offers an excellent, although dated, examination of national economic issues. Specific economic data may be drawn from the Economist Intelligence Unit's quarterly *Country Profile: Ecuador* and the annual reports of Ecuador's Central Bank. (For further information and complete citations, see Bibliography.)

Chapter 4. Government and Politics

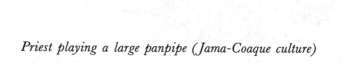

Priest playing a large panpipe (Jama-Coaque culture)

ONE OF THE LEAST POLITICALLY stable of the South American republics for most of its history, Ecuador had 86 governments and 17 constitutions in its first 159 years of independence. Only twenty of those governments resulted from popular elections, and many of the elections were fraudulent. José María Velasco Ibarra, who completed only one of his five terms as president, often stated, "Ecuador is a very difficult country to govern."

Ecuador had four successive democratic elections from 1948 to 1960, but the country did not experience relative political stability under democratic rule again until the 1980s. Seven years of military dictatorship ended with the presidential inauguration of Jaime Roldós Aguilera on August 10, 1979. After Roldós died in an airplane crash on May 24, 1981, Vice President Osvaldo Hurtado Larrea assumed the presidency. The completion of the Hurtado/Roldós administration and the constitutional and orderly transfer of power—the first such transfer in twenty-four years—to conservative León Febres Cordero Ribadeneyra (1984–88) in August 1984 seemed to affirm the restoration of democracy in Ecuador. Nevertheless, as Roldós himself had cautioned shortly before taking office, the nation had only a formalistic and ritualistic democratic tradition.

Indeed, Ecuador has been shaken periodically since 1984 by bitter conflicts between the executive branch on the one side and the unicameral legislature and the judiciary on the other. These clashes were particularly pronounced during Febres Cordero's polemical administration. His authoritarian rule also provoked military mutinies and even his brief abduction by rebellious troops. Although battered, Ecuador's democratic system survived, and Febres Cordero transferred power to his long-time rival, Rodrigo Borja Cevallos, in August 1988. Whereas Febres Cordero, a millionaire businessman from Guayaquil, had advocated a free-market economy, strong executive control, and close alignment with the United States, Borja, a social democrat from Quito, espoused a mixed economy, a pluralist government, and a nonaligned foreign policy. In his first two years, Borja succeeded in softening the impact of his predecessor's legacy of political, economic, and social crises.

Despite a decade of civilian democratic rule marked by three peaceful transitions of government, analysts generally agreed that the political system remained vulnerable. Political scientist John D. Martz noted, for instance, that the transition to a third democratic

155

government in 1988 provided "little reason to believe that the fragile democratic system in Ecuador had been strengthened, nor that the historic pattern of instability had been fundamentally reversed or modified."

The destabilizing conflicts among the executive, legislative, and judicial branches of government resulted primarily from idiosyncrasies of Ecuador's institutional structure. For example, the judiciary, despite being independent, lacked the authority needed to serve as an effective check on the abuse of presidential powers. Although the Supreme Court of Justice (Corte Suprema de Justicia—CSJ) carried out many judicial duties normally expected of a nation's highest court, it did not rule on constitutional issues. A nonjudicial appendage of the National Congress (Congreso Nacional—hereafter, Congress), the Tribunal of Constitutional Guarantees (Tribunal de Garantías Constitucionales—TGC), exercised that function, thereby giving the legislative body the power to, in effect, control interpretation of the Constitution.

The traditional, deep-seated division between the liberal, trade-oriented, tropical Costa (coastal region) and the conservative, agrarian-oriented Sierra (Andean highlands) also helped explain Ecuador's bitter infighting over political and economic affairs. This fundamental division pitted the Pacific port city of Guayaquil, the country's principal economic center, against the highland capital of Quito. The enmity between natives of Guayaquil and of Quito was reflected in the alignment of the country's sixteen registered political parties in the 1988 elections, as well as in the refusal of outgoing President Febres Cordero, a native of Guayaquil, to speak to his successor, Rodrigo Borja, a native of Quito, or even to personally pass the presidential sash to him on August 10, 1988. According to political scientist and former president Hurtado, rivalry among provinces and regions for central government attention in the form of development projects, principally road construction, also was a major source of political conflict.

Although Ecuador's political parties and its free and partisan press participated in a lively and contentious democratic political process, parties suffered from factionalism, weak organization, lack of mass participation, and blurred ideologies, as well as from the competing influences of populism and militarism. Analysts generally agreed that the proliferation of small parties and the need to negotiate alliances contributed significantly to political instability in the 1980s.

Constitutional Background

The tension between civilian and clerical authority dominated Ecuador's constitutional history for much of the nineteenth and early twentieth centuries. This issue provided one of the bases for the lasting dispute between Conservatives, who represented primarily the interests of the Sierra and the church, and the Liberals, who represented those of the Costa and anticlericalism.

Ecuador's first constitution of 1830, when the country seceded from the Confederation of Gran Colombia, followed the precedents of other independence documents: the Quito State Charter (1812) and the Gran Colombia constitutions of Cúcuta (1821) and Bogotá (1830). The Quito State Charter, framed before independence, called for a unicameral legislature and a popular and representative state established through indirect elections by its citizens. The term "popular," however, meant in practice participation by only wealthy and influential persons. Succeeding constitutions clearly defined the stringent property, professional, and literacy requirements for citizenship and distinguished between citizens and Ecuadorians. Only a small, white, male minority (initially those over twenty-one years of age) met these requirements and therefore enjoyed the impressive rights guaranteed under these and other nineteenth-century constitutions (see The Struggle for Independence, ch. 1).

Ecuador's first constitution as a republic, that of 1830, also became known as the Floreana constitution, after the new nation's first president, General Juan José Flores (1830–45). It established a unitary and centralized presidential system of government and separation of powers, with the executive power predominating in practice. The 1830 constitution also established a unicameral congress, elected by indirect suffrage and made up of an equal number (ten) of deputies from each of the three districts—Quito, Azuay, and Guayaquil—and a Council of State to assist the executive in administering the government and to substitute for Congress during the recess.

The five constitutions framed between 1830 and 1852 had much in common. Voting was made indirect, through electors, in both congressional and presidential elections. The presidential term was four years, with the exception of the 1843 constitution (the so-called "Slavery Charter"), which provided for an eight-year term. The 1843 constitution also recognized Roman Catholicism as the state religion. Only the constitutions of 1830 and 1851, however, provided for a unicameral legislature; the others established a bicameral Congress, composed of a Senate and a Chamber of Deputies. The 1843 constitution also made an exception to indirect congressional elections by extending popular suffrage to the election of senators. The 1845 constitution declared that sovereignty resides in the people, although it extended suffrage only to all male citizens.

157

The constitution of 1861, promulgated by President Gabriel García Moreno (1859–75), eliminated the financial requirements for citizenship and the franchise; introduced direct and secret suffrage for electing all members of a bicameral Congress, the president and vice president of the republic, and the provincial authorities; and established proportional representation for Ecuador's provinces in the Chamber of Deputies (each province elected two senators). These innovations made the 1861 constitution the most representative in Ecuador's constitutional evolution in the nineteenth century. It also reintroduced the strong presidency, whose chief executive was elected by "universal suffrage" for a four-year term. Although it retained Roman Catholicism as the only legal religion, the 1861 constitution guaranteed free expression of thought.

Nearly all of the constitutions prohibited the immediate reelection of the president, but this provision was often violated in spirit. Despite a strong sentiment against long-term monopoly of the presidency, generals Flores, García, and Eloy Alfaro (1895–1912) managed to rule behind the scenes between their terms of office. In 1869 García, a conservative, intensely devout Catholic, promulgated a more authoritarian constitution, referred to as the Garciana constitution or Carta Negra (the Black Charter), which extended the presidential term to six years (see The Era of Conservatism, 1860–95, ch. 1). It introduced the religious factor into politics by making membership in the Roman Catholic Church a requisite for citizenship, and it also required being at least twenty-one years of age, married, and able to read and write. The 1884 Elections Law, however, eliminated the requirement of being Catholic in order to be a citizen.

The Liberal period from 1895 to 1925 had two constitutions, those of 1897 and 1906. The first, promulgated by General José Eloy Alfaro Delgado, prohibited religious orders, abolished privileges of the Catholic Church, and reduced the male voting age to eighteen (or marital status). The second, the country's twelfth and most durable charter, provided unprecedented protection of civil and political rights and guarantees, including abolition of the death penalty, introduced new individual freedoms, and prohibited arbitrary imprisonment for debts. It also established the separation of the church and state and strengthened the Council of State (see The Role of the Liberals, 1895–1925, ch. 1). The 1906 Elections Law gave women the right for the first time to participate in political and administrative life.

The 1929 constitution combined quasicorporate features drawn from many different models. Described as a semiparliamentary charter, it reorganized the Senate into a body consisting of fifteen senators elected to represent specific interest groups. Ecuadorian judicial scholar Hernán Salgado Pesantes notes that the 1929 constitution was the only one that weakened presidential powers by, for example, disallowing successive presidential reelection and introducing a Council of Ministers and a vote of no confidence. Congress was even able to impeach an incumbent president in 1933. The 1929 document also introduced various social, economic, and political rights, including the right of literate women of at least twenty-one years of age to have citizenship and to vote, and the right of minorities to elect deputies and provincial councillors (*consejeros provinciales*). The traditional social and ethnic stratification continued, however, as did the constitutional distinction between citizens and Ecuadorians. Consequently, the 1929 charter, coinciding as it did with the worldwide economic crisis, failed to improve political stability significantly.

A Constituent Assembly, dominated by the leftist Ecuadorian Democratic Alliance, deliberated almost six months before adopting the country's fourteenth constitution, promulgated by President Velasco on May 3, 1945. Although Velasco had opposed the assembly's efforts to strengthen the legislature, the new constitution imposed a number of important checks on the president, especially regarding the executive's use of emergency and veto powers. The 1945 constitution also provided for a unicameral legislature, rendered the cabinet partially responsible to Congress, replaced the Council of State with the TGC, and established the Supreme Electoral Tribunal (Tribunal Superior Electoral—TSE). In addition, the 1945 constitution smoothed over the religious issue by stating that the nation did not recognize any official religion and that citizens could practice any faith.

Although Velasco signed the 1945 constitution, his immediate rejection of it prompted the adoption of another, promulgated in 1946, that restored the bicameral legislature (consisting of a forty-five-member Senate and a sixty-four-member Chamber of Deputies) and the Council of State (replacing the TGC) and greatly increased the executive's authority. Velasco's constitution also reintroduced the office of vice president, for which no provision had been made in the constitutions of 1869, 1906, 1929, and 1945. The constitution made autonomous the institutions responsible for supervising the electoral process: the TSE and the Provincial Electoral Tribunals (Tribunales Provinciales Electorales—TPEs) (see The Electoral Process, this ch.).

The most extensive of Ecuador's constitutions, the 1967 document, drafted by a popularly elected constituent assembly, legitimized political parties recognized by the TSE; made voting obligatory for women as well as for men; and made Congress bicameral, meeting twice a year in ordinary sessions (from March 6 to May 4 and from August 10 to October 9). In addition, the TGC again replaced the Council of State.

The 1967 constitution, however, contained provisions that displeased Velasco, who as of June 2, 1968, was in his fifth term as president. For example, it restricted powers to call a state of siege. On June 22, 1970, Velasco, in an *autogolpe* (self-seizure of power), assumed extraconstitutional powers and began ruling by decree. He suspended the 1967 constitution, which he charged had destroyed executive control, amputated the Senate's power, divested the police of all authority, and dismembered the administrative organization.

After General Guillermo Rodríguez Lara deposed Velasco in a military coup in February 1972, the armed forces issued a decree reinstating the 1945 document. Rodríguez suspended it in 1974, however, and cancelled plans for holding an election. In January 1976, a military junta ousted Rodríguez and again reinstated the 1945 constitution. In a measure unprecedented in Ecuador's constitutional history, the junta held a popular referendum on January 15, 1978, to decide between a reformed version of the 1945 document and a new charter; 44 percent of the voters cast their ballots for the latter, and 31 percent for the former. Nullified votes totaled 23 percent.

By allowing for a considerable amount of state intervention and providing for a large number of economic and social rights, the new Constitution (promulgated on August 10, 1979) is much more progressive than the reformed document, which had favored the status quo. Framed along the lines of the 1945 and 1967 charters, the 1979 Constitution, the country's seventeenth, contains several innovations, including granting citizenship and suffrage to all Ecuadorians over eighteen years of age, including illiterates; and requiring candidates in popular elections to affiliate with a legally recognized party. It also creates a unicameral Congress (for the fourth time in Ecuador's constitutional history) and four legislative commissions, which form the Plenary of Legislative Commissions (Plenario de las Comisiones Legislativas—PCL). In addition, it requires the selection of the president and vice president in the same election, prohibits either from seeking a successive term, authorizes Congress to elect a new vice president if the incumbent resigns, and allows the president to declare a state of national emergency and to finance the public debt without prior legislative authorization. Although the Constitution initially extended the presidential term to five years, an amendment later reduced it to four. The Constitution also creates the National Development Council (Consejo Nacional de Desarrollo—Conade), headed by the vice president, to plan state policies.

To help compensate for numerous deficiencies in the 1979 Constitution, amendments were approved in 1983. These reforms, which went into effect in August 1984, give more power to the TGC; reduce from five to four years the term of the principal officials of the state, including the president (with the exceptions of TGC and TSE members, who serve two years); shorten the terms of the judges of the CSJ, Fiscal Tribunal, and Contentious Administrative Tribunal (Tribunal Contencioso Administrativo—TCA) from six years to four; and make the president and vice president of the republic subject to trial only for treason, bribery, or other infractions that seriously compromise the national honor.

The Constitution prohibits discrimination based on race, sex, religion, language, or social status. Nevertheless, in the late 1980s Indians and blacks constituted a disproportionate share of those living in poverty, although there was no legally sanctioned discrimination against them. Moreover, there were still few highly placed women in the political structure. Fewer than 15 percent of the candidates in the 1984 elections were women, and only three of the seventy-one congressional deputies elected that year were female. Women still suffered some discrimination under civil law and usually received lower wages than men employed in similar positions. In 1987, however, changes in laws concerning divorce, property distribution, and inheritance gave women equal rights with their husbands in these areas as required by the Constitution.

According to the United States Department of State, the following individual rights were respected in the late 1980s: the freedom of peaceful assembly and association; the freedom of religion (although the country was overwhelmingly Roman Catholic); the freedom of movement within the country, of foreign travel, and of emigration and repatriation (persons from other Latin American countries readily found asylum in Ecuador); and the freedom to exercise political rights. Worker rights that were generally respected included the right of association, the right to strike, and the right to organize and bargain collectively. Although forced or compulsory labor and employment of children under the age of eighteen were prohibited, Indians often worked for near-starvation wages, and many children in rural areas were active in the work force.

Governmental Structure

Under the 1979 Constitution, Ecuador is a democratic and unitary state with a republican, presidential, elective, and representative government. Although the presidency is mainly a political office, it and the rest of the executive branch are responsible for the governmental process. Congress is responsible for the legislative process. The Supreme Court of Justice, which supervises the Superior Courts, is, along with other judicial organs, responsible for serving justice. Relations between the executive and legislative branches are based on the principle of the separation of powers, although there are several points of contact. In the 1980s, there also have been numerous points of friction between the executive and legislative branches, particularly during the Febres Cordero administration. As political scientist David Corkill observed in 1985, "Politics became locked in a familiar cycle of executive-legislative conflict, protracted political deadlock, and military intervention to break the impasse."

The Executive

The executive branch of government consists of the president, the vice president, the ministers of state and their subordinate officials, and Conade (see fig. 16). The office of the president is located in the National Palace (Palacio Nacional) in Quito, and the offices of the vice president and ministers at various other locations in the capital. The president serves a four-year term and may not run for reelection.

To be president, one must be Ecuadorian by birth, in full possession of the rights of citizenship, and at least thirty-five years of age at the time of the election. Election requires an absolute majority of the votes cast by direct, universal, and secret ballot. A candidate may not be a current or former president, a spouse or relative of an incumbent president, vice president in the term immediately prior to the election, a minister of state at the time of the election, a member of the Public Forces (composed of the armed forces and National Police) within six months prior to the election, a minister of any religious denomination, a government contractor, or a legal representative of a foreign company.

The president's duties and powers include the following: to comply with and enforce the Constitution, laws, decrees, and international conventions; to approve, promulgate, carry out, or challenge the laws enacted by Congress or the PCL; to maintain domestic order and national security; to freely appoint and remove ministers, chiefs of diplomatic missions, governors, and other public officials, as provided by law (the president sends a list of three candidates for high-level state positions to Congress, which selects one); to determine foreign policy and direct international relations; to enter into treaties and other international agreements, and to ratify treaties and agreements after their approval by Congress; to contract loans; to serve as commander in chief of the Public Forces; to appoint, confer promotions on, or remove officials of the Public Forces; to mobilize or demobilize the Public Forces and assume command of them in wartime, and to approve their organization; to declare a state of national emergency and to assume emergency powers as needed in times of crisis; to submit an annual report to Congress on the general state of the government and the republic; and to call a popular referendum on important questions.

The president may declare a state of emergency in general situations involving imminent foreign aggression, international war, or serious internal strife or catastrophe. A state of emergency empowers the president to decree the anticipated collection of taxes; to invest fiscal funds designated for other areas (with the exception of health and social services) in the defense of the state or the solution of a catastrophe, but not in the case of an internal conflict; to move the seat of the government; to close or open ports; to censor the media; to suspend observance of constitutional guarantees, with the exception of such basic human rights as the right to life, personal integrity, and freedom from expatriation or confinement (except under certain conditions); and to declare a security zone in the national territory. In order to prevent arbitrary presidential declarations, Congress or the TGC may revoke the state of emergency at any time if the circumstances justify such action.

The president has important legislative powers as well. The principle of "legislative coparticipation" allows the chief executive to participate in the formation as well as the execution and application of laws. The president may present before Congress or the PCL any proposed law, including constitutional amendments. Congress or the PCL must invite the head of state or a representative to participate, without voting rights, in the discussions of the proposed law. Within fifteen days, Congress or the PCL must approve, amend, or reject urgent presidential proposals on the economy. In the absence of any congressional action, the president may promulgate any such proposal as a decree-law, which the Congress may overrule or amend. Any bill approved by Congress or the PCL must be submitted to the president, who has ten days to approve or to object partially or totally to it. The legislature may override a presidential veto by a two-thirds majority. The chief executive, once signing a bill into law, must promulgate it by publishing it in the *Registro Oficial del Estado* (Official Register of the State) and issue regulations within ninety days.

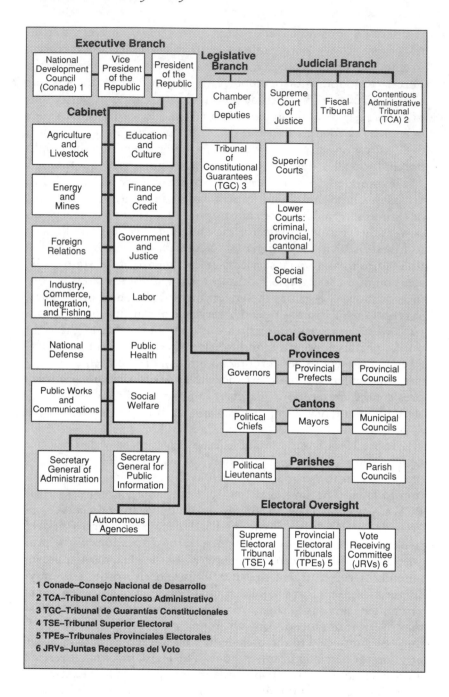

Figure 16. Organization of the Ecuadorian Government, 1989

The president may call Congress into extraordinary session to consider exclusively matters put before it by the head of state. In practice, however, these sessions have not always worked to the president's advantage. For example, although President Febres Cordero convoked extraordinary sessions of Congress in March and April 1985, the legislature suspended the first one after rejecting a presidential bill to increase the monthly minimum wage by 30 percent, and the president of Congress unilaterally, and some claimed illegally, suspended the second session without completing its agenda. Although the Constitution does not specifically give Congress the power to suspend an extraordinary session called by the president, the legislative body may interpret the charter and the laws as it sees fit.

The presidency may be declared vacant following the incumbent's death, resignation, physical or mental incapacitation, or removal from office by the legislature for having been absent from Quito for thirty consecutive days or for having left the country without congressional authorization. Under these circumstances, the Constitution provides for subrogation or substitution of the president. The order of presidential subrogation is the vice president, the president of Congress, and the president of the CSJ. The presidential order of subrogation also serves for the temporary replacement of the vice president. In the definitive absence of the vice president, Congress may designate a successor by an absolute majority.

The 1979 Constitution establishes that the vice president be elected simultaneously with the president on the same party slate by an absolute majority and meet the same requirements and restrictions. The vice president also serves as president of Conade, which plans the various policies of the state.

The ministers of state, who comprise the cabinet, discharge the affairs of state and represent the president in matters relating to their respective ministries. To be a minister, one must be Ecuadorian by birth, in full possession of the rights of citizenship, and at least thirty years of age. In 1989 the Borja cabinet had twelve ministers and also included two secretaries of state—the secretary general of administration and the secretary general for public information—with ministerial rank. All ministries also had deputy ministers, who were, with the usual exception of the deputy minister of defense, civilians. In addition, the president supervised more than 700 autonomous agencies, including the national planning board, Conade.

Conade determines the general economic and social policies of the state and prepares development plans for presidential approval. The eleven-member Conade consists of the vice president, four ministers of state appointed by the president, the president of the Monetary Board, and one representative each of Congress, the mayors (*alcaldes*), and provincial prefects (*prefectos provinciales*), organized labor, the Commercial Associations (Cámaras de Producción), and the polytechnical universities and schools. In the event of a tie, the matter is resolved by the vote of whoever is presiding over the meeting. Once approved by the president, the policies adopted by Conade must be implemented by the appropriate ministers and by government agencies.

Under a restructuring directive issued by Vice President Luis Parodi in January 1990, Conade created the offices of undersecretaries of Economic Planning and Decentralized Planning and Social Development. In addition, seven general directorates were established: Short-Range Planning, Medium- and Long-Range Planning, Decentralized Planning, the Costa Social Development, Technical and Financial Cooperation, and Administration. The changes resulted from a desire to emphasize the role of planning as a tool of the government, thus necessitating modernization and institutional consolidation of the council.

The Legislature

Although a bicameral organization of Congress had been predominant in Ecuador's republican history, the 1979 Constitution establishes a unicameral legislative body, the Congress. Two classes of deputies—the nationals and the provincials—are elected. The twelve national deputies are elected through a national vote, are at least thirty years of age at the time of election, and serve four years; they may be reelected after sitting out a legislative period. Provincial deputies serve two years and may be reelected after waiting out one legislative term. They are elected in the twenty-one provinces under a system of proportional representation. The provincial deputies must be at least twenty-five years of age at the time of their election and be either natives of the province they are to represent or residents of that province for at least three years prior to the election. National and provincial deputies must be Ecuadorian by birth, in full possession of the rights of citizenship, and affiliated with one of the political parties legally recognized by the TSE.

Those prohibited from serving as members of Congress or even from participating in the electoral process include virtually all members of the executive and judicial branches, public employees,

Presidential Palace, Quito
Courtesy Martie B. Lisowski Collection,
Library of Congress

officials of banks and other credit institutions, holders of active state contracts, military personnel on active duty, ministers of any denomination and members of religious communities, and representatives of foreign companies. In addition, no candidate may be economically dependent on the state or have had any connection with it at least six months prior to the election. Ninety days prior to an election, a legally recognized political party must register its candidates for Congress with the TSE.

Once elected, a deputy may not hold any other public post, with the sole exception of a university teaching position. Likewise, deputies are prohibited from exercising their profession while Congress and its commissions are in session. While performing their legislative duties or even carrying out acts outside of these functions, deputies are protected by parliamentary immunity from prosecution for common law penal infractions. They may be prosecuted only if Congress votes to lift their immunity.

Congress usually meets once a year for a period of seventy working days beginning on August 10 and ending on October 8. When Congress convenes in an ordinary period of sessions, it elects from among its members a president and vice president to serve one-year terms. In addition, two secretaries are elected who are not

167

members of the legislature. The holders of these one-year appointments may be reelected.

Congress also must name, from among its national deputies, seven legislators and seven substitutes (*suplentes*) to each of the four legislative commissions. These commissions cover civil and penal issues; labor and social issues; tax, fiscal, banking, and budgetary issues; and economic, agrarian, industrial, and commercial issues. Congress may also designate or form other commissions to deal with specific issues, such as constitutional reform. When Congress recesses, the four established commissions continue operating with certain powers, and in some matters certain state organs may substitute for Congress. To discuss and approve laws or other legislation, the four commissions meet under the direction of the president of Congress and form the PCL (see table 19, Appendix). The PCL may approve or reject proposals of law; codify the laws; prosecute the judges of the CSJ, the Fiscal Tribunal, and the TCA for infractions of the law; reject treaties or international agreements; and, when Congress is in recess, make the final decision on the legality of laws, decrees, regulations, orders, or resolutions suspended by the TGC for reasons of unconstitutionality.

The Constitution gives Congress important powers in legislation and in political and judicial control. Only Congress, or in its recess the PCL, may enact legislation or interpret the Constitution. The executive may only work out regulations for the application of the laws, without interpreting or altering them. Specific congressional powers include reforming the Constitution and interpreting ambiguous provisions; expediting, modifying, reforming, repealing, and interpreting the laws; establishing or replacing taxes, rates, or other public revenues; and approving or rejecting public treaties and other international conventions entered into by the executive. High officials of the state—including the president, the presidents of the CSJ, TSE, TGC, and Fiscal Tribunal, as well as the comptroller general and the attorney general—must also present their annual reports to Congress.

The legislature may also prosecute the president and vice president; the ministers of state; the ministers of the CSJ, TCA, and Fiscal Court; the members of the TGC and TSE; the comptroller general; the attorney general; the fiscal general minister; and the superintendents of banks and companies for infractions committed during the exercise of their duties or up to one year after leaving office. The president may be prosecuted only for serious charges, such as betrayal of the nation, bribery, or other infractions severely affecting the national honor.

Utilizing the interpellation procedure, one or more legislators draw up a list of questions to an official or judge who is to be prosecuted by Congress. The secretary of Congress must deliver the list to the person at least five days prior to the date of *interpelación* (interpellation procedure), when the individual must appear before Congress to answer the questions. If during the proceeding the person is determined to be guilty by an absolute majority, Congress may censor the subject and dismiss him or her from the post; the case then passes on to the appropriate judges.

Congress also appoints a number of high-level government officials, including the comptroller general, the attorney general, the fiscal minister, and superintendents of banks and companies. These appointments are made from lists submitted by the president, each containing three proposed names. Only Congress may remove these individuals from their four-year posts. Congress also appoints the ministers or judges of the CSJ, the Fiscal Tribunal, and the TCA. Should any of these posts become vacant when Congress is in recess, it remains unoccupied until the next session.

The political nature of judicial appointments became a matter of considerable controversy in the 1980s. For example, in October 1984 a dispute broke out between the legislative and executive branches following Congress's appointment of sixteen CSJ judges opposed by Febres Cordero. He used military and security forces to prevent the newly elected judges from entering the Supreme Court of Justice building. The controversy was resolved that December, however, when Congress agreed to waive its prerogative to select all of the judges and allow Febres Cordero to appoint eight of them.

Congress also designates the seven members who make up the TSE, as well as their substitutes. It elects three TSE members on its own accord and elects the remaining four from two sets of names: two members from one set provided by the president and two members from another list sent by the CSJ. In addition, Congress selects three of the eleven members of the TGC and their substitutes and nominates the remaining members and their alternates from lists of candidates submitted by the president, the CSJ, the Electoral College, the Electoral College of Provincial Prefects, the National Federation of Workers, and the Commercial Associations.

Congress also has a role in budgetary matters. One of its legislative commissions reviews the budget submitted by the executive branch through the Ministry of Finance and Credit. Only in the case of budgetary discrepancies does Congress intervene. Once Congress resolves any discrepancies, its approval is final, and the executive may not object. If Congress wishes to repeal or modify laws that increase public expenditures, it must seek other sources of financing, create new substitute revenues, or increase the existing ones.

Other congressional powers include installing the president and vice president once the TSE proclaims them to be elected, and electing the vice president, if that post becomes vacant. Congress also handles resignations of the president, the vice president, and certain other officials. Congress grants or denies permission to the president and vice president to be absent from the country, grants them general amnesty for political crimes, and imposes fines on them for common crimes.

Congress may dismiss cabinet ministers by majority vote. During the Febres Cordero presidency, the opposition majority in Congress dismissed the finance and credit minister in late 1986 for alleged abuse of tariff, exchange, and public spending laws; forced the resignation of the energy and mines minister in August 1987 for allegedly violating Ecuador's sovereignty in negotiating an oil trade agreement; and impeached the government and justice minister that October for alleged complicity in arbitrary arrests, torture, and disappearances.

To deal with important matters that cannot wait until the next ordinary session, the legislature may convene in extraordinary session. This session may be called by two-thirds of the legislators, the president of Congress, or the president. It may consider only the specific matters for which it was called. If another important issue arises or is introduced by the president, it cannot be considered until the assembly ends and another is called.

The Judiciary

The Court System

The judicial branch consists of three organs of equal status and importance: the Supreme Court of Justice (CSJ); the Fiscal Tribunal, which recognizes and resolves controversies arising between the revenue-collecting administration and the taxpayers and determines tax obligations; and the Contentious Administrative Tribunal (TCA), which is primarily responsible for recognizing and resolving controversies arising in public administration. Located in Quito, these judicial bodies have jurisdiction over all of the national territory. Their judges or ministers of justice must be Ecuadorian citizens by birth, be at least forty years of age, hold a doctorate in jurisprudence, and have at least fifteen years of professional experience as a lawyer, judge, or university professor in jurisprudence. The appointment of the CSJ's sixteen justices is the constitutional prerogative of Congress.

In practice, Congress and the executive branch have frequently manipulated the supposedly independent judiciary for political purposes. Congress appoints the judges of the three judicial organs to serve four-year terms. If vacancies later arise, these are filled by the organs themselves until Congress nominates official replacements. Occasionally, the president may intervene (on his or her own accord and without any specific constitutional authorization to do so) in the process of nominating CSJ justices by presenting a list of candidates, and the Council of State (a body whose bureaucratic organization and powers are unclear) may intervene by endorsing the candidates suggested by the president.

At the apex of the court system is the CSJ, consisting of five chambers of three judges each, as well as the court's president. When they meet, the members of the five chambers constitute the plenary tribunal. The tribunal selects the court's president, who represents the entire judicial branch for a two-year period and may not be reelected until after five periods have elapsed.

The three judicial organs have certain powers with respect to reforming the Constitution and initiating legislation. The CSJ may initiate reforms of the Constitution, and all three judicial organs may initiate proposals of law. In an arrangement similar to the "legislative coparticipation" enjoyed by the president, the justices of the three judicial bodies may meet with Congress or its legislative commissions to intervene, without voting rights, in the discussion of bills. The CSJ has a very secondary role in controlling matters of constitutionality. Although any of its chambers, as well as the Fiscal Tribunal and the TCA, may declare a law or regulation unconstitutional, the plenary session of the CSJ must affirm such a declaration, in which case the matter is reported to the TGC.

The CSJ supervises the superior, lower, and special courts and prepares regulations to ensure that judicial employees function properly. The CSJ examines the statistics of the cases submitted annually by the superior courts, hears or resolves questions raised by these courts, and suspends or removes lawyers who violate legal statutes. It also removes criminal, provincial, and cantonal judges and attorneys for misconduct while in office or for incapacitation. Finally, it publishes the semiannual *Gaceta Legal* (Legal Gazette), as well as the court's diary.

Each province has a Superior Court, whose judges are named by the CSJ. Within its jurisdiction, each Superior Court nominates penal, civil, labor, traffic, and tenancy judges, as well as fiscal agents, public defenders, notaries, registers of property and merchandise, and other judicial officials. Superior courts have first-instance jurisdiction in criminal cases involving provincial governors, mayors, members of electoral tribunals, customs officials, provincial judges, and police officials. They hear appeals from lower courts in both criminal and civil cases. They also resolve questions raised by lower-court judges and supervise their activities, as well as those of attorneys and notaries public. In addition, they appoint provincial and cantonal judges and attorneys.

Lower courts included thirty-five criminal and forty-two provincial courts in the late 1980s. They have first-instance jurisdiction in civil cases where the amount involved exceeds 8,000 sucres (for the value of the sucre—see Glossary). They must consult the higher courts on the interpretation of the law. When ordered by higher courts, lower courts must have representatives visit the jails in the provinces to hear the complaints of inmates, correct any abuses caused by prison personnel, and secure the release of any person arrested or detained in an illegal manner. To be a provincial judge, a person must be a citizen and a lawyer with three years of service.

The eighty-seven cantonal courts have jurisdiction in civil cases where the amount involved is between 200 and 8,000 sucres. Cantonal judges also may fine political lieutenants (*tenientes políticos*), who are responsible for the administration of justice in each parish (*parroquia*), for negligence of duty. Finally, special courts try cases involving juveniles, and labor disputes.

The Fiscal Tribunal, consisting of three chambers and nine judges named by Congress, resolves tax controversies. The TCA, which consists of two chambers of three judges each who are named by Congress, resolves controversies originating in the public administration and monitors the application and fulfillment of the law by entities of the state and their officials.

The justices of the three judicial organs—CSJ, Fiscal Tribunal, and TCA—are subject to prosecution by Congress or, in its recess, the PCL. The Constitution prohibits the judges and fiscal officials from carrying out leadership functions in the political parties, or intervening in elections. They are also prohibited from serving as lawyers or holding other public or private positions, with the exception of university professorships.

The Tribunal of Constitutional Guarantees

The TGC, rather than the CSJ, interprets and monitors compliance with the Constitution. Located in Quito, the TGC consists of eleven members and their substitutes, who serve for a two-year period, without the possibility of reelection. Congress appoints three TGC members who are nonlegislators and selects eight others from lists submitted by the president, the CSJ, the mayors and provincial prefects, the legal labor unions, and the Commercial

Associations. TGC members selected to represent the legislative, executive, and judicial branches must not already be government officials; they must be citizens by birth, in possession of their rights of citizenship, over forty years of age, and doctors of jurisprudence; and they must have fifteen years of professional experience as lawyers, judges, or university professors in jurisprudence. TGC members representing the workers, the Commercial Associations, and the citizenry (such as the mayors and provincial prefects) are required only to be citizens by birth and in possession of their citizenship rights. The ministers of state, the comptroller general, and the leaders of recognized political parties may participate in TGC deliberations without voting rights.

The TGC's role has been secondary and temporary, and its decision-making power weak. Salgado points out that the control of constitutionality has been, in effect, entrusted to a largely political organ, Congress, which lacks the requisite impartiality for debating the unconstitutionality of laws, decrees, or resolutions enacted by Congress itself. Although the 1979 Constitution failed to give the TGC enforcement authority, the 1983 constitutional reforms partly rectified this deficiency. Under the 1983 reforms, the TGC may demand the dismissal of officeholders who violate TGC decisions, and the violators' superiors are obligated to comply; request judges to initiate penal action; or report its decision to Congress, which may act on it. The TGC may also suspend those laws, decrees, accords, regulations, ordinances, or resolutions that violate the Constitution. Nevertheless, it must submit its decision to Congress or, in its recess, to the PCL, for final resolution of the case of unconstitutionality. The PCL, for its part, has had relatively broad powers to control constitutionality.

The TGC has several other powers as well. During the recess of Congress, the TGC is empowered to authorize any foreign travel by the president and to revoke a state of national emergency. The Law of Municipal Regime allows the TGC to rule on cases involving the disqualification of municipal councillors (*concejales municipales*), vacancies, or unconstitutional ordinances that the Provincial Councils were unable to resolve. The Law of Political Parties of 1978 and the Law of Elections of 1987 also grant the TGC some electoral powers.

Public Administration

The Public Ministry is one of the autonomous agencies and is headed by the attorney general. The ministry consists of the state's only judicial representative, the attorney general (who may delegate this representation), and the ministers, fiscal agents, and other

173

officials who determine the law and establish the ministry's powers, rights, reasons for dismissal, and replacement procedures. The attorney general, who serves four years, must meet the same requirements as the members of the CSJ. The office of the attorney general of the state is an autonomous organ headed by the attorney general.

The autonomous office of the comptroller general of the state manages the public funds and the property of public-sector entities. Its oversight extends to the private-sector entities that receive state subsidies. The comptroller general and the superintendents of banks and companies all serve for four years.

Local Government

The republic is divided administratively into provinces, cantons (municipalities), and parishes. Provinces are governed by a governor, cantons by a political chief (*jefe político*), and parishes by a political lieutenant. These officials all answer to, and are appointed by, the president or the executive branch. The Ministry of National Defense administers the Galápagos Islands.

Each of the twenty-one provinces has an autonomous provincial council, headed by a prefect who has only a deciding vote in case of ties in the council. The council, which has jurisdiction throughout the province and a seat in its capital, maintains public services, carries out public works, coordinates municipal activities, and informs the central government of budget expenditures. A municipal council, presided over by a mayor empowered to cast a deciding vote in case of ties, is responsible for the government of each canton, of which there were 103 in the late 1980s.

All provincial and municipal officials are elected for a four-year period by direct and secret popular vote. In elections for mayor, president of the municipal council, and provincial prefect, the candidates who obtain the greatest number of votes are elected. Councils at both levels have functional, financial, and administrative autonomy. Their legislative decisions are issued in the form of ordinances.

The 746 parishes that existed in the late 1980s were predominantly rural areas governed by a political lieutenant and a parish council within its area of responsibility; over 100 were classified as urban parishes. Although the urban parishes were mainly voting districts, the rural ones also had municipal functions. The parish council is responsible for improving public services, executing public works, investing revenues, and carrying out any other duties required by law. Its members are elected by direct popular vote to serve a four-year term.

Municipal building, Guayaquil
Courtesy Embassy of Ecuador,
Washington

The Electoral Process

Under the 1987 Law of Elections, all citizens have the right to vote or be elected, except active-duty members of the Public Forces and anyone whose citizenship rights have been suspended. Electoral registrars (*padrones electorales*) determine citizens' qualifications to vote. The franchise is obligatory for those entitled to vote, with the exception of illiterates, persons over seventy-five years of age, those certified as sick or physically disabled, individuals who suffered a domestic calamity on election day or from one to eight days before, and citizens who are absent from the country or who arrived on the day of the election.

The 1979 Constitution establishes several innovations in the system for designating the president and vice president. Whereas previously they were elected by a plurality, the Constitution requires that they be elected by an absolute majority of votes. This stipulation usually requires a second electoral round between the two leading candidates. The three organs responsible for overseeing the electoral process, with the aid of the Public Forces, are the TSE (Supreme Electoral Tribunal), TPEs (Provincial Electoral Tribunals), and the Vote Receiving Committees (Juntas Receptoras del Voto—JRVs).

As the highest of these bodies, the TSE is responsible for appointing and supervising TPE members, overseeing the electoral registrars, convoking elections and the entities that form the electoral

175

colleges, counting electoral votes, resolving appeals of rulings made by the TPEs, and issuing regulations governing the political parties. The TSE must convoke elections at least 120 days in advance of the casting of ballots. If this deadline is missed by more than forty-eight hours, the TGC may convoke the elections or a popular referendum and replace the TSE members with their substitutes, although in 1989 the constitutionality of this arrangement remained an issue. The TSE must resolve within ten days appeals raised about TPE decisions not to register candidates, to nullify votes, to invalidate or annul the vote counting, or to impose penalties for electoral infractions. The TSE also resolves electoral complaints made against civil authorities.

The TPEs are formed by the TSE in each province. The seven TPE members, who serve two years, represent the various political parties. TPE members direct and oversee the electoral process in their own jurisdiction and see that the orders of the TSE are carried out. The TPEs also appoint the members of the JRVs, conduct vote counting in their jurisdiction in a popular referendum or in elections for mayor, and resolve complaints by citizens and political parties over electoral irregularities.

The JRVs receive ballots at a public polling place on the election days. For each election, the TPEs designate a number of JRVs in accordance with the electoral registrars. The JRVs each have three principal members, three substitutes, and a secretary, all of whom are selected by their respective electoral registrar. The various political parties must be represented in the JRVs. Parties submit suggested candidates to the TPE at least sixty days before elections. The principal powers and duties of the JRVs are to provide each citizen with ballots and later a certificate of having voted; to conduct partial vote counting immediately after the polls have closed; to determine the number of valid, blank, or null votes; and to remit the ballots to the TPEs.

Only legally recognized political parties may declare candidates and register them. Registration must be completed ninety days before the date of the elections. A citizen may not be a candidate in a national and provincial election simultaneously. The president and vice president of the republic, mayors, presidents of municipal councils, provincial prefects, and most of the councillors, council members, and national and provincial deputies are elected in the first electoral round every four years. The second electoral round is held two years after the first round. Provincial deputies, whose term lasts two years, and some replacements for councillors and council members are elected at that time.

The Constitution provides for a popular consultation (*consulta popular*), which the Law of Elections refers to more specifically as a plebiscite (generally held as a vote of confidence on an action of a government) or a referendum (generally held to approve the text of a law). Either the executive or the legislative branch of government may call on the electorate to resolve a divisive issue, although the former has greater prerogatives to hold a popular consultation.

The decision adopted by a popular consultation is final. Febres Cordero became embroiled in a constitutional row in early 1986 when he formally called for an election-day plebiscite on whether independent candidates should be allowed to run for elective office. The opposition, believing that the proposed reform was designed to concentrate political and economic power in the presidency, contended that Febres Cordero's action violated Article 78, which allows the president to call plebiscites on "issues of national transcendence," but not on constitutional amendments. The opposition also claimed that Febres Cordero violated a provision giving the president recourse to a plebiscite only if Congress votes against a constitutional reform proposed by the executive. Although Febres Cordero had his way and the plebiscite on the constitutional amendment was held in June 1986, he lost the vote by a margin of 58 to 26 percent.

Political Dynamics
Political Parties

The 1967 constitution was the first to introduce provisions for political parties. The 1979 Constitution attempts to strengthen the party-based system by giving parties state protection and financial assistance. For a party to receive state financial aid, it must have obtained at least 5 percent of the votes in elections for national and provincial deputies, councillors, and council members. In these elections, the parties are prohibited from forming alliances; each party is obliged to run its own candidates. Alliances are allowed, however, in elections for president and vice president, mayors, and prefects.

The Constitution apportions state financial aid to legally recognized parties as follows: 60 percent in equal parts to each party and the remaining 40 percent according to the votes obtained in the last national elections. Although the parties also receive contributions from their affiliates, they may not receive, directly or indirectly, financial donations from individuals or groups that have contracts with the state or from companies, institutions, or foreign states.

177

Article 37, which was widely debated prior to the holding of a popular referendum in June 1986, gives legally recognized parties a type of monopoly because only they can run candidates in an election. Whereas the Constitution gives any citizen the right to be elected, Article 37 prohibits a citizen from running as an independent candidate and requires candidates to be affiliated with a political party. Salgado observed that the party affiliation requirement probably strengthens the party system, but it does so by compromising the political right of any citizen to run for office.

Although Ecuadorians over eighteen years of age may join a political party, under the Law of Political Parties this right does not apply to active-duty members of the armed forces and National Police, ministers of any religious denomination, or anyone sentenced to jail for defrauding the state (at least until after a period double that of the prison sentence). The law also prohibits more than one party affiliation. The penalty of violating this law is loss of citizenship rights for one year.

The Constitution sets out the organizational requirements for a political party. It must have a party doctrine and a program of political action that are in accord with the national interest. A party must keep count of the number of its members and be organized on a national level; that is, its organization must extend to no fewer than ten provinces, including two of the three most populated provinces (which in the late 1980s were Guayas, Pichincha, and Manabí). The Law of Political Parties also establishes that the membership of a party must constitute no fewer than 1.5 percent of the registered voters in the last electoral turnout.

A grouping or political movement must seek TSE recognition as a party according to a procedure laid out in the Law of Political Parties. To participate in elections, a party must have been legally recognized six months before the holding of these elections. In the late 1980s, Ecuador had sixteen legal parties.

Any changes in the higher leadership of a party or in its statutes must be reported to the TSE within eight days. The principal leader of a party and the members of its higher leadership body serve two-year terms. The principal leader may be reelected only once, after a two-year period, for another term. When a party splits and two directorates are formed, the TSE must determine which faction is legitimate. To that end, each faction has a thirty-day period in which to present its case. The TSE then has fifteen days in which to decide on the case, and its decision is final. Other party problems generally are resolved internally and in accordance with the party's statutes and regulations. The party's national leadership or the elements in conflict may, however, submit their problem to the decision of the TSE.

According to the Law of Political Parties, the TSE may abolish a party that decides to dissolve itself, incorporates or joins with another party, does not participate in general elections in at least ten provinces, forms paramilitary organizations, or does not respect the required nonpolitical character of the active-duty armed forces and National Police. As originally formulated, the Law of Political Parties also provided that if a party failed to obtain at least 5 percent of the votes in each of two successive elections, the TSE could dissolve it by withdrawing its legal recognition. That provision was not in effect in 1988, however, having been declared unconstitutional because of a technicality; whereas the Law of Political Parties spoke of a required "electoral percentage," the Constitution refers only to an "electoral quotient."

Unless it is dissolving itself, a party being abolished by the TSE has sixty days in which to present documentation in its own defense. Notice of the abolishment of a party and the cancellation of its registration are published in the *Registro Oficial del Estado* and sent to the news media.

The Law of Political Parties guarantees parties the right to organize meetings, marches, and public demonstrations. A party must submit a written request to hold a public march or demonstration at least forty-eight hours in advance. The authority may reject a request only if another demonstration will be held at the same place, day, and hour, but will approve another date and hour and must act on the request within twenty-four hours. A rejection may be appealed to the TPE. Any march or public demonstration must also be authorized by the police authority in the provincial capitals, by the national commissioner (*comisario nacional*) in the cantons, and by the political lieutenant in the parishes. Parties do not require authorization to hold nonpublic meetings, but are obligated to inform the aforementioned authorities in advance. Counter-demonstrations are prohibited.

The Law of Political Parties also guarantees the right of parties to propagandize their programs. If, however, political propaganda or statements disseminated by news media impugn the honor or good name of someone, that individual may demand that the offender publish a retraction. If necessary, the individual may appeal to the TPE to have this demand carried out. Under the law, all means of social communication not owned by a party must provide access to all parties and may not enter into exclusive political propaganda contracts. Lastly, political proselytism in schools and colleges is prohibited, as is coercing someone to join a party, to vote for a candidate, to participate in marches or demonstrations, or to make financial contributions.

Traditional Parties

Middle- and upper-middle class professionals and businessmen have led Ecuador's two traditional parties, the Conservative Party (Partido Conservador—PC) and the Radical Liberal Party (Partido Liberal Radical—PLR), also commonly referred to as the Liberal Party (Partido Liberal) (see The First Century of the Republic, ch. 1). García Moreno established the PC in 1869 as a loosely structured party and gave it a rightist ideological base. The Conservative Party promoted close cooperation between church and state, a strong, centralized government, and private property. Its regional stronghold was the Sierra, particularly Quito and Cuenca (capital of Azuay Province). The PC monopolized political power from 1860 until 1895, when the PLR seized power as the outcome of a civil war. The PC steadily lost ground thereafter. Although neither party held the presidency between 1944 and 1989, the PC supported the successful presidential candidacy of Camilo Ponce Enríquez in 1956. The PC also consistently made a strong showing in municipal and congressional elections in the 1960s.

Like the Conservatives, the Liberals were slow to develop a formal party structure. According to Osvaldo Hurtado, although the Liberal political movement had strengthened organizationally and ideologically by the 1880s, especially in Guayaquil, it still lacked a formal political party and remained factionalized into two main groups. The original ''civilist'' faction consisted of doctrinaire intellectuals who opposed the Conservative governments through the press and legislature. In 1884 the six-year-old radical faction of the Liberals led by Eloy Alfaro and his revolutionary *montoneros* (guerrillas) proclaimed itself the true Liberal Party and took up arms on the Costa against the Conservative government. After the temporary defeat of the radicals in 1887, the civilist faction again assumed the leadership of the Liberals. The Liberal Party was formally organized as a political entity with the holding of its first assembly in Quito in July 1890. Nevertheless, party factionalism continued. In 1892 a ''fusionist'' faction broke away and joined the Conservatives. Liberal opposition to Conservative rule became so bitter, however, that Alfaro was able to consolidate the various factions into the Radical Liberal Party (PLR) by 1895, when it took power.

The PLR was the principal ruling party between 1895 and 1944, although the coup of July 9, 1925, marked the beginning of a gradual decline in the two-party structure and in Liberal hegemony.

Modern Quito
Courtesy Embassy of Ecuador, Washington

Since its founding, the PLR had been strongest in the Costa, but in the 1960s it also won a significant following in Quito. Since the 1920s, the PLR's platform has included anticlericalism and agrarian reform. The Radical Liberals traditionally aligned themselves with the armed forces and commercial interests. The armed forces, discredited by their association with the party, distanced themselves after 1942, but trade and banking interests continued to finance the PLR. Like the PC, the PLR garnered nearly a third of the vote in congressional elections in the decades prior to 1972.

The traditional parties depended to a considerable extent on the largess of wealthy individuals or economic interest groups. It was customary, moreover, for most donors to expect large returns on their investment, and most of them assumed the role of *patrón* (patron) toward the dependent party leaders, who were expected to assume a properly subservient attitude. Corruption was widely assumed to be an institutionalized attribute of partisan activities, and party platforms enjoyed little credibility.

Other Parties

The two-party structure began to decline in the early twentieth century as leftist parties emerged and the country experienced a

181

quarter-century of political instability. Ecuador had at least four communist and socialist parties. The oldest was the Ecuadorian Socialist Party (Partido Socialista Ecuatoriano—PSE), founded in 1925 as a section of the Communist International. Consisting of a small group of intellectuals, the PSE was influential only through coalitions either with groups on the left, including the Communists, or more often, with the PLR. The PSE was one of the few parties that was neither regionally based nor personalist in character. Although it depended on wealthy groups and individuals for support, the PSE played a major role in formulating social welfare legislation.

The PSE gave birth to both the Moscow-oriented Ecuadorian Communist Party (Partido Comunista Ecuatoriano—PCE), which broke away in 1928, and the pro-Cuban Revolutionary Socialist Party of Ecuador (Partido Socialista Revolucionario del Ecuador—PSRE), which broke away in 1962. The PCE, a legal party, generally has concentrated on enhancing its position within organized labor, student organizations, and the educational bureaucracy; it had little voter appeal. By the 1970s, the PSRE had become the strongest advocate of revolution in the country. The PSRE and PCE, along with Christian leftists and Maoists, joined in 1977 to form a Moscow-line leftist front called the Broad Left Front (Frente Amplio de la Izquierda—FADI). Another PCE splinter group, the pro-Chinese Communist Party of Ecuador—Marxist-Leninist (Partido Comunista del Ecuador—Marxista-Leninista—PCE–ML) was formed in 1972.

Several noncommunist and Christian Democratic parties also emerged in the twentieth century. The Ecuadorian Nationalist Revolutionary Action (Acción Revolucionaria Nacionalista Ecuatoriana—ARNE), founded in 1942, was a highly nationalistic, anticommunist, quasi-fascist group with its strongest appeal among youths in the Sierra. The center-right Social Christian Party (Partido Social Cristiano—PSC) was established in 1951 and became the ruling party when Febres Cordero assumed the presidency in 1984. The Christian Democratic Party (Partido Demócrata Cristiano—PDC), founded in 1964, affiliated with the International Christian Democratic Association. Its center-left platform attracted a small but growing following among workers, students, and young professionals.

In 1970 Rodrigo Borja broke away from the PLR and formed, in 1977, a Quito-based Social Democratic party, the center-left Democratic Left (Izquierda Democrática—ID). The ID became Ecuador's largest party and the voice of a new generation of reformist, professionally trained political leaders. The Alfarist Radical

Front (Frente Radical Alfarista—FRA), a populist and centrist party, was established in 1972. Popular Democracy (Democracia Popular—DP), an affiliate of the Christian Democratic International, was founded in 1978 as a coalition of the PDC and the Progressive Conservative Party (Partido Conservador Progresista—PCP) and a breakaway faction of the PC. Because of its Christian Democratic membership, DP often was referred to as Democracia Popular—Democracia Cristiana.

Personalist Movements

According to Hurtado, political parties were always relatively insignificant in the Ecuadorian political process, whereas individuals transformed into caudillos played the dominant role. None of the personalist movements, however, had more than a temporary impact on politics, usually only as long as their leader enjoyed popularity. Major personalist movements have included the National Velasquista Party (Partido Nacional Velasquista—PNV), organized in 1952 by Velasco; the Social Christian Movement (Movimiento Social Cristiano—MSC), founded in 1951 by former president Camilo Ponce Enríquez; the Democratic Institutionalist Coalition (Coalición Institucionalista Democrática—CID), founded in 1965 by former provisional president Otto Arosemena Gómez; and the Concentration of Popular Forces (Concentración de Fuerzas Populares—CFP), a Guayaquil-based, populist, and center-right party organized in the late 1940s as a splinter of the *velasquista* movement by Carlos Guevara Moreno, a former interior minister. In 1980 a *roldosista* faction broke away from the CFP and formed People, Change, and Democracy (Pueblo, Cambio y Democracia—PCD), which dissolved after the death of its leader Jaime Roldós Aguilera in 1981. The populist Ecuadorian Roldosist Party (Partido Roldosista Ecuatoriano—PRE), led by Abdalá Bucaram Ortiz (nephew of Asaad Bucaram Elmhalim, a staunchly anti-Marxist former mayor of Guayaquil and former leader of the CFP), was founded in Guayaquil in late 1982.

In order to participate more effectively in elections, personalist movements often joined ad hoc coalitions of parties. Every president elected to office since 1944, with the exception of Velasco, owed his victory to a coalition rather than to a single party. Although most of these coalitions were unstable and short-lived, a few had a semipermanent character, emerging from dormancy at each election and representing roughly the same groups and interests each time. One of the most important was the National Democratic Front (Frente Democrático Nacional—FDN), which usually formed around the nucleus of the PLR, frequently along with the PSE.

Often more successful than the moderate FDN was the conservative Popular Alliance (Alianza Popular—AP), usually composed of Conservatives, *arnistas* (members of ARNE), and MSC members. The AP was responsible for Ponce Enríquez's victory in 1956 and congressional victories in 1958 and 1962.

Party Politics in the 1980s

Ecuadorian politics in the 1980s constituted an increasingly bitter struggle among conservative, center-left, and far-left parties and their leaders. Political scientist Catherine M. Conaghan, commenting on the declining standards of Ecuadorian political discourse in the late 1980s, noted that "in the absence of strong institutions and new ideas, Ecuadorian politics has devolved into a highly personalized and often trivialized arena of intra-elite struggle."

Party competition in the 1980s was mainly between the PSC (Social Christian Party) and the ID (Democratic Left). Many blamed the heightened interparty friction on Febres Cordero, the PSC leader who won the presidency by polling 52.2 percent in the second round of voting in May 1984. Febres Cordero narrowly defeated Borja, who polled 47.8 percent as the ID candidate. Febres Cordero's conservative National Reconstruction Front (Frente de Reconstrución Nacional—FRN) coalition consisted of seven parties, including the traditional PC and PLR. The FRN held only twenty-nine of the seventy-one seats in Congress, however, and the opposition effectively controlled the remaining forty-two. The resulting political infighting threatened the stability of the country's fragile democracy on several occasions.

Febres Cordero promised an honest public administration and a revival of market principles in managing the economy. Nevertheless, his government suffered from a succession of political and economic crises. Ruling more in the style of a caudillo than an elected politician, Febres Cordero used his executive powers boldly, creating a number of constitutional conflicts with the other two branches of government. For example, in late 1985 he promulgated a controversial bill changing the electoral law and postponing the legislative elections scheduled for early 1986. The proposed reform, which was defeated in the plebiscite held on June 1, 1986, would not only have given the executive extraordinary economic powers, but would also have limited the right of habeas corpus, set a four-year term for all members of Congress, and allowed independents to be elected. Febres Cordero's authoritarian rule and strongly pro-United States policies were blamed for his government's major political defeat in the mid-term congressional elections by allied center-left and Marxist parties, which captured forty-three of the legislature's seventy-one seats.

Certain high-ranking military officials posed a challenge to Febres Cordero in 1986. He dismissed the armed forces chief of staff, Air Force Lieutenant General Frank Vargas Pazzos, for accusing the minister of national defense and an army commander of corruption. Vargas subsequently staged a week-long double revolt—first at the Eloy Alfaro Air Base in Manta on the Pacific Coast and then at Quito's Marshal Sucre International Airport—and demanded the resignations of the two military leaders. A bloody battle in March ended the second revolt and resulted in Vargas's arrest. Although Congress granted Vargas amnesty that October, a decision upheld by the TGC, Febres Cordero refused to honor the decision, sparking a constitutional controversy.

During a presidential visit to the Taura Air Base outside Guayaquil in January 1987, paratroop commandos loyal to Vargas abducted Febres Cordero and his defense minister. They were released eleven hours later after Febres Cordero personally granted amnesty to Vargas and signed a written guarantee that no reprisals would be taken against either the rebellious former general or his commandos. A few days later, however, the army arrested the ninety-four paratroopers, who were then expelled from the air force. A military tribunal sentenced fifty-eight of them to prison sentences ranging from six months to sixteen years.

Rather than rallying around the president following the near overthrow of the democratic system, the leftist-dominated Congress called a special session to consider impeaching Febres Cordero for allowing himself to be kidnapped and then negotiating his release by freeing Vargas. Although the opposition was unable to obtain the two-thirds majority needed to impeach the president, it approved a nonbinding demand that Febres Cordero resign for "disgracing" the national honor.

Running as both a Socialist and a populist, Vargas participated in the first round of the 1988 presidential elections as the representative of the People's Patriotic Union (Unión del Pueblo Patriótico—UPP). To the surprise of many, Vargas placed fourth by garnering over 12 percent of the vote. In that election, Vargas's UPP also allied itself with the PSE (Ecuadorian Socialist Party), the Ecuadorian Revolutionary Popular Alliance (Alianza Popular Revolucionaria Ecuatoriana—APRE), and FADI (Broad Left Front).

Also running as a center-left candidate was Jamil Mahuad Witt, a DP protégé of former president Osvaldo Hurtado. Mahuad won 11.5 percent of the vote. On the far left, Jaime Hurtado ran as the candidate of the Maoist-oriented Democratic Popular Movement (Movimiento Popular Democrático—MPD), with the backing of the FADI, but collected only 5 percent of the vote, behind the CFP's Angel Duarte, with nearly 8 percent.

Another contender was PRE leader Abdalá Bucaram Ortiz, who returned from Panama, where he had fled in 1985 after criticizing the armed forces, to participate in the first round of the presidential elections. Febres Cordero allowed the flamboyant, mercurial Bucaram to return in the belief that his candidacy would help weaken the center-left and unite the right. The 18.4 percent of the vote Bucaram garnered shocked all the candidates and their parties, especially those on the disunited right, whose prime contender, the PSC's Sixto Durán Ballén, placed third with not quite 15 percent of the vote. A high voter turnout (nearly 78 percent) throughout the country and particularly in Guayaquil contributed to Bucaram's impressive showing. He suddenly became a major challenger by edging out Durán and placing second to Rodrigo Borja who, as expected, was in first place, with 24.5 percent.

Accordingly, the second round of the presidential elections in May 1988 was a contest between Borja and Bucaram. Despite their lack of substantive policy differences—both favored economic nationalism and import substitution—their campaigns were characterized by hard-hitting personal attacks that, Conaghan notes, "brought the level of political discourse to a new low." Borja won, as expected, with 1.7 million ballots, or 47.4 percent of the vote. Bucaram, with the aid of the Lebanese community in Guayaquil, polled 40.3 percent, totaling about 1.45 million votes. (Of the approximately 3.8 million ballots cast, 425,000 were null and 45,000 blank.) This was a much better showing than expected, especially considering the failure of his PRE to win the support of any of the other major registered parties. Bucaram subsequently fled the country again to avoid an arrest order issued by the president of Guayaquil's Superior Court for alleged malfeasance when he was mayor of Guayaquil in 1985. Nevertheless, according to Conaghan, the electoral results legitimized Bucaram as a national leader and assured him a future role as a presidential contender.

Although Borja lost in the five coastal provinces, he carried the fourteen provinces of the Sierra and Oriente (eastern region), as well as the Galápagos Islands. (Sucumbíos, the twenty-first province, was not created until 1989.) He also made an important showing in Guayas Province and adjacent Los Ríos Province, winning about 33 percent of the vote. Borja's ID became the majority party by winning twenty-nine of the seventy-one seats in Congress and entering into a coalition with the Popular Democratic Union (Unión

President Borja
Courtesy Embassy of Ecuador,
Washington

Democrática Popular—UDP) and DP (Popular Democracy), with seven seats, and FADI, with two seats. FADI was joined by the Movement for the Unity of the Left (Movimiento para la Unidad de la Izquierda—MUI) and the Revolutionary Movement of the Christian Left (Movimiento Revolucionario de la Izquierda Cristiana—MRIC). Borja also had the support of the FRA (Alfarist Radical Front), the Maoist MPD, and CFP (Concentration of Popular Forces).

Borja took office in August 1988 promising to reverse completely the policy course of Febres Cordero. He called for a "pluralist cabinet" and a "government of consensus," meaning a national understanding (*concertación*) among workers, employers, and the government. His cabinet included seven ID members, four independents, and one DP member, as well as the two secretaries general, who belonged to the ID. Borja, a former professor of constitutional law at the Central University, made respect for legal guarantees a central theme in the selection of his ministers. His government energetically investigated alleged civil abuses perpetrated by Febres Cordero's government and secured several convictions.

The Borja government also took a new direction by making moves to appease opposition elements within military and guerrilla ranks. In November 1988, with the approval of the CSJ and several other institutions, including the military, Borja pardoned the air force paratroopers who had kidnaped Febres Cordero and

187

had become, in jail, heroes among left-wing and populist parties. In early 1989, the Borja government negotiated an agreement with the Eloy Alfaro Popular Armed Forces (Fuerzas Armadas Populares Eloy Alfaro—FAP-EA), popularly known as the Alfaro Lives, Damnit! (¡Alfaro Vive, Carajo!—AVC), a guerrilla/terrorist group founded in 1982 (see Internal Security, ch. 5). Borja also pardoned a number of imprisoned former air force members (see Political Forces and Interest Groups, this ch.). In mid-1989, his legislative coalition with Hurtado's Christian Democratic party ended by mutual accord: Hurtado had opposed it from the start, and Borja no longer needed the agreement with the Christian Democrats, having won the support of other small parties.

Political Forces and Interest Groups

Interest groups able to influence regime changes traditionally have included the church, the military, the agrarian elite, the largely Guayaquil-based commercial community, foreign commercial interests, the urban working class, the politically active peasantry and rural workers, and the middle class (including students). Some of these groups have formed alliances with or have manipulated less influential groups. Motivated primarily by parochial concerns, many of these interest groups, like the political parties themselves, have provided little impetus to national development. Other smaller interest groups have included the myriad of governmental autonomous agencies, which generally controlled their own funds and followed their own policies. Illegal political extremist organizations, such as the AVC and a nascent narcotics-trafficking mafia, may, in a sense, constitute additional, unconventional interest groups.

The Roman Catholic Church

The role of the Roman Catholic Church in society was the most divisive political issue in Ecuador for more than a century after independence. Despite the confiscation of its land by the Alfaro government at the beginning of the twentieth century, the church in the Sierra retained its preeminent position in social and economic life. In the more remote villages and small towns of the Sierra, the parish priest was often seen as the ultimate temporal, as well as spiritual, authority. The church gave religious and moral legitimacy to the actions of its defender, the PC. By contrast, the Costa was the base of the PLR, whose major platform traditionally had been anticlericalism. PLR policies caused the clergy and many devout laymen to rise to the defense of the church and its prerogatives. Nonetheless, by 1945 the church-state conflict had ceased to be a significant political issue on the national level.

In the 1960s, the church hierarchy, influenced by reform-oriented papal encyclicals, endorsed land reform, a more just system of taxation, and workers' rights. The church underwent a process of significant internal transformation and ideological renovation and found itself cast in the role of an advocate of far-reaching change and innovation (see Religion, ch. 2). Nevertheless, Thomas G. Sanders noted that the Catholic Church in Ecuador had become firmly committed to nonpartisanship by the late 1970s. According to Sanders, the Ecuadorian church's more neutral role contributed to political stability and strengthened pluralism by emphasizing national unity and the need to promote social justice.

The Military

Historically, the military establishment alternated between direct or indirect control over the executive functions in general and a more limited role of exercising a veto over policies considered to fall within the area of its corporate interests (see Involvement in Politics and Government, ch. 5). In contrast with the pattern found in the majority of Latin American countries, the Ecuadorian military, which traditionally was allied with the PLR, early on became more closely identified with the merchant class than with the landholding elite. After the decline of the traditional parties in the early twentieth century and the rise of ad hoc political coalitions, however, the military acquired greater autonomy as an institutional political force.

Constitutions between 1945 and 1979 have legitimized the role of the military in policy making by allotting to the officer corps an official seat in the Senate. Interventions between 1945 and 1963 arose most often over issues considered basic by the military leadership. For example, in 1962 the military pressured President Carlos Julio Arosemena Monroy to sever relations with Cuba and other socialist countries. When they ousted him in 1963, it was only after more than a year of encouragement by various political factions and economic interest groups, all of which were concerned over the chaotic drift in national affairs and over Arosemena's personal conduct (see Instability and Military Dominance, 1960–72, ch. 1). After assuming power, however, the military became increasingly confident of its ability to rule better than civilians. The changing attitude of the officer corps, coupled with its declining trust in civilian leaders, was attributed in part to a new emphasis in military training on technical and managerial skills and to extensive foreign training in general.

Factionalism within the armed forces has helped to account for the propensity of military plotting against civilian governments, as well as the difficulties encountered by the military establishment in its attempts to govern on its own. Civilian contenders for political power often sought the support of dissident elements of the military in order to topple an administration or to forestall an electoral outcome unfavorable to them. At the same time, factions within the military aligned themselves with civilian groups in order to strengthen their own positions vis-à-vis other military factions. For example, when widespread civilian discontent boded ill for the continuation of government by junta in 1966, important elements of the armed forces joined the civilian opposition and contributed to the fall of the junta.

On numerous occasions, the military applied its influence to ward off political developments that it opposed or to intervene indirectly. For example, when the leftist opposition in Congress undertook to impeach Febres Cordero in January 1987, armed forces representatives warned the president of Congress that the military would shut down the legislature if impeachment proceedings were not halted. Febres Cordero's interference in internal military matters, however, created resentments, as demonstrated dramatically by the military rebellions in March 1986. In June 1987, a group of about a dozen army and naval officers met with the defense minister and suggested that Febres Cordero resign. The military also reportedly threatened to intervene if Bucaram won the 1988 presidential election.

The Economic Elite

In popular usage, the term oligarchy referred to the old Quito upper class, whose fortunes were amassed originally through ownership of land, and to prominent commercial groups in Guayaquil. Although members of the wealthiest families historically seldom participated personally in politics—except for serving in diplomatic posts in Europe or the United States or as foreign ministers—the economic elite often appeared to manage political affairs to its own advantage.

Since the mid-twentieth century, associational interest groups representing the upper class have proliferated. Commercial, industrial, and agricultural associations became increasingly important, even in provincial capitals where informal connections were previously considered sufficient. After the constitution of 1967 allowed agricultural, commercial, and industrial associations to elect one senator each from the Sierra and one each from the Costa, the Senate became dominated by representatives of employer groups (see Elite, ch. 2).

A view of the Northern Sierra
Courtesy Patricia Mothes

Although lacking the claims to aristocracy of the Quito upper class, Guayaquil's commercial and financial elite was the wealthiest in the country. Its members espoused liberal principles, such as the expansion of political participation, but generally seemed even less disposed toward economic reforms than did its counterparts in Quito. The coastal elite participated in the political process by financing the campaigns of various parties and factions. It was well organized, principally through the Guayaquil Chamber of Commerce, and was capable of raising the banner of regional autonomy whenever its interests were threatened.

The provincial landowners formed the most conservative of all significant political groups. Their strength was much greater in the Sierra than on the Costa, and they were especially powerful in provincial and municipal affairs in the south. Until the dissolution of Congress in 1970, hacendado associations were strongly represented in that body, both through the regional senators and deputies representing the southern highland provinces and through the senators elected by the associations themselves. There was broad sympathy and support for the hacendado viewpoint among those who monopolized most instruments of power.

Labor

Disunited and poorly organized for most of its history, the labor movement developed only slowly and had only a marginal political impact. Precise figures on unionization in the late 1980s were practically nonexistent, even within the unions themselves. The organized labor movement was divided into four confederations and a number of independent federations. At the local level, labor organizations also took the form of artisan guilds, cooperatives, and neighborhood associations. In addition to representing only a minority of the workers in all sectors of employment (approximately one-fifth), the labor movement traditionally was weakened by rivalry and government repression. Nevertheless, it had influence disproportionate to its numbers as a result of the concentration of labor unions in urban areas, mainly Quito and Guayaquil, its organizational power, and the political impact of strikes and demonstrations on governments that did not enjoy strong support.

Professional or employee associations (*cámaras*), composed of middle-class, white-collar workers, constituted about 25 percent of all labor unions. Representing the dominant economic groups in the country, these associations exercised a predominant influence on economic policy; their representatives frequently held cabinet posts and other top government positions dealing with economics. The support of the associations proved crucial to most governments.

Although union organizations began forming in Ecuador early in the twentieth century, organized workers did not begin to acquire any influence until the late 1930s. Key events in Ecuador's labor history took place in 1938 with the promulgation of the Labor Code and the founding of the first labor confederation, the Ecuadorian Federation of Classist Organizations (Central Ecuatoriana de Organizaciones Clasistas—CEDOC). Between 1938 and 1949, some 550 labor organizations were formed. These included the country's second confederation, the Confederation of Ecuadorian Workers (Confederación de Trabajadores Ecuatorianos—CTE), which began operating in 1944. A total of 3,093 unions were established between 1950 and 1973.

CEDOC was never an effective articulator of worker interests, being more concerned with religious causes, combating efforts to eliminate exclusion of ecclesiastical control and influence in labor organizations, and curtailing communist infiltration in the labor sector. Although of Catholic origin, CEDOC rejected its Christian Democratic leadership in 1976 and adopted a socialist orientation. The old leaders retained the support of a few grassroots organizations and formed a parallel organization. Approximately 80 percent of CEDOC'S membership came from the Ecuadorian Federation of Peasant Organizations (Federación Ecuatoriana de Organizaciones Campesinas—FEDOC). In the mid-1980s, CEDOC had unions in fifteen of the twenty provinces; its estimated membership of 130,000 was largely composed of artisans, with almost no industrial worker membership. After twelve years of political division, the two CEDOC branches united in 1988 and formed the Ecuadorian Confederation of Classist Organizations for Workers' Unity (Confederación Ecuatoriana de Organizaciones Clasistas para la Unidad de los Trabajadores—CEDOCUT).

Through militant activities, such as petitions, collective conflicts, and general strikes, the CTE—composed predominantly of industrial workers and led by members of the communist and socialist parties—emerged as the principal labor organization in Ecuador in the late 1970s. Although the CTE had become the largest of the three national confederations by the 1970s, its hegemony declined in the 1980s as a result of the growth of rival confederations, internal conflicts and splits, and governmental repression. In 1987 only a shadow remained of its peasant federation, the Ecuadorian Indian Federation (Federación Ecuatoriana de Indios—FEI). The CTE still included a number of industrial unions and various public-sector unions, and was organizing autonomous workers. It encompassed an estimated 55,000 members in 200 affiliated unions.

The Communist Party of Ecuador—Marxist-Leninist established a small federation, the General Union of Ecuadorian Workers (Unión General de Trabajadores Ecuatorianos—UGTE), in an attempt to rival the CTE. Apart from the powerful National Union of Teachers (Unión Nacional de Educadores—UNE), which had about 100,000 members, the UGTE had little success in affiliating unions. Together with student unions and a few other groups, the UGTE formed the Popular Front (Frente Popular—FP), which in the 1980s was attempting to rival the United Workers Front (Frente Unitario de Trabajadores—FUT) in organizing protest action.

The Inter-American Regional Organization of Workers (Organización Regional Interamericana de Trabajadores—ORIT) tried to unify the non-Marxist unions by founding the Ecuadorian Confederation of Free Trade Union Organizations (Confederación Ecuatoriana de Organizaciones Sindicales Libres—CEOSL) in 1962. The CEOSL became the third-largest confederation, with membership consisting almost exclusively of urban white- and blue-collar workers. It included fourteen provincial and thirteen national federations made up of a large proportion of industrial workers, a number of members from the service sector, and a small number of agricultural workers, peasants, and craftsmen.

FUT emerged in 1971 and eventually united the three main confederations—CEDOC, CEOSL, and CTE—plus a number of independent unions, including the Catholic Federation of Workers (Central Católica de Obreros—CCO), making FUT the country's largest workers' confederation. By the 1980s, FUT totaled an estimated 300,000 members and emerged as the leader of a massive movement that arose spontaneously to protest the economic crisis, and that greatly outnumbered the ranks of unionized workers. FUT nearly toppled President Hurtado in 1982 when he introduced austerity measures in the face of the debt crisis. In June 1988, FUT, together with the National Coordinator of Workers (Coordinadora Nacional de Trabajadores—CNT), the Confederation of Indigenous Nationalities of Ecuador (Confederación de Nacionalidades Indígenas del Ecuador—Conaie), and FP, staged a one-day national strike aimed at obtaining a large increase in the minimum wage and a freeze on the prices of basic goods. It was the seventh general labor action against the Febres Cordero government and coincided with an ongoing strike by the UNE for a rise in monthly wages. The impact of FUT remained limited, however, because the federation tended to maintain its working-class orientation, based on wage claims, and in practice gave relatively little importance to the claims of other sectors that looked to it for leadership.

Students

Beginning in the first decade of the twentieth century, students took to the streets on a number of occasions in defense of public freedoms, university autonomy and reform, separation of church and state, and opposition to dictatorship. Following the establishment in 1944 of the Federation of University Students of Ecuador (Federación de Estudiantes Universitarios del Ecuador—FEUE), the student movement, spurred by campus representatives of the political parties, became increasingly politicized and one of the most influential pressure groups in the country, playing a role in every nonconstitutional change of government. Both the FEUE and the Federation of High School Students of Ecuador (Federación de Estudiantes Secundarios del Ecuador—FESE) contributed significantly to the downfall in 1966 of the military junta, which had abolished university autonomy and student-faculty government. Student federations were organized at Catholic universities in 1966 and at the polytechnic schools in 1969. In the early 1970, the FEUE represented some 40,000 student at five public and two Catholic

Broadcasting in Quichua
over Radio Latacunga in Cotopaxi Province
Courtesy Inter-American Foundation (Miguel Sayago)

universities, one non-Catholic private university, and the polytechnic schools (see Education, ch. 2).

During the late 1960s, the student movement, heavily influenced by the Cuban Revolution, had assumed a militantly anti-oligarchy, anti-military, and anti-imperialist orientation. Student radicalism prompted the military government to intervene brutally in the Central University in 1966 and to close it in 1970. In the late 1970s, the student movement, seriously weakened as a result of endemic factionalism and the increasing isolation of the FEUE leadership, faced invincible shortcomings. With few exceptions, the political action of the university federations in the 1970s had gone no farther than press statements, graffiti, revolutionary pamphlets, street demonstrations, meetings, strikes, and work stoppages. Consequently, the groups had lost their traditional political prestige and the support of important segments of the student population.

The Media

Although the 1979 Constitution accords Ecuadorians the right to freedom of opinion and expression of thought, media ownership has remained concentrated in the hands of a few large interests. In the late 1980s, all media were privately controlled, except the

National Radio (Radio Nacional), which was operated by the government's ministerial-level National Communications Secretariat (Secretaría Nacional de Comunicaciones—Senac), previously called the National Secretariat for Public Information (Secretaría Nacional de Información Pública—Sendip) under the Febres Cordero administration. The government, however, controlled the allocation of radio and television frequencies. Historically, most media owners endorsed the political status quo and gave tacit support to right-wing governments and even to dictatorships. In the 1980s, however, conservative interests were less dominant in radio than in television and the written press.

The Febres Cordero government used the media systematically in an effort to gain media support for its free-market economic policies, and in the process it infringed on press freedom. For example, in late 1984 the government temporarily closed five radio stations—four in Guayaquil and one in Quito—after they broadcast Guayaquil mayor Abdalá Bucaram's censure of Febres Cordero. The government also used economic means of pressure, such as suspending its substantial public-sector advertising in the center-left daily *Hoy* and the monthly magazine *Nueva*, as well as pressuring private banks and companies not to advertise in these publications. As a result, the independent media initially omitted or toned down criticism of the government. However, two prestigious inter-American media associations criticized the Febres Cordero government for alleged violations of press freedom. In a report released in March 1985, the Inter-American Press Association accused the government of intolerance toward the independent press and a lack of objectivity in government press releases. In addition, many opposition journalists complained that the government was using legal or pseudo-legal devices and pretexts to reduce further the already limited space available to the minority press. In 1987 opposition radio and television stations continued to experience government attempts to stifle the media. The ability of the government to pressure state and private companies to discriminate against the independent media diminished following the erosion of Febres Cordero's standing and influence.

On taking office in August 1988, Borja vowed to uphold freedom of the press and appointed various journalists to high-level governmental posts. Senac, composed of new members appointed by Borja, undertook efforts to make the government accessible to the media and to promote freedom of the press. Senac also abolished the progovernment simulcasts initiated by the Febres Cordero administration and allowed Channel 5 in Quito to resume broadcasting in August 1988, after being closed for four years.

Ecuador had ten principal television stations in the late 1980s. The country's commercial radio stations numbered over 260, including 10 cultural and 10 religious stations. The ''Voice of the Andes'' station had operated for more than fifty years as an evangelical Christian shortwave radio service supported largely by contributions from the United States.

Ecuador had only thirty daily newspapers in the late 1980s. The newspapers with the largest circulations, *El Comercio* and *El Universo,* were published in Quito and Guayaquil, respectively. Founded in the 1920s, they were closely connected with each city's small but powerful business community in the 1980s. Quito and Guayaquil each had four dailies. Quito's largest newspaper, *El Comercio,* was conservative and had a circulation of 130,000. *El Comercio* also owned an evening newspaper, *Últimas Noticias.* The Quito-based *Hoy,* founded in the early 1980s, had a circulation in 1987 of between 35,000 and 40,000. Guayaquil's *El Universo* was independent and had a circulation of between 120,000 and 190,000 on weekdays and 225,000 on Sundays. Guayaquil's second newspaper, *Expreso,* published evening newspapers in both cities: *Extra* in Guayaquil and *La Hora* in Quito. Some ten international news agencies had bureaus in Quito.

The principal weekly periodicals that covered political and economic affairs were Quito's *La Calle,* with a circulation of 20,000, and Guayaquil's *Análisis Semanal* and *Vistazo. Nueva,* with a circulation of between 12,000 and 14,000, was founded in the early 1970s as an alternative magazine oriented to those sectors of the population that were under-represented by the traditional press, such as trade union workers, intellectuals, and Indians.

Among Ecuador's ten principal publishers, only Editorial Claridad and Pontificia Universidad Católica del Ecuador, published books on politics. According to the United States Department of State in the late 1980s, there was no political censorship of domestic or foreign books, films, or works of art, and no government interference with academic inquiry.

Foreign Relations

According to the United States Department of State, Ecuador's principal foreign-policy objectives have included defense of the national territory from external aggression and internal subversion; support for the objectives of the United Nations (UN) and the Organization of American States (OAS); defense of its claim to 320 kilometers of territorial and fisheries jurisdictions off its coast; and revision of the 1942 Protocol of Peace, Friendship, and Boundaries (Rio Protocol), which ended, at least officially, open warfare

197

between Peru and Ecuador over a territorial dispute. Although Ecuador's foreign relations traditionally have centered on the United States, Ecuador's membership in the Organization of Petroleum Exporting Countries (OPEC) in the 1970s and 1980s allowed some Ecuadorian leaders to exercise somewhat greater foreign policy autonomy. Ecuador's international foreign policy goals under the Borja government in the late 1980s were more diversified than those of the Febres Cordero administration, which closely identified with the United States. For example, Ecuador was more active in its relations with the Third World, multilateral organizations, Western Europe, and socialist countries.

The United States

The United States maintained good relations with Ecuador's democratically elected governments in the 1980s. These close ties were based on trade, investment and finance, cooperation in Ecuador's economic development, and participation in inter-American organizations and treaties, including the Western Hemisphere's regional mutual security treaty, the Inter-American Treaty of Reciprocal Assistance (Rio Treaty) of 1947. The United States provided US$48 million in assistance to Ecuador in 1988 and was its main commercial partner. The United States provided economic assistance through its Agency for International Development program in Ecuador and multilateral organizations, such as the Inter-American Development Bank and World Bank (see Glossary). In addition, the United States Peace Corps operated a sizable program in Ecuador.

Three irritants in particular affected bilateral relations in the 1970s and 1980s. One was the United States Foreign Trade Act of 1974, which denied (until the 1980s) favorable tariff treatment to all OPEC members, even though neither Ecuador nor Venezuela participated in the 1973 oil boycott of the United States. Ecuador also reacted indignantly in early 1977 when the United States prohibited Israel from selling a dozen Kfir fighter-bombers to Ecuador because the aircraft contained licensed General Electric engines. In 1981, however, the United States lifted the prohibition (see Equipment Sources, ch. 5). An additional aggravation was a dispute over the extent of the territorial sea claimed by Ecuador since 1953 and its rights over highly migratory fish traveling through these waters. In the early 1970s, Ecuador seized about 100 tuna boats flying the United States flag and collected fines and fees totaling more than US$6 million. No additional seizures occurred until November 1980, when ten tuna boats were detained while fishing and fined. That action provoked a United States embargo on the importing of tuna from Ecuador. Although still unresolved, the territorial sea and fishing issues did not adversely affect bilateral relations for most of the 1980s.

Febres Cordero's foreign policy was characterized by a marked preference for bilateralism and closer ties to the United States. His foreign and economic policies mirrored those advocated by the administration of President Ronald Reagan, particularly on matters related to Central America and Latin America's international debt. During Febres Cordero's week-long state visit to Washington in January 1986, United States and Ecuadorian officials repeatedly underlined their two presidents' total agreement on economic and political matters.

Ecuador was almost alone in its enthusiastic reception of the 1986 Baker Plan (named after then United States secretary of the treasury James A. Baker III) for alleviating Third World debt, which called for fresh infusions of capital into the debt-ridden countries, contingent on structural reforms. Febres Cordero advocated bilateral negotiation rather than the use of a regional "cartel" to renegotiate the debt and strongly favored an "understanding" between debtor and creditor nations. (Nevertheless, Ecuador stopped paying interest on its debt in 1987.) The Febres Cordero government also ignored petroleum production quotas set by OPEC and threatened to withdraw from the cartel as well.

Febres Cordero approved "Operation Blazing Trails," a United States-sponsored civic-action project to repair bridges and roads in the earthquake-devastated province of Napo. The project involved rotating contingents of 600 United States troops through the country at fifteen-day intervals beginning in May 1986, until an Ecuadorian congressional resolution in July called for their immediate withdrawal. Marxist and centrist leaders alike had denounced Febres Cordero's approval of the project as a violation of national sovereignty.

United States secretary of state George P. Shultz attended Borja's swearing-in ceremony on August 10, 1988. During his first year in office, Borja remained on good terms with the United States. In his meeting with United States vice president Daniel Quayle in Caracas in February 1989, Borja stressed the need for good relations within the framework of mutual respect and nonintervention in Ecuador's domestic affairs. The Borja government expressed satisfaction with the proposal presented in March 1989 by United States treasury secretary Nicolas Brady regarding the Latin American debt problem. The Brady Plan called for the creditor banks to write off a portion of a poor country's indebtedness in return for guaranteed repayment of the remaining debt. Nevertheless,

Borja favored a Bolivian-style policy of holding back payments because of poverty.

Other Nations and International Organizations

Ecuador and the Soviet Union established diplomatic relations in 1969, but it was not until 1972, when Ecuador joined OPEC, that the Soviets showed much interest in Ecuador. By the mid-1970s, the Soviet Union maintained an embassy in Quito rivaling in importance that of the United States.

Ecuador traditionally favored multilateral approaches to international problems. It belonged to the UN, the Nonaligned Movement (NAM), the OAS, and other regional integration groupings, such as the Latin American Economic System (Sistema Económico Latinoamericano—SELA), the Latin American Energy Organization, the Latin American Integration Association, and the Andean Pact. Ecuador—along with Bolivia, Chile, Colombia, and Peru—signed the Andean Pact and the Cartagena Agreement in 1969, creating an Andean Common Market. In 1978 Ecuador and seven other South American countries signed the Amazon Pact treaty for the joint development of the Amazon River Basin.

Febres Cordero, however, took exception to Ecuador's traditional multilateralism. Impatient with regional and multilateral arrangements, he opposed the clause in the Andean Pact that restricted foreign investment, and sought to have it liberalized. To that end, Ecuador threatened several times to withdraw from the Andean Pact. It did not send a representative to the 1986 meeting of the group's foreign ministers in Uruguay. The Febres Cordero government also kept a low profile in the OAS, SELA, and the Cartagena Group.

Praised as "realistic and pragmatic" by some, Febres Cordero's foreign policy was criticized as "erratic and incongruous" by others. Evidence supporting both these views could be found in his government's relations with Cuba and Nicaragua and his positions on Latin American issues. On April 16, 1985, Febres Cordero became the first conservative Latin American president to visit Cuba since Fidel Castro Ruz took power twenty-six years earlier. The Ecuadorian president reportedly talked at length with Castro about ways to ease the region's foreign debt burden and bring peace to Central America.

The Febres Cordero government kept its distance, however, from most of the region's initiatives to promote Latin American solidarity. In October 1985, Ecuador joined the so-called Lima Group of four South American nations—Argentina, Brazil, Peru, and Uruguay—supporting the search for peace in Central America initiated by the Contadora Group (consisting of Mexico, Venezuela, Colombia, and Panama, whose ministers first met in 1983 on Contadora Island in the Gulf of Panama). Nonetheless, Ecuador not only withdrew from the Lima Group later that month, but also became the first Latin American nation to break diplomatic relations with Nicaragua. The break in relations, which came suddenly after Febres Cordero and Nicaraguan president Daniel Ortega Saavedra traded public insults, had the unintended effect of isolating Ecuador from other Latin American countries. Some observers also viewed it as Febres Cordero's response to the United States' request for a blockade of international aid to Nicaragua.

In his inaugural address, Borja vowed to pursue an independent, nonaligned foreign policy based on the principles of self-determination and nonintervention. He believed that Latin American unity should take priority over ideological differences. Accordingly, he invited both Ortega and Castro to his inauguration ceremony on August 10. Castro attended the event, but Febres Cordero refused to allow Ortega into the country, except as a tourist. Consequently, Ortega delayed his arrival in Quito until August 11, by which time Borja, in one of his first official acts as head of state, had restored diplomatic relations with Nicaragua. Borja also expanded the relationship that Febres Cordero had initiated with Cuba, allowing some Cuban and Nicaraguan advisers to assist in Ecuador's National Literacy Program. In addition, he criticized the policy of isolating Cuba from international forums, such as the UN and OAS.

Borja also endorsed the establishment of an OPEC common front to defend oil prices, to fulfill the obligations that Ecuador assumed in the modifying protocol of the Cartagena Agreement, and to reincorporate Ecuador into the group of Latin American countries supporting the Central American peace process. The Borja government anticipated good relations with Venezuela, another OPEC member whose president, Carlos Andrés Pérez, was Borja's closest associate in the region. In early 1989, however, the Group of Eight (the eight democratic Latin American countries which belonged to the former Contadora or Lima Groups) rejected Ecuador's bid for membership. Nevertheless, in June 1989 Colombian president Virgilio Barco Vargas invited Ecuador to replace Panama in the Group of Eight. In September 1989, Borja stated publicly his belief that General Manuel Antonio Noriega, Panama's de facto leader as commander of the Panama Defense Forces, should step down, but added that he opposed United States military intervention to depose him.

A protracted border dispute continued to strain relations between Ecuador and Peru. The approximately 200,000-square-kilometer area of the Amazon (the Marañón district), which Ecuador had claimed since the nineteenth century, contained the city of Iquitos on the west bank of the Amazon River and also Peru's main jungle petroleum-producing region. Since 1960, when Ecuador's president Velasco declared invalid the Rio Protocol, under which the area was recognized as Peru's, Ecuador had continued to assert its right to the disputed region and to emphasize its need for an outlet to the Atlantic via the Amazon River (see Reform, Chaos, and Debacle, 1925–44). A small border war with Peru broke out on January 28, 1981, in the Condor mountain range, which runs along the border between the Amazon Basin and Ecuador. After Peruvian forces drove Ecuadorian troops back from the border posts, a cease-fire came into effect on February 1. A commission composed of the military attachés of the United States, Argentina, Brazil, and Chile, who helped negotiate the cease-fire, was charged with supervising the border area. Most Ecuadorians, however, supported their government's efforts to obtain a revision of the 1942 protocol.

As a vice president of the Socialist International, Borja enjoyed good relations with several West European countries. He was particularly close to Portuguese president Mário Lopes Soares, who attended his inauguration. The French-speaking Ecuadorian president was also a long-time admirer of France's president François Mitterrand, whose wife Danielle attended the installation ceremony on behalf of France. The deputy prime minister of Spain also attended, as did representatives from the Federal Republic of Germany (West Germany), the German Democratic Republic (East Germany), and Sweden. The Soviet Union and China were also represented at the inauguration. The Borja government reaffirmed Ecuador's support for the rights of the Palestinian people and for a peaceful, just, and lasting solution to the Middle East conflict within the framework of UN Security Council Resolutions 242 and 338 and an international conference under UN auspices. Borja attended the NAM summit in Yugoslavia in September 1989.

* * *

The scholarly literature in English on Ecuador's political system is limited. A pioneering study of Ecuador's political system is George I. Blanksten's *Ecuador: Constitutions and Caudillos*. John D. Martz's *Ecuador: Conflicting Political Culture and the Quest for Progress* is a somewhat dated but still useful historical study of the political system. Former president Osvaldo Hurtado's *Political Power in Ecuador* is a very informative and insightful academic study of Ecuadorian politics. Although some of the data in the revised version remains outdated or inconsistent, Hurtado's book is nevertheless widely considered to be one of the best and most original studies of the country's political, economic, and intellectual history. An authoritative study of Ecuador's constitutional history and political system in the 1980s by one of the country's leading judicial scholars is Hernán Salgado Pesants's *Instituciones Políticas y Constitución del Ecuador.* Other up-to-date, scholarly books include David W. Schodt's *Ecuador: An Andean Enigma, Ecuador: Fragile Democracy* by David Corkill and David Cubitt, and Catherine M. Conaghan's *Restructuring Domination: Industrialists and the State in Ecuador.*

Insightful political analyses in academic journals include Martz's "Instability in Ecuador" and Conaghan's "Ecuador Swings Toward Social Democracy" in *Current History.* A detailed and well-informed analysis (in French) of voting patterns in Ecuador's 1984 and 1988 presidential elections is "Équateur de León Febres Cordero à Rodrigo Borja (1984–1988)," by Yves Saint-Geours. (For further information and complete citations, see Bibliography.)

Chapter 5. National Security

Military chief clutching a club (Bahía culture)

ALTHOUGH MODEST IN SIZE AND operational capacity, the Ecuadorian armed forces (Fuerzas Armadas—FF.AA.), have been sufficient to deal with the nation's limited external and domestic security concerns. The only outside hostilities Ecuador has experienced have been with Peru in 1941 and 1981, when the two nations engaged in brief encounters over disputed claims in the Amazon River Basin. On both occasions, the Ecuadorian army proved little match for the larger and better equipped Peruvian forces. As of 1989, the distant prospect of some renewed confrontation with Peru remained the primary justification for the purchase of modern military armaments. In the late 1980s, organized domestic terrorism was not the challenge in Ecuador that it was in neighboring Peru and Colombia. The security of the northern frontier area against drug traffickers and insurgent groups originating in Colombia was, however, a continuing problem.

The president of the republic functioned as commander in chief of the armed forces. The National Security Council (NSC) and the Joint Command, the chief of which was the senior military officer, advised the president on defense issues. A ranking military officer, either active or retired, customarily held the position of minister of national defense. The army, the dominant branch of the military with about 40,000 troops, included five infantry brigades, two jungle brigades, an armored brigade, and a special forces brigade. The navy, with two submarines and a number of missile-armed surface vessels, was capable of protecting territorial waters and communications with the Galápagos Islands. Analysts regarded the air force's three squadrons of modern fighter planes as effective in both air defense and ground support roles.

The military employed a conscription system requiring young men to serve for one year at the age of nineteen. Those able to meet stringent requirements could remain as career personnel. Officers entered by way of one of the three military academies. Advancement was based on merit, coupled with successful performance in service schools at various levels.

In the early years of Ecuadorian independence, individual military leaders frequently dominated the political system. The political involvement of the military institution, however, was a phenomenon of the twentieth century. Although the armed forces assumed power only three times—in 1925, 1963, and 1972—those were extended periods and the military's influence and interests loomed continuously over the political scene. In 1979, following seven years of reformist military rule that was only partially successful in bringing about economic modernization, the armed forces oversaw the enactment of a new constitution and voluntarily returned to the barracks. During the 1970s, however, the armed forces had nearly doubled in size, and defense spending rose accordingly. Acquiring its own business enterprises and profiting from the oil bonanza, the military assembled a considerable inventory of modern weapons, including armored vehicles, combat aircraft, and naval units. The country's mounting economic crisis and the sharp drop in oil revenues in the 1980s, on the other hand, brought an abrupt halt to the equipment modernization efforts.

Although not in sympathy with most of the civilian governments of the 1980s, the armed forces refrained from intervention. Indeed, the other service chiefs considered the revolt by the air force commander in 1986 as damaging to internal discipline and order and did not support him. In spite of the blow to the prestige and unity of the armed forces caused by this episode and the subsequent brief kidnapping of the president by air force commandos, cooperative civil-military relations remained an important ingredient in Ecuadorian political life.

Military Heritage

Ecuador's military history dates from the first attempt to secure freedom from Spain in 1811. The rebel forces of the newly declared independent state of Quito attempted to extend their control to other parts of Ecuadorian territory but proved little match for the army dispatched by the viceroy of Peru. In the Battle of Ibarra in December 1812, Spanish forces easily reasserted control of the country. When the independence movement began again in 1820, Ecuadorian forces assembled in Guayaquil, combining with contingents of revolutionary soldiers from Colombia commanded by Antonio José de Sucre Alcalá, a close collaborator of the Venezuelan liberator, Simón Bolívar Palacios. After a successful invasion of the Sierra (Andean highlands), the rebels scored a decisive victory over the royalist army in 1822 at the Battle of Pichincha (see The Struggle for Independence, ch. 1).

In 1828, as a member along with Colombia and Venezuela of the Confederation of Gran Colombia, Ecuador fought against Peru to block the latter's attempt at annexation. Confederation forces, fewer than half of which were Ecuadorians, defeated the much larger Peruvian invasion force at a second Battle of Pichincha in February 1829.

At the dissolution of Gran Colombia in 1830, most of Ecuador's senior army officers and many of its troops were Venezuelans, as was the country's first president, Juan José Flores. The army of 2,000 men consisted of three infantry battalions and one cavalry regiment. Even as late as 1845, when Flores was forced from his second term of office, only four of fifteen general officers were Ecuadorian. Non-Ecuadorians comprised most of the officers and noncommissioned officers (NCOs) of the elite cavalry units as well. Upon taking office as president in 1851, General José María Urbina freed the black slaves and recruited many of them into the military.

Beginning in the 1860s, successive governments attempted to professionalize the armed forces. Gabriel García Moreno, who dominated the political scene from 1860 until 1875, reduced the army in size and depoliticized it. Further improvements in the army occurred during the relatively prosperous period of the 1880s and 1890s under the military dictator Ignacio de Veintemilla and successor civilian governments. French officers arrived to provide training on a newly acquired arsenal of weapons. By 1900 the army was able to repel an attack from Colombia by Ecuadorian political opponents of the government in power.

In 1905 the government established military education and training institutions and divided the country into four defense zones. Immediately preceding World War I, the army had nine infantry battalions, three cavalry regiments, three artillery regiments, and three engineering battalions. By the mid-1920s, it had expanded to fifteen infantry battalions. Later, under the influence of an Italian military mission, the infantry was reduced to ten battalions, although each battalion now consisted of four rather than the previous two or three rifle companies. In 1930 the army had a total strength of about 5,500 men of all ranks.

Despite the military's continual growth, in July 1941, when conflict broke out over the Amazonian region disputed with Peru, the Ecuadorians were ill-prepared to resist invasion. The much larger Peruvian army of 13,000, supported by a battalion of Czech-manufactured tanks, together with artillery and air power, moved quickly into the southern coastal province of El Oro, threatening Guayaquil (see fig 1). The fewer than 1,800 Ecuadorian troops in the area lacked air cover and could offer only limited resistance. Peruvian forces also moved into the disputed Amazonian territory without significant opposition. After a campaign lasting only three weeks, an armistice was arranged. The subsequent Protocol of Peace, Friendship, and Boundaries (Rio Protocol) in early 1942 imposed on Ecuador acceptance of Peru's claims in the Amazonian region in return for Peruvian withdrawal from Ecuador's coastal provinces.

Ecuador declared war on the Axis powers and began to receive military aid from the United States in 1942. This aid consisted at first of light weapons, mortars, light tanks, and armored scout cars. Under a military assistance agreement with the United States in 1952, the Ecuadorian armed forces, which now totaled approximately 15,000 troops, received additional equipment, including howitzers, tanks, and armored personnel carriers. Revenue coming from the oil discovered in the late 1960s financed the purchase of considerable additional ground forces weaponry as well as fighters for the small air force (see Armed Forces, this ch.).

Occasional clashes with Peru occurred in the border area lost by Ecuador in the 1942 settlement. These clashes flared into an outbreak of serious fighting in January 1981. Ecuadorian troops had apparently established an outpost on Peruvian soil but were driven back in an engagement lasting five days at a reported cost to Ecuador of 200 deaths. The Peruvians made effective use of helicopters, air strikes, and commando teams specially trained for jungle operations. In 1983 and again in 1984, shooting incidents occurred when patrols of both countries met in the territory still claimed by Ecuador.

Strategic Perspective

The predominant military concern remained, as of late 1989, Ecuador's refusal to accept the boundary settlement of 1942 as final (see Other Relations and International Organizations, ch. 4). The southern deployment of many Ecuadorian army and air force combat units reflected the nation's preoccupation with the possibility of future tensions in the disputed area, although the units were not in forward positions. Peru's armed forces were far stronger than those of Ecuador, but analysts regarded the likelihood of an unprovoked Peruvian attack as remote. From a Peruvian perspective, there was no unsettled border problem. Peru regarded the Rio Protocol as fixing the boundary permanently and subsequent confrontations and clashes in the area as simply Ecuadorian efforts to reopen the issue.

As the 1941 conflict had demonstrated, Ecuador was in a vulnerable position in the event of a serious conflict with Peru. Its coastal areas in the south were exposed to penetration, and the port of Guayaquil could be subjected to both land attack and blockade from the sea. In addition, observers noted that Ecuador had been unwilling to risk the commitment of its modern fighter aircraft during the 1981 hostilities, presumably out of fear that Ecuador's air

An artillery unit in Quito in 1944
Courtesy Prints and
Photographs Division,
Library of Congress

force would suffer a crippling blow at the hands of the stronger Peruvian air power.

Ecuador did not believe it necessary to take special military precautions against Colombia, its neighbor to the north, except to limit the infiltration of terrorists and narcotics traffickers. Like the northeastern border with Peru, the border area with Colombia consisted of heavily canopied jungle that greatly limited surveillance by ground patrols or air reconnaissance. The jungle was inhabited only sparsely by Indian tribes. Ecuador and Colombia had cordial official relations and no outstanding disputes. The Colombian armed forces, although somewhat larger than those of Ecuador, were not geared for offensive operations. Moreover, Colombia was preoccupied with serious internal security problems, notably narcotics trafficking and guerrilla insurgencies. Although one of these guerrilla organizations—the 19th of April Movement (Movimiento 19 de Abril—M-19)—had helped train an Ecuadorian underground group, terrorism imported from Colombia remained primarily a police rather than a military problem (see Internal Security, this ch.).

As a nation facing the Pacific Ocean, Ecuador had important maritime resources to protect, as well as protecting the security of the Galápagos Islands, 1,000 kilometers distant from the mainland (see Geography, ch. 2). The navy therefore patrolled the 320-kilometer zone claimed as territorial waters, both off the coast of the mainland and around the Galápagos Islands.

211

Involvement in Politics and Government

With the exception of García Moreno, the most powerful Ecuadorian political figures of the nineteenth century arose from the military. Chronically threatened by revolts and insurrection, leaders employed force to defend their authority. The distinction between civilian and military spheres of action was blurred, and the institutional identity of the military had not become wholly established.

Reformist Liberal governments of the early part of the twentieth century codified military law, regularized promotions, and banned soldiers from joining political parties or clubs. The establishment of a military academy in Quito in 1901 helped professionalize the armed forces. In addition, the military recruited an increasing proportion of its officer corps from the middle rather than the upper class. By 1916 officers had begun to regard themselves increasingly in institutional terms.

In 1925 the army as an institution intervened in national politics. A group of young officers, objecting to the political domination of the Guayaquil business oligarchy, revolted against civilian rule (see The Rule of the Liberals, 1895–1925, ch. 1). Ambivalent over imposing direct military rule, the officers appointed a civilian-dominated junta, followed, in 1926, by a civilian as provisional president. The army continued to intervene in political affairs until 1948, removing numerous presidents. Yet the military refrained from governing directly.

In 1963 the army high command deposed President Carlos Julio Arosemena Monroy, perceiving him to be overly tolerant of the communist threat against Latin America and a national embarrassment because of his reported public drunkenness (see Instability and Military Dominance, 1960–72, ch. 1). In contrast to previous patterns, however, the army assumed direct control, claiming the need to "end the chaos and rectify mistaken paths" and promising to introduce a new socioeconomic structure. Over the next three years, the military junta adopted a moderate program of fiscal, agrarian, and industrial reforms aimed at eliminating structural obstacles to development. The military failed to mobilize support from the intended beneficiaries of its reforms, however, and stirred strong opposition from elite groups, especially Guayaquil business interests. Shaken by the lack of popular backing and an economic downturn and fearful of damage to military prestige, the armed forces relinquished power to a civilian interim president in 1966.

The longest period of direct control by the armed forces occurred between 1972 and 1979. In 1970 President José María Velasco Ibarra, unable to win congressional approval for his budget, had assumed dictatorial power with agreement of the military. Concerned over Velasco's cumulative political misjudgments and his interference in military promotions and assignments, however, the armed forces seized power in 1972 (see Direct Military Rule, 1972–79, ch. 1). General Guillermo Rodríguez Lara launched an era of military authoritarianism with a program of state-led development more ambitious than any during previous interventions by the armed forces. Ranking officers held many cabinet posts or became deputies in ministries and agencies headed by civilians. In spite of being divided into reformist and traditionalist elements, the military government brought banking, basic industries, agriculture, and fisheries under public-sector control. It also nationalized several large unprofitable enterprises. In addition, the government created new mixed-ownership firms and public enterprises, notably the Ecuadorian State Petroleum Corporation (Corporación Estatal Petrolera Ecuatoriana—CEPE). Some enterprises served the military's own equipment requirements and brought revenue to the armed forces. After powerful large landholders diluted an ambitious effort to recast agriculture by redistributing income to the peasantry, however, the military's reformist thrust gradually lost momentum.

Although key capital garrisons successfully foiled a coup attempt against Rodríguez Lara by the chief of staff of the armed forces in 1975, discontent simmered among senior military and influential civilian political elements. Early the following year, a Supreme Council of Government composed of the commanders of the army, navy, and air force replaced Rodríguez Lara. The triumvirate disagreed as to the advisability of an early restoration of civilian government, but the commitment to gradual military withdrawal espoused by its head, Admiral Afredo Poveda Burbano, prevailed, and constitutional rule was restored in 1979. The incoming civilian government inherited serious economic problems, however, because of the Supreme Council's unwillingness to make unpopular decisions on wages and consumption.

The military attempted to limit its withdrawal by retaining a veto power over undesirable candidates, parties, and coalitions. Outmaneuvered by civilian politicians, however, the armed forces could not prevent the electoral victory of a left-leaning coalition that it found distasteful. Nonetheless, the seven years of military rule had strengthened the position of the armed forces. They controlled the membership of the boards of major state corporations; operated air and sea transportation lines; became major industrial shareholders through investments made by the Directorate of Army Industries (Dirección de Industrias del Ejército—Dine); and received a portion of petroleum revenues for military requirements. The armed forces reportedly controlled at least fourteen major business enterprises, ranging from an automotive assembly plant and a profitable shrimp-farming project owned by the army to a dredging company owned by the navy, and a domestic airline operated by the air force. In addition, several prominent retired officers had turned to politics or management positions in private or government-owned businesses.

During the 1980s, the military as a whole remained loyal to the constitutional system. Nonetheless, civilian politicians could never safely ignore the reactions of the military to their proposed actions and accepted a degree of military autonomy in matters of national defense. Indeed, the outbreak of hostilities with Peru in 1981 was fundamentally a military affair; the elected civilian government had little choice but to support the initiatives taken by the high command.

During the conservative administration of President León Febres Cordero Ribadeneyra (1984–88), a series of episodes inflamed relations between the military and the executive branch. Matters reached a crisis point in March 1986 when Lieutenant General Frank Vargas Pazzos, the air force commander and chief of the Joint Command of the armed forces, accused the minister of national defense and an army commander of corruption and demanded their dismissal. When the president reneged on his commitment to remove the two officers and bring them to trial, Vargas and his supporters took control of the Quito air force base. The brief rebellion was put down at the cost of several lives, and Vargas was court-martialed and put under house arrest at an army base. In January 1987, air force paratroop commandos loyal to Vargas seized Febres Cordero at the Taura Air Base near Guayaquil. In return for his freedom, the president pledged that no reprisals would be taken against his kidnappers and agreed to Vargas's release. Vargas later presented himself as a candidate for president and came in fourth in the first-round election in January 1988, winning over 12 percent of the vote (see Political Dynamics, ch. 4).

When the Congress initiated moves to impeach Febres Cordero, the military warned congressional leaders that it would shut down the legislature if a formal impeachment action were brought against the president. Military authorities also backed Febres Cordero in proceeding with the court-martialing of the rebellious paratroopers in spite of his promise of immunity. Nevertheless, the episode shook military unity and tarnished its prestige as an institution (see Political Forces and Interest Groups, ch. 4).

Armed Forces

The Constitution of 1979 defines the armed forces as a nondeliberative body and an instrument of civil authority—an inaccurate reflection of the true civil-military relationship in Ecuador. According to the Constitution, the president is the commander in chief of the armed forces and the only one authorized to grant military ranks. The mission of the Public Forces (the armed forces and the National Police) is to preserve national sovereignty, to defend the integrity and independence of the republic, and to guarantee its legal order. The Constitution further enjoins the Public Forces, in a manner to be determined by law, to lend their cooperation in national economic and social development.

National Security Act Number 275 of 1979 authorized the president to mobilize forces during threats of aggression and to declare a state of national emergency at times of imminent aggression, major disturbances, and domestic disasters. This law also established the NSC, chaired by the president, to make recommendations on, and supervise execution of, national security policies. NSC members included the president of the National Congress (Congreso Nacional, hereafter Congress); the president of the Supreme Court of Justice; the chairs of the National Development Council and the Monetary Board; the ministers of foreign relations, national defense, government and justice, and finance and credit; and the chief of the Joint Command.

The Secretariat General, the NSC's operational arm, coordinated and helped shape national security planning. Secretariat personnel primarily consisted of active-duty or retired officers. Analysts considered it to be a subordinate arm of the Joint Command, whose chief nominated the head of the secretariat, ordinarily an army general. The secretariat directly supervised the National Directorate of Mobilization, the National Directorate of Civil Defense, the Institute of Higher National Studies, and the National Directorate of Intelligence. Although the latter body was designed to coordinate all intelligence activities, its head had a lower rank than the chief of army intelligence.

The Joint Command, consisting of its chief and chief of staff of the Joint Command as well as the commanders of the three service branches, also directly advised the president. The Joint Command had its own staff organized into functional departments. Each of the three services had staffs organized along similar lines (see fig. 17). The minister of national defense was normally a senior active-duty or retired officer. His influence on national defense policy generally depended on his rank relative to the chief of the Joint Command and his personal relationship to the president.

All retired career personnel and all conscripts had reserve status until the age of fifty. The armed forces maintained a skeleton reserve organization at the national level, directly under the Ministry of National Defense, as well as cadre organizations staffed by

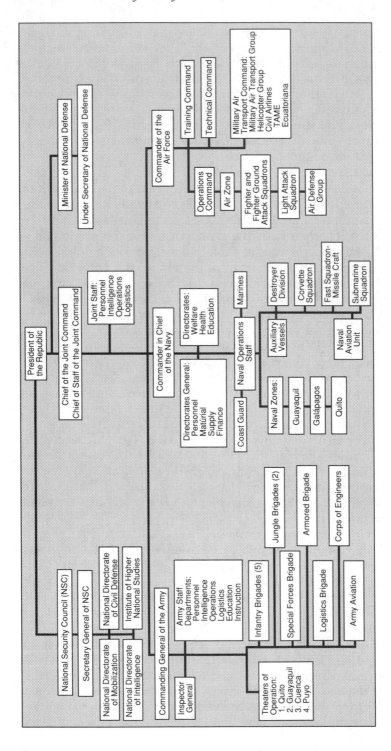

Figure 17. Organization of National Security, 1989

retired officers and NCOs in various areas of the country. Training exercises were not generally held, but former conscripts assigned to reserve units could expect to be called up for annual weekend musters.

Army

Organization and Equipment

The army was the dominant service; its personnel strength of approximately 40,000 in 1989 was nearly four times the combined strength of the navy and air force, and its commander normally held the rank of four-star general. The army had four theaters of operation, commonly known as defense zones, with headquarters in Quito, Guayaquil, Cuenca, and Puyo, respectively (see fig. 18).

The army's principal operational units consisted of twelve brigades, all odd-numbered, running in sequence from the first to the twenty-third. The first ("El Oro"), third ("Portete"), fifth ("Guayas"), seventh ("Loja"), and thirteenth ("Pichincha") brigades were infantry units with headquarters at Machala, Cuenca, Guayaquil, Loja, and Quito, respectively. The army deployed two jungle brigades in the Oriente (eastern region): the seventeenth ("Pastaza"), with headquarters at Mera, and the nineteenth ("Napo"), based at Puerto Napo. The ninth Special Forces brigade ("El Patria")—an outgrowth of a special paratroop detachment formed in 1960 to combat leftist guerrillas in the Oriente—had its headquarters at Latacunga. The eleventh armored brigade ("Galápagos") deployed from Riobamba. Three other specialized brigades, the twenty-first (logistics), the twenty-third (corps of engineers), and the fifteenth (army aviation), operated out of Quito. Originally confined to transport, communications, training, and geographic survey duties, the fifteenth brigade expanded into battlefield logistic support following the delivery in 1981 of French Puma, Super Puma, and Gazelle helicopters.

Combat brigades generally consisted of three battalions. Although not all brigades were at full strength, key units such as the Loja brigade near the Peruvian border had full complements or even additional reinforcements. States of readiness varied because personnel primarily consisted of one-year conscripts, some of whom received minimal training. Brigade commanding officers generally held brigadier general rank, although some were led by senior colonels. The commanders of the Pichincha, Guayas, Portete, and Pastaza brigades served concurrently as commanders of their respective theaters of operation.

The army's standard infantry weapons consisted of the Belgian FN FAL 7.62mm rifle and the Israeli Uzi 9mm submachine gun,

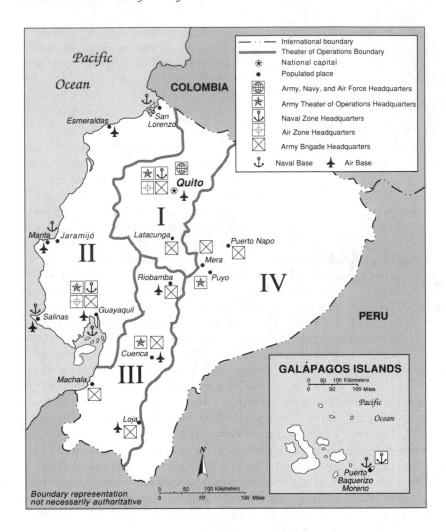

Figure 18. Major Military Installations and Deployments, 1989

the latter employed for counterinsurgency operations. The FN
MAG 7.62mm was the standard machine gun, although the army
still had .30- and .50-caliber machine guns of United States origin
and 81mm mortars in its inventory. Armored vehicles included
French-origin light tanks and four-wheeled reconnaissance vehicles, as well as Cascavel armored cars from Brazil (see table 20,
Appendix). Most of the army's approximately 100 armored personnel carriers were French and Brazilian wheeled models, although
it also had some tracked M–113s from the United States. A large

order for obsolete medium tanks and armored personnel carriers from Argentina had to be cancelled in 1988 because of the deepening financial crisis.

Training and Education

Army conscripts received their training in the units to which they were assigned. The quality of basic training depended greatly on the importance attached to it by the brigade commander. In an effort to standardize unit training, the Department of Instruction was created in army headquarters in 1988. Special ranger, underwater demolition, parachute, and other similar courses were given at brigade level. Upon attaining the rank of corporal, conscripts accepted for enlistment for further service could apply to one of several NCO schools. Each school included a core curriculum accompanied by training in a military occupational specialty at such facilities as the armor school at Riobamba or the engineers' school at Esmeraldas. The intense competition and the difficulty of the courses produced a high dropout rate among NCO candidates.

Cadets preparing for commissioning as army second lieutenants studied at the Eloy Alfaro Advanced Military School (Escuela Superior Militar "Eloy Alfaro") in Parcayacu, approximately fifteen kilometers north of Quito. Candidates had to complete the ninth grade of school and pass a battery of written examinations, interviews, and psychological screening. In 1987 approximately 130 cadets graduated from the school's three-year course of study, which corresponded to the final three years of high school. The Eloy Alfaro school offered separate curricula for cadets opting for combat arms (infantry, armor, artillery, engineers, and signals), service branches (administration, supply, transportation), and service support branches (health, military justice, cartography). Observers considered the school's quarters, sports facilities, and training areas to be excellent. Additional construction was expected to allow enrollment to climb from 500 in 1987 to 800 cadets by 1989.

Prior to promotion, lieutenants and captains each attended separate nine-month courses at the Advanced Training Institute (Escuela de Perfeccionamiento). Courses covered tactical operations, integration of the various service arms, and branch-oriented training. Total enrollment was about 165.

The Army War Academy (Academia de Guerra del Ejército), located in a southern suburb of Quito, prepared majors for command and general staff posts or for assignments to service elements at brigade and higher echelons. The study material corresponded to that of the United States Army Command and General Staff College at Fort Leavenworth, Kansas. The academy offered a two-year program for officers of combat arms and a one-year program for service and service support officers. Enrollment in 1987 was forty-five in the combat arms track and seventy in the service tracks.

The Army Polytechnic Institute (Escuela Politécnica del Ejército— Espe), located in Quito, combined the functions of a technical training school, a technical college, and a postgraduate scientific and engineering university. Espe included undergraduate departments of civil, mechanical, and electronic engineering as well as geography. A graduate-level program consisted of industrial and systems engineering. Although administered along quasi-military lines, Espe had a largely civilian faculty and student body. Military attendees ranged from soldiers from the enlisted ranks through mid-level officers. Several Espe dependent institutes offered nondegree courses in basic sciences, languages, computer programming and systems analysis, and industrial administration. One Espe branch at Latacunga, the Advanced Technical Institute of the Armed Forces, offered practical training in automotive mechanics, electronics, telecommunications, and automatic data processing.

The Institute of Higher National Studies at Quito offered a one-year course for ranking military officers of all three services and for civilian officials. Comparable to the National Defense University in Washington, the institute offered a curriculum focused on the planning and execution of policies at the highest levels of government. The NSC supervised the operation of the institute.

Each of the services operated a number of schools for children in the first through the ninth grades. Although originally intended to help families of military personnel avoid difficulties arising from divergent school calendars in the Costa (coastal region) and the Sierra, the schools also accepted children of civilians on a tuition basis. Ecuadorians rated these schools highly; as a result, competition for admission was keen. Graduates of the armed forces schools had an advantage in applying for admission to one of the service academies.

Navy

The origin of the Ecuadorian navy can be traced to the independence era when British officers in the service of Bolívar assembled a small squadron at Guayaquil. An 1832 congressional decree formally established the navy.

Organization and Equipment

As of 1988, the navy had a personnel complement of approximately 5,000, including 1,000 marines. Its varied missions included

preparing and maintaining the fleet during peacetime for naval operations in wartime; controlling ocean and river communications; protecting territorial waters, the coastline, and rivers; participating in operations in conjunction with other branches of the armed forces; regulating the merchant marine; promoting the development of the naval construction industry; overseeing the installation and maintenance of aids to navigation; and preparing hydrographic charts.

The country was divided into three naval zones. The first, headquartered at Guayaquil, had jurisdiction over the southern provinces and the territorial waters adjacent to the coastal provinces of Manabí, Guayas, and El Oro. The second had authority over the Galápagos archipelago and surrounding territorial seas and operated from Puerto Baquerizo Moreno on San Cristóbal Island. The third, with headquarters at Quito, had jurisdiction over the northern provinces and the territorial seas adjacent to the coastal province of Esmeraldas. The navy also had bases at Guayaquil, San Lorenzo, Salinas, and Jaramijó.

Operationally, the navy was organized into a destroyer division, a squadron of fast-missile craft, a squadron of corvettes, a submarine squadron, and auxiliary vessels and transports. A naval aviation unit, equipped mainly with light reconnaissance and liaison aircraft, supported the fleet by patrolling territorial seas and coastlines, combating smuggling, and performing logistical tasks. A small coast guard, formed in 1980, controlled maritime traffic, interdicted drug and contraband traffic, and enforced Ecuadorian maritime law. Equipped with twenty coastal patrol craft, most of which were twelve to fifteen meters in length, the coast guard had a personnel strength of 200 as of 1988.

The marines conducted amphibious operations, maintained security of naval bases and detachments, and protected the Trans-Ecuadorian Pipeline terminal and shipping point at Esmeraldas (see fig. 11). Directly subordinate to the naval operations staff, the marines had their headquarters at Guayaquil and were organized into three battalions, consisting of a commando group, a security force, and a support group, based at Guayaquil, in the Galápagos, and in the Oriente. In addition to small arms, the marines were armed with 81mm mortars and 106mm recoilless rifles.

At the time of the navy's formal establishment, naval equipment consisted of one frigate and seven gunboats. During the turbulent years that followed, however, the fortunes of the navy often suffered, and equipment was reduced to a single vessel in 1880. Four years later, the armed forces took the first step in the creation of a modern navy with the launching of the *Cotopaxi,* a 300-ton gunboat. Well into the twentieth century, the navy's only seagoing units remained the *Cotopaxi* and the 750-ton torpedo gunboat, *Libertador Bolívar.*

Ecuador acquired a number of armed yachts and miscellaneous craft from the United States in return for having granted the latter base rights in the Galápagos Islands and at Salinas during World War II. In 1955 Ecuador purchased two older Hunt-class destroyers from Britain; these became the most formidable vessels in the Ecuadorian fleet. A significant expansion took place during the 1970s with the purchase of missile attack craft and two small submarines from the Federal Republic of Germany (West Germany). In the early 1980s, Ecuador acquired corvettes equipped with Exocet missiles from Italy. The Hunt-class destroyers were retired and were replaced in 1980 by a United States-manufactured Gearing-class destroyer, renamed the *Presidente Eloy Alfaro.* This destroyer remained the principal surface vessel as of 1989 (see table 21, Appendix).

Training and Education

Training of enlisted naval personnel took place primarily at the Center of Naval Instruction at the Salinas Naval Training Base. In addition to basic training, the center provided a variety of basic and advanced specialized courses, such as electronics, radio operation, gunnery, and administration.

Naval cadets attended the Advanced Naval Academy (Escuela Superior Naval) at Salinas in a four-year program that stressed the humanities, scientific subjects, naval science, and physical training. Cadets also completed practice cruises on board a three-masted sailing vessel.

Located in Guayaquil, the Naval War College was the service's senior instructional institution and prepared officers, generally at the level of commander, for higher ranks and general staff duty. The two-year course of study covered such topics as strategy and tactics, logistics, geopolitics, operational planning, intelligence, and international maritime law, together with sociology, economics, and other nonmilitary subjects.

The marines operated their own instructional program, including a basic school for recruits and more advanced courses in amphibious operations, communications, intelligence, and weaponry, plus special courses in frogman and paratroop skills. The navy also administered the Merchant Marine School, whose cadets received some military training and formed part of the naval reserve after graduation as merchant marine officers.

Air Force

The origins of the air force (Fuerza Aérea Ecuatoriana—FAE) date to the early 1920s when, under the guidance of an Italian military mission, Ecuador acquired several planes and established a flying school near Guayaquil. During the 1930s, the air force, still subordinate to the army, came under growing United States influence as it purchased a number of Curtis Wright training planes and employed United States advisers. By the time of the brief war with Peru in 1941, the air force had forty-eight pilots but, lacking modern combat aircraft, did not present a serious threat to the Peruvians.

During World War II, the United States transferred a number of training aircraft to Ecuador, provided advanced training to Ecuadorian pilots, and operated the air base at Salinas. The first combat squadron was formed with seven obsolescent Seversky P–35 fighters. After becoming independent from the army in 1944, the FAE received additional planes under the United States Military Assistance Program, including twenty F–47 Thunderbolts to replace the P–35s, Catalina maritime patrol aircraft, and a number of C–47 transports. During the 1950s, the air force purchased its first jet fighters, Gloster Meteors, from Britain, along with Canberra B–6 jet-engined bombers. The FAE deactivated the bomber squadron in 1981; although it retained the three surviving Canberras in reserve status, they were no longer flyable by 1987. Sixteen F–80s supplied by the United States in 1958–60 permitted creation of a second jet fighter squadron.

During the 1970s, new oil revenues enabled the FAE to modernize its combat fleet by purchasing British Jaguars to replace the Meteors and F–80s in the ground attack role, as well as Cessna A–37Bs suitable for training and counterinsurgency operations. After the United States licensed the export of General Electric engines, Ecuador purchased twelve Israeli Kfir fighters in the early 1980s. The FAE also placed an order for sixteen French-manufactured Mirage F–1s, plus two Mirage trainers, deliveries of which began in early 1979. All combat aircraft were equipped with French- or Israeli-origin air-to-air missiles. Total personnel strength was believed to be somewhat less than 5,000 in 1988.

As of 1989, Jaguars, Kfirs, and Mirages provided the FAE's three fighter squadrons with a small but modern and effective combat air arm. The FAE had also received a number of Lockheed At-33 Shooting Stars from United States stocks, refurbished for light attack and advanced training roles (see table 21, Appendix). The jet pilots were a highly select group, well-trained and competent. The quality of other FAE personnel varied, and the mixture of equipment sources presented a maintenance and training problem. The FAE as a whole had only a marginally satisfactory safety record.

The FAE divided Ecuador into two air zones, the first covering the coastal areas from its headquarters at Taura near Guayaquil and the second covering the remainder of the country from Marshal Sucre International Airport at Quito. These two facilities also functioned as the FAE's principal air bases. The first-line combat squadrons operated from Taura, although they were regularly deployed to other air bases in various parts of the country. The Mera airfield—developed by the Texaco-Gulf oil consortium—was the only one in the Oriente long enough to accept jet aircraft. The air force paratroop squadron, a combat commando unit, was disbanded after its involvement in the kidnaping of the president in 1987. It was replaced by a special police unit, wearing a distinctive uniform, with responsibility for air base security.

The Military Air Transport Command incorporated the civil airline operated by the military, Ecuadorian Military Air Transport (Transportes Aéreos Militares Ecuatorianos—TAME), as well as the international civil airline, Ecuatoriana. TAME had both military and civilian crews, including many retired FAE pilots. The passenger and cargo fleet with dual civil-military markings consisted mainly of Boeing 707s, 720s, and 727s.

Israeli teams under contract carried out major overhaul for many aircraft, including commercial planes flown by TAME. FAE technicians working under Israeli supervision maintained and carried out some overhaul of Kfirs, T–34s, and A–37s at Cotopaxi Air Base at Latacunga. In addition to serving as Ecuador's principal maintenance and training center, Cotopaxi had the country's longest landing strip.

The Air Force Academy, located at Salinas, provided a three-year course for aspiring FAE officers. Cadets received basic flying instruction mainly on T–34s. After commissioning, those officers selected for jet training attended the Military Aviation School and received instruction on the At–33, the A–37, and the Strikemaster. Future helicopter pilots trained at Manta. A specialists' school in Guayaquil offered nonflight instruction for technicians and engineers. The eighteen-month program consisted of six months of basic military instruction followed by training courses in maintenance of jet and reciprocating engines, air frames, hydraulics, electronics, radar, and aerial photography. The Air War College at Quito offered a general staff course of two academic years' duration, qualifying field-grade officers for promotion to senior ranks and general staff assignments.

Military Justice

Military justice followed procedures prescribed in the armed forces' penal code. A trial for a nonserious offense was held in the military unit of the accused, with the case usually prosecuted by a member of the judge advocate corps and decided by the unit commander and two officers of captain rank. The accused had the right to representation, to speak in his or her own defense, and to be defended by a qualified individual. Trials for more serious offenses were held in the headquarters of the military zone or the navy or air force district in courts known as military discipline councils. A member of the military accused of serious crimes was subject to court-martial. All members of such a court were senior in rank to the accused.

Military law could be implemented in cases of serious civil disorder. Such law authorized trials of civilians in military courts. Civilians could also be tried for infractions of military regulations or acts against military installations. In practice, few civilian detainees were placed under military control, and these were generally persons accused of terrorism or subversion.

The procedures and penalties in military trials closely approximated those of civil courts. The maximum penalty was sixteen years for most serious crimes, such as murder. A person convicted of the military offense of treason, however, could be punished by life imprisonment. An individual guilty of insubordination could receive from three months to two years of military confinement. In cases of absence without leave, sentences ranged from eight days to two years, depending in part on the reasons for the transgression.

Ranks, Insignia, and Uniforms

The rank structure of the armed forces generally conformed to that used in the United States, except that Ecuador did not employ all of the ranks found in the United States military. The army and air force had nine officer ranks ranging from second lieutenant to general. The navy had eight officer ranks from ensign to vice admiral (see fig. 19). Army enlisted personnel had seven grades ranging in level from private to sergeant major, air force enlistees had seven grades ranging from airman to chief master sergeant, and naval enlistees had eight grades from the equivalent of seaman to master chief petty officer (see fig. 20).

Rank insignia for officers of the army and air force were a series of five-pointed stars on shoulder boards. Insignia for general, lieutenant general, and major general consisted of four, three, and two gold stars, respectively, with gold-braided borders and the national crest. Field-grade officers wore gold stars, and company-grade officers wore silver stars on shoulder boards. Naval officers wore gold stripes indicating rank on the lower sleeve of the blouse. Army and air force enlisted personnel wore red and yellow stripes, respectively, and the navy red or yellow stripes, as appropriate, on shoulder boards or upper sleeve of the uniform.

The three services had dress, semi-dress, service, and field uniforms for officers and dress, service, and field uniforms for enlisted personnel. The army winter service uniform consisted of a gray blouse and trousers, white shirt, and black tie. Air force winter service uniforms were light blue, whereas those for the navy were navy blue and white. The armed forces also had summer uniforms.

Recruitment and Conditions of Service

According to the Constitution, all Ecuadorians are subject to a military service obligation. In practice, conscription applied only to males, who were liable for call-up at age nineteen for one year of service. Only a small number of women had been recruited as specialists in the enlisted grades; some received commissions in a few categories, such as medicine and dentistry. As of 1988, there were approximately 1,834,000 males in the eighteen to forty-nine age bracket, about 80,000 of whom reached the age of eligibility each year. Analysts considered this figure ample for service needs even though approximately 50 percent could not meet minimum physical or educational standards.

There was little active opposition to the conscription system. Those undergoing military service enjoyed a measure of respect. In a country with chronic underemployment, many poorer youths improved their educational, housing, health-care, and dietary situations by joining the armed forces. Ambitious young men with few opportunities in the civilian labor market might be successful candidates for further service and training, thereby learning valuable skills and finding an avenue for upward mobility. Selective service boards in provincial capitals chose conscripts and liberally granted exemptions for family reasons, such as being the only son or the breadwinner. Students in good academic standing received deferments.

Since the 1960s, the army had assigned many conscripts with peasant backgrounds to the Army Agrarian Military Conscription (Conscripción Agraria Militar del Ejército—CAME). The CAME program sought to enable youths from rural areas—often with a minimum education—to meet their service obligation by working in army-operated dairy, livestock-raising, vegetable- or fruit-farming, and shrimp enterprises. The conscripts received a limited amount of military training and were exposed to modern farming practices that might benefit them when they returned to civilian life. The military used CAME products directly or sold them commercially.

Virtually all officers graduated from one of the three military academies. In an analysis of the social origins of the officer corps based on cadets entering the military academies between 1960 and 1966, political scientist John Samuel Fitch determined that more than 60 percent came from the middle segment of the middle classes (see Middle Class, ch. 2). Fitch assumed each cadet's class background from his father's occupation; this group had fathers who were mainly civil servants, military officers, teachers, and merchants. Those of working-class or lower middle-class origins, whose fathers were artisans, military NCOs, or workers, constituted approximately 20 percent. Approximately 17 percent had fathers who were members of the property-owning upper class or professionals from the upper middle class. Fitch's research confirmed a definite trend toward democratization of the officer corps. In 1928 and 1929, for example, more than 44 percent of entering cadets came from the upper and upper middle classes, whereas some 55 percent were from the middle class and none from the lower classes. The number of sons of military officers remained constant at about 20 percent of the entering cadets, although a growing number of sons of NCOs had qualified for the service academies since 1956.

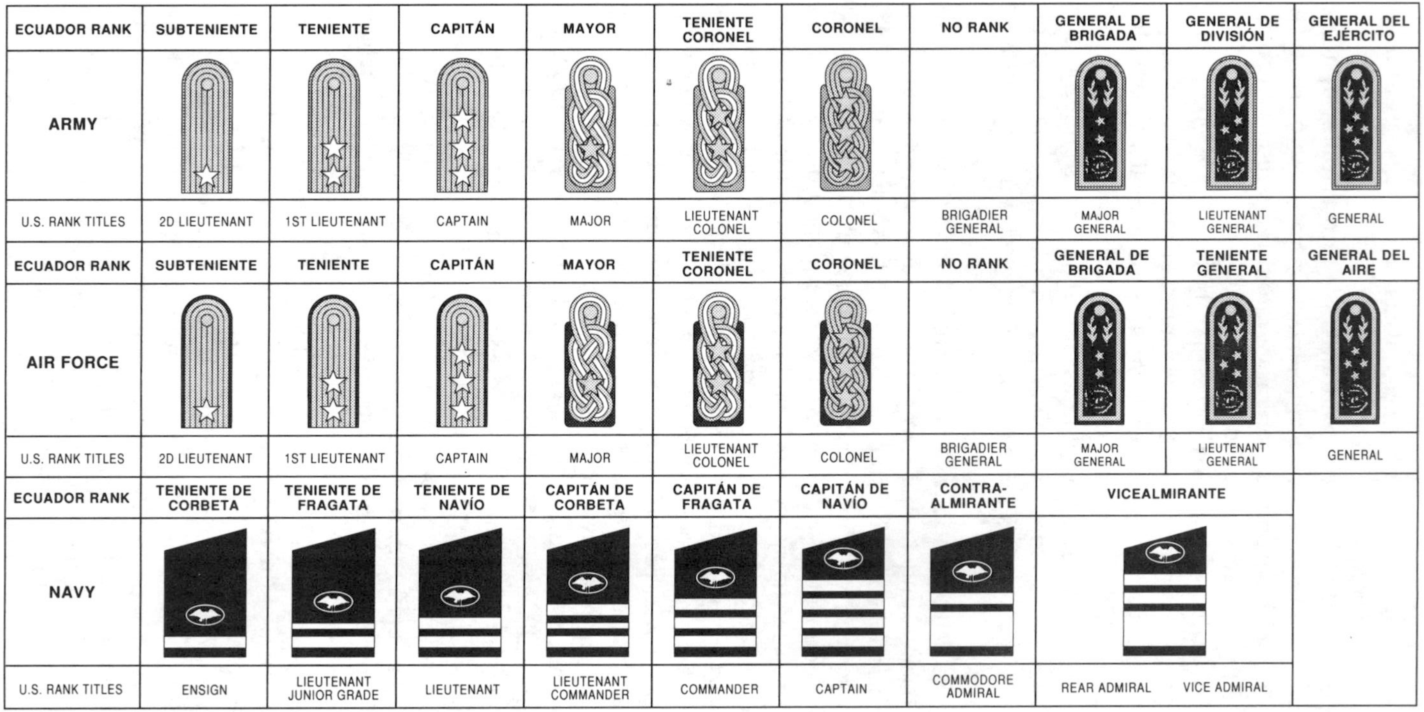

ECUADOR RANK	SUBTENIENTE	TENIENTE	CAPITÁN	MAYOR	TENIENTE CORONEL	CORONEL	NO RANK	GENERAL DE BRIGADA	GENERAL DE DIVISION	GENERAL DEL EJÉRCITO
ARMY										
U.S. RANK TITLES	2D LIEUTENANT	1ST LIEUTENANT	CAPTAIN	MAJOR	LIEUTENANT COLONEL	COLONEL	BRIGADIER GENERAL	MAJOR GENERAL	LIEUTENANT GENERAL	GENERAL
ECUADOR RANK	SUBTENIENTE	TENIENTE	CAPITÁN	MAYOR	TENIENTE CORONEL	CORONEL	NO RANK	GENERAL DE BRIGADA	TENIENTE GENERAL	GENERAL DEL AIRE
AIR FORCE										
U.S. RANK TITLES	2D LIEUTENANT	1ST LIEUTENANT	CAPTAIN	MAJOR	LIEUTENANT COLONEL	COLONEL	BRIGADIER GENERAL	MAJOR GENERAL	LIEUTENANT GENERAL	GENERAL
ECUADOR RANK	TENIENTE DE CORBETA	TENIENTE DE FRAGATA	TENIENTE DE NAVIO	CAPITÁN DE CORBETA	CAPITÁN DE FRAGATA	CAPITÁN DE NAVIO	CONTRA-ALMIRANTE	VICEALMIRANTE		
NAVY										
U.S. RANK TITLES	ENSIGN	LIEUTENANT JUNIOR GRADE	LIEUTENANT	LIEUTENANT COMMANDER	COMMANDER	CAPTAIN	COMMODORE ADMIRAL	REAR ADMIRAL	VICE ADMIRAL	

Figure 19. Officer Ranks and Insignia, 1989

228

ECUADOR RANK	SOLDADO	NO RANK	CABO SEGUNDO	CABO PRIMERO	SARGENTO SEGUNDO	SARGENTO PRIMERO	SUB-OFICIAL SEGUNDO	SUB-OFICIAL PRIMERO
ARMY	NO INSIGNIA							
U.S. RANK TITLES	BASIC PRIVATE	PRIVATE	PRIVATE 1ST CLASS	CORPORAL	SERGEANT	STAFF SERGEANT	SERGEANT 1ST CLASS / MASTER SERGEANT	COMMAND SERGEANT MAJOR
ECUADOR RANK	SOLDADO	NO RANK	CABO SEGUNDO	CABO PRIMERO	SARGENTO SEGUNDO	SARGENTO PRIMERO	SUB-OFICIAL SEGUNDO	SUB-OFICIAL PRIMERO
AIR FORCE	NO INSIGNIA							
U.S. RANK TITLES	AIRMAN BASIC	AIRMAN	AIRMAN 1ST CLASS	SERGEANT	STAFF SERGEANT	TECHNICAL SERGEANT	MASTER SERGEANT / SENIOR MASTER SERGEANT	CHIEF MASTER SERGEANT
ECUADOR RANK	SOLDADO	MARINERO	CABO SEGUNDO	CABO PRIMERO	SARGENTO SEGUNDO	SARGENTO PRIMERO	SUB-OFICIAL SEGUNDO	SUB-OFICIAL PRIMERO
NAVY	GRUMETE / NO INSIGNIA							
U.S. RANK TITLES	SEAMAN RECRUIT	SEAMAN APPRENTICE	SEAMAN	PETTY OFFICER 3D CLASS	PETTY OFFICER 2D CLASS	PETTY OFFICER 1ST CLASS	CHIEF PETTY OFFICER / SENIOR CHIEF PETTY OFFICER	FLEET FORCE MASTER CHIEF PETTY OFFICER

Figure 20. Enlisted Ranks and Insignia, 1989

Fitch's study found a striking pattern of recruitment to the officer corps from the interior highlands, which had persisted in spite of the shift of population toward the coastal provinces (see Migration and Urbanization, ch. 2). In 1963, when the total population of the Sierra and Oriente barely exceeded that of the Costa, merely 7 percent of the entering classes came from the Costa. Guayas Province, with over 20 percent of the nation's population, supplied less than 1 percent of the new cadets.

Strict regulations determined promotion of officers, taking into account such factors as seniority; attendance and performance at service schools, both in Ecuador and abroad; assignments held; and demonstrated administrative effectiveness. At the highest levels, boards of admirals and generals of the three services screened officers for promotion, subject to the approval of the president, the minister of national defense, and the chief of the Joint Command. The president appointed the commanding officer of each service. During the 1980s, attempts by President Febres Cordero to circumvent the established procedure for promotion caused serious tensions in his relations with the military.

Observers considered basic salaries for officers adequate by comparison with civilian government employees. In 1988 a major general received a base salary of about US$600 a month. Benefits and allowances added at least 50 percent to this salary. In addition to the excellent medical care and post exchange and commissary privileges available to all military personnel, a general officer had the use of a car and driver, gasoline, a cook, and other allowances. Per diem allowances for travel abroad were extremely generous. A high-ranking officer attending frequent meetings or courses in other countries could supplement his salary with savings from this source.

Corruption within the military reportedly was fairly widespread. In the case of senior officers, this often took the form of "commissions" on arms purchases. Lower-ranking officers had fewer opportunities to benefit by improper means but might be guilty of such minor abuses as the unauthorized use of official equipment for personal purposes.

Most officers were subject to retirement after twenty years of service unless they reached the rank of general. Time spent in attendance at a military academy was included in calculating retirement benefits. In addition to receiving a relatively high percentage of their base pay, retired career personnel also received severance pay that was often used to begin business careers.

Defense Budget

A series of unfavorable economic developments in the second half of the 1980s, beginning with the decline in oil revenues in 1986 and a devastating earthquake in March 1987, curtailed national government outlays, including spending on the armed forces. The precipitous drop in the value of Ecuadorian currency meant an escalation of the cost of imported weapons, on which the armed forces almost entirely depended. In September 1988, the new administration of Rodrigo Borja Cevallos (1988–) cancelled a US$106-million contract with Argentina for the purchase of armored vehicles and other equipment. Even prior to this, other planned procurements, such as the purchase of planes for an additional fighter squadron, had to be postponed.

In 1987, the most recent year for which such data were available in late 1989, the Ecuadorian government reported that defense expenditures totalled 32.0 billion sucres—equivalent to US$188 million at the prevailing rate of exchange (for the value of the sucre—see Glossary). The defense budget for 1987 did not reflect the cut that followed the earthquake. The corresponding figure for defense in 1986 was 20.4 billion sucres, equivalent to US$166.2 million.

Although defense expenditures apparently declined after the end of military rule in 1979, it was difficult to draw conclusions about trends in defense spending owing to a number of factors, including variations in the dollar-sucre exchange rate. Analysts believed that the true cost of defense exceeded the officially budgeted figures by a considerable amount because of unreported nonbudgetary spending. The armed forces covered these costs, which observers believed to have been as high as the official defense expenditures in some years, through profits from business enterprises owned by the military and receipts from the sale of petroleum abroad. A portion of revenues from petroleum production above a stipulated level was allocated to a special military account, but the amount involved and the formula by which it was calculated remained confidential. Low oil production levels and depressed prices in the late 1980s necessitated a sharp curtailment of imports of military equipment.

The United States Arms Control and Disarmament Agency (ACDA) estimated Ecuador's military expenditures at US$250 million in 1987. ACDA noted, however, that this estimate omitted most arms acquisitions. According to ACDA, annual defense spending had risen over a ten-year period from US$150 million in 1978. If defense expenditures for 1978 were converted to 1987 dollars, however, they would come to US$245 million—nearly equal to the 1987 expenditures in purchasing power. The lowest levels of defense spending during the decade were in 1983 and 1984, when military outlays fell below US$160 million, calculated in 1987 dollars.

According to ACDA's analysis, based on 1987 data, Ecuador's annual defense expenditures of US$25 per capita were lower than the average for Latin America as a whole (US$36 per capita), although well above comparable figures for Brazil and Colombia. The defense budget of its larger neighbor and rival, Peru, was four times as great per capita. The number of persons in military service per 1,000 population (4.4 in 1987) almost mirrored the average for Latin America as a whole, although it was higher than the figure for Brazil or Colombia and lower than that for Peru. Military expenditures constituted 15.3 percent of central government expenditures in 1987 and 2.6 percent of gross national product (GNP—see Glossary). These ratios compared to 10.4 percent of central government expenditures and 2.0 percent of GNP for Latin American countries as a whole, but were again well beneath the corresponding figures for Peru.

Civil Defense

Article 82 of National Security Act Number 275 of 1979 established a civil defense structure composed of the National Directorate of Civil Defense, provincial boards (*juntas*), and various local bodies. A military officer of colonel or higher rank held the position of civil defense national director. Chaired by governors, the provincial boards included representatives of the military, the National Police, the Roman Catholic Church, and provincial officers of various ministries.

The National Directorate of Civil Defense was subordinate to the NSC. Essentially a planning organization, the directorate prepared guidelines and coordinated preparations for possible disasters and subsequent relief operations to be carried out by other national, provincial, municipal, and private agencies.

Participants in actual disaster relief operations included the armed forces; the Ecuadorian Social Security Institute; the ministries of Public Health, Social Welfare, and Public Works and Communications; the National Police; local fire departments; the Red Cross; and Catholic relief agencies. In the event of an emergency, the National Directorate of Civil Defense normally assigned a local agency to take the lead in resource mobilization.

The massive floods in 1982 and 1983 and the earthquake of 1987 severely tested the capabilities of the civil defense organizations. During these crises, compliance with leadership from the national level tended to be haphazard, with political considerations often receiving priority in the allocation of efforts. Relief projects were delayed because the national directorate lacked the power to resolve questions of jurisdiction among other agencies. The armed forces repeatedly demonstrated their effectiveness in responding to emergencies, but in many instances they did not coordinate their efforts with other civil defense authorities.

During the 1982–83 flood disaster, the national directorate formed an emergency operations center in Guayaquil to supervise the logistics of relief assistance. It subsequently established a flood commission to coordinate the efforts of nongovernment organizations, and a high-level committee to assess infrastructure damage and reconstruction needs. Following the 1987 earthquake, the government set up the National Emergency Relief Center in Quito to coordinate the dispensing of assistance from public and private sources, including foreign governments, international charities, and personal donations of money, goods, and services. The FAE, assisted by the air forces of Italy, Argentina, Brazil, and Venezuela, established an ''air bridge'' of supplies from Quito to the Oriente.

Civic Action

The armed forces actively engaged in various civic-action programs. Army engineer battalions played a leading part in road construction between the remote areas of the Oriente and the more populated regions of the country (see Transportation, ch. 3). They repaired and restored roads and bridges damaged during natural calamities and built various public buildings such as schools. Army medical teams periodically conducted examinations and provided medicines, inoculations, and dental services in remote settlements lacking civilian medical facilities. The military also engaged in health, education, and construction projects in the slums and shantytowns of the cities.

The army trained officers and selected enlisted men to provide literacy training to conscripts and to civilians living in areas where the military were assigned. In January 1989, the government reported that the armed forces and the National Police would provide security, transportation, lodging, and food to teachers sent to conduct a new literacy campaign in remote areas (see Education, ch. 2).

Foreign Influence

Although French officers comprised the first foreign military mission to Ecuador in the 1890s, the Ecuadorian armed forces relied primarily on Chilean and Italian assistance throughout the early years of the twentieth century. In 1903 the German-trained Chilean armed forces furnished a military mission and opened Chile's military academy to Ecuadorian cadets. The Chilean navy also provided sea training to Ecuadorian midshipmen, and Chilean officers staffed the Army War Academy until 1962. In 1922 an Italian military mission organized a system of army training schools in aviation, cavalry, infantry, and engineering. Beginning in 1935, United States specialists operating under private contracts gradually replaced Italian flight instructors. Italy withdrew its entire military mission in 1940 when it entered World War II.

Military Relations with the United States

Ecuador declared war on Japan immediately after the latter's attack on United States forces at Pearl Harbor. Ecuador granted the United States base rights in the Galápagos Islands, primarily for the defense of the Panama Canal against possible Japanese attack; and United States influence on Ecuadorian military policy subsequently became significant. The United States constructed an air base on one of the Galápagos Islands, manned it until the end of World War II, and then turned it over to Ecuador. The FAE later took over the Salinas base, which the United States had also manned during the war. Agreements signed in 1940 and 1944 also provided for the transfer of military equipment. In 1952 an agreement between the two governments resulted in the establishment of a United States Military Group that incorporated the already existing army, navy, and air force missions and led to the delivery of significant amounts of United States military matériel. The United States withdrew the military group in 1971 as a consequence of a dispute over fishing rights but subsequently reestablished it.

Between 1950 and 1988, almost 8,000 Ecuadorian officers and NCOs received training sponsored by the United States. Ecuadorian military personnel attended training programs in the former Panama Canal Zone and in the United States, including programs offered by the United States Naval Academy.

Deliveries of United States military assistance to Ecuador between 1950 and 1988, including credit sales, totaled almost US$123 million. United States budgetary cutbacks limited military assistance financing to only US$4 million in grant form in fiscal year (FY— see Glossary) 1989. Proposed aid in FY 1990 was limited to US$3 million in credit financing. The United States tailored much of the assistance in the late 1980s to the efforts to control the northern border and the eastern jungle areas frequently crossed by terrorist groups and narcotics traffickers. With the exception of the credit sale of At-33 trainer aircraft, assistance consisted largely of vehicles, medical equipment, communications items, small arms, and support for existing inventories.

Between May and December 1987, almost 6,000 United States National Guardsmen, reservists, and active-duty personnel rotated

Relief operations following the 1987 earthquake
Courtesy United States Agency for International Development,
Office of United States Foreign Disaster Assistance (LeVonne Harrell)

to Ecuador at two-week intervals to assist in earthquake reconstruction. The United States initially regarded the project as a field-training exercise in road and bridge building. Although plans originally called for restoration of roads in the Costa, the earthquake resulted in a United States-Ecuadorian decision to shift the project to the Oriente. United States forces encountered severe weather problems affecting the movement of heavy equipment over the Andes, carving a road through tropical jungle, and combating health hazards. In addition, the presence of United States troops became a source of political contention, as opposition forces in the Ecuadorian Congress passed a resolution demanding the troops' immediate departure. President Febres Cordero rejected the resolution but nevertheless terminated the project earlier than planned.

Equipment Sources

Historically, Ecuador depended on a wide variety of foreign suppliers for virtually all of its equipment needs. Only in the 1980s did it begin to develop a modest domestic arms industry as the Directorate of Army Industries manufactured rifle ammunition, uniforms, boots, and other consumable items.

Prior to World War II, Italy supplied a substantial amount of military matériel to Ecuador. During and after World War II, the United States became the predominant supplier, although by the 1950s Ecuador had also turned to World War II-vintage weapons from European countries, notably aircraft from Britain. During the 1960s and 1970s, France became a leading supplier of tanks and aircraft. Ecuador purchased submarine and patrol boats from West Germany and rifles and machine guns from Belgium.

Ecuador became a substantial customer for Israeli arms in the 1970s, purchasing Arava aircraft, Gabriel missiles for arming naval patrol craft, Uzi submachine guns, and other munitions. Under technical assistance contracts, Israel serviced Israeli planes in the air force inventory as well as Boeing civilian aircraft flown by TAME and Ecuatoriana Airlines. Ecuador reportedly also employed Israeli security specialists as consultants in the fight against terrorism.

In 1976 Ecuador became the first foreign country to order the Kfir, an advanced jet fighter equipped with the General Electric J–79 engine produced in Israel under license. The transaction, which required United States government approval because of the engine technology, was rejected by the administration of President Jimmy Carter in order to discourage the proliferation of sophisticated military equipment in the Third World. The action caused

236

an uproar in Israel where the sale was regarded as an important breakthrough in Israel's efforts to develop international markets for the Kfir. In 1981, after the inauguration of President Ronald Reagan, Washington removed its objection to the sale. Although the contract called for the purchase of twelve Kfirs and an option to purchase an additional twelve, Ecuador acquired only the original group, at a price estimated at US$196 million.

According to ACDA, Ecuador was a relatively heavy importer of arms in the late 1970s and early 1980s, averaging US$150 million annually and reaching a peak of US$280 million in 1982. These imports declined sharply to an average of only US$50 million annually between 1985 and 1987, presumably as a result of a dramatic reduction in oil revenues and the precipitous drop in the value of the sucre, which made imported arms extremely expensive. Between 1983 and 1987, Ecuador imported an estimated US$460 million of arms, primarily from Italy, France, the United States, and Britain. Ecuador did not receive military equipment from the Soviet Union or other communist countries.

Internal Security

In spite of the volatile nature of Ecuadorian politics during the 1980s, the country did not encounter major disruptions of internal security and successfully contained localized episodes of public disorder, such as riots and demonstrations. Since 1985, strikes and demonstrations to protest economic austerity measures and increases in living costs had been frequent. The Febres Cordero administration regularly declared such activities to be illegal and broke up street demonstrations with tear gas and arrests. Although police actions proved effective, critics often accused the police of excesses in dispersing public marches and rallies. In January 1986, several hundred Quito students clashed with police during a three-day period of demonstrations. This outbreak, in which 100 students were jailed, coincided with Febres Cordero's visit to the United States and was in part a protest against United States policies toward Ecuador.

As of late 1989, no subversive or terrorist group posed a serious threat to domestic order. A small leftist group, Alfaro Lives, Damnit! (¡Alfaro Vive, Carajo!—AVC), periodically carried out acts of terrorism and insurgency. Even though the AVC had a low potential for subversive action and numbered only 200 to 300 activists, Ecuador was determined to avoid a situation like that in the neighboring nations of Peru and Colombia, where large, well-organized, and violent guerrilla organizations presented a grave challenge to the authority of the state. An intensive police campaign in the 1986–87 period resulted in the death or capture of most of the AVC leadership.

The AVC had come to national attention in 1983 when it broke into a museum in Guayaquil and stole state swords used by the Ecuadorian national hero, José Eloy Alfaro Delgado. The AVC claimed to be non-Marxist and adopted a vague program to combat social injustice. Analysts believed that AVC members were primarily university-educated middle- or upper-class youths without close links to other domestic political movements. Some of its leaders, however, reportedly had ties with Cuba and Nicaragua. In addition, police found evidence of Libyan involvement in the training of some AVC members. AVC activists also traveled to Colombia for training and participation in M–19 military operations.

Between mid-1986 and mid-1987, the AVC kidnapped two journalists, killed four policemen in a rescue operation to free one of its members being treated in a hospital, robbed five banks and a factory, and took over several radio stations, forcing them to broadcast AVC manifestos. In August 1986, the AVC also kidnapped a prominent Guayaquil businessman; both the prisoner and his kidnappers died during a massive police assault. After this incident, police infiltration, raids, and arrests dealt heavy blows to the AVC. By the beginning of 1987, sixty-one of its members were in prison and many others had been killed, including most of the leadership.

Disorganized and essentially leaderless, the AVC had carried out few terrorist actions since mid-1987. The remnants of the organization entered into an agreement with the government in April 1989 to lay down their arms, renounce violence, and integrate themselves within the democratic system.

A small splinter group of the AVC, Guerrillas for a Free Homeland (Montoneros Patria Libre—MPL), which made its appearance in 1986, did not take part in the negotiations with the government and vowed to continue its armed resistance. Estimated to have a membership of only 100, the MPL was suspected of a series of bank robberies to amass funds for its operations.

The Ecuadorian Communist Party (Partido Comunista Ecuatoriano—PCE) grew out of the Socialist Party, which had been formed in 1926. The PCE gradually gained in importance; in 1944 the PCE won fifteen out of eighty-five seats in the National Assembly and had one of its members appointed minister of education. In 1946 the government outlawed the PCE and jailed many of its members. The PCE was legalized during the 1948–52 term of President Galo Plaza Lasso, but was banned again when the military junta held power in 1963–66. Thereafter, the PCE was a legally constituted political party, although it had only an estimated 500 members in 1988. The PCE participated in congressional and presidential elections as part of the coalition of the Broad Left Front (Frente Amplio de la Izquierda), which gained thirteen seats in Congress in 1986. The PCE also controlled the Confederation of Ecuadorian Workers (Confederación de Trabajadores Ecuatorianos—CTE), which comprised about 20 percent of organized workers (see Political Forces and Interest Groups, ch. 4).

A pro-Chinese faction, the Communist Party of Ecuador, Marxist-Leninist (Partido Comunista del Ecuador, Marxista-Leninista—PCE–ML), broke away from the PCE in 1963. With a membership estimated at only 100, the PCE–ML nevertheless published its own newspaper and contested elections as part of the Democratic Popular Movement (Movimiento Popular Democrático—MPD), a coalition that won four seats in the 1986 congressional election. Both the PCE and PCE–ML were legally recognized as of 1989 but had little political impact and were not regarded as constituting an internal security risk.

Police

Primary responsibility for the preservation of public order rested with the National Police functioning under the supervision of the minister of government and justice. According to Article 136 of the Constitution, the police are an auxiliary body of the armed forces and have the mission of guaranteeing internal order and individual and collective security.

The congress established by the constitution of 1830 decreed that the separate municipal councils would create their own police departments and would have appropriate regulations for law enforcement. For the first thirty years after independence, the police systems were either under the control of the separate municipalities or dominated by the army. The police developed slowly under a system of provincial organizations until the formation of the first national police organization in 1937. In 1951 the name was changed from the National Civil Guard to the National Civil Police and in 1979 to the National Police.

In 1988 the National Police had about 18,000 members grouped in a highly centralized structure organized along military lines. A clear line of demarcation existed between officers and troops with little or no opportunity for troops to advance to officer rank. The National Police was headed by a commanding general of the police who reported directly to the minister of government and justice. The organization consisted of a number of support directorates, as well as technical operations directorates (see fig. 21). The country

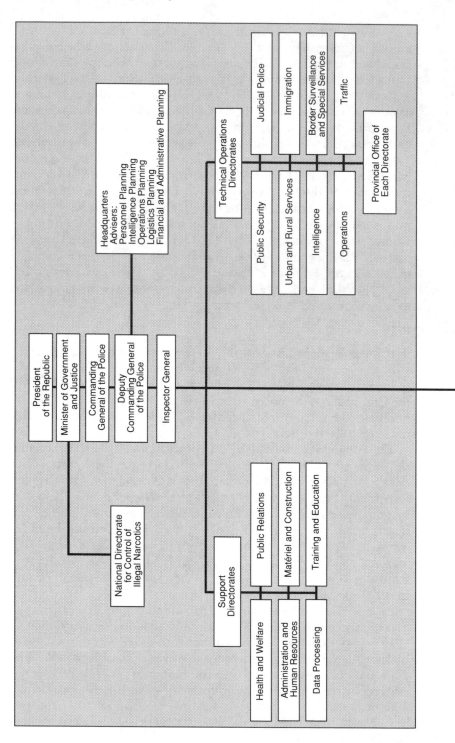

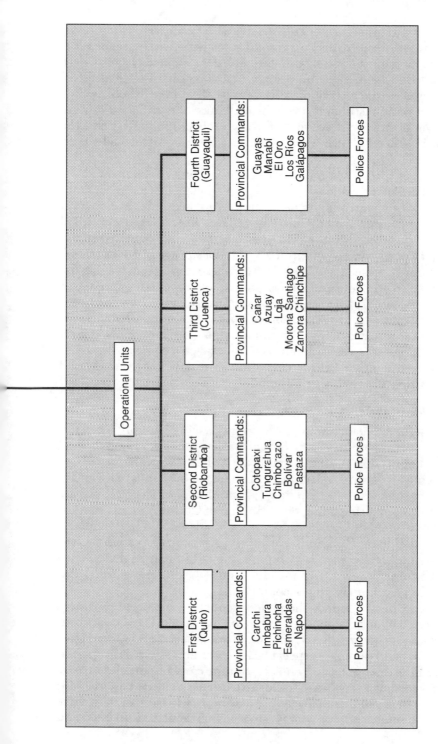

Figure 21. Organization of the National Police, 1988

was divided into four police districts, with headquarters in Quito, Riobamba, Cuenca, and Guayaquil, each with five commands corresponding to provincial boundaries. The Galápagos Islands were included in the Guayaquil district. The National Police also had three instructional facilities: the Troop Training School, which offered basic instruction for enlisted ranks; the Officer Training School, a three-year academy for high school graduates; and the Police Officers' Higher Training School, which provided advanced courses.

Several specialized and local police services supplemented the operations of the National Police. The National Directorate for Control of Illegal Narcotics reported directly to the minister of government and justice. The Customs Police, with fewer than 2,000 officers under the Ministry of Finance and Credit, countered smuggling at ports and airports, supervised the storage of goods in customs, and checked baggage of individuals entering and leaving the country. Both Quito and Guayaquil had metropolitan police forces of several hundred members with a number of low-level functions, such as enforcing local ordinances, controlling public vendors, assuring the removal of trash, and maintaining order in public places. Most other cities also had some type of local police, generally poorly organized and led, whose contribution to law enforcement and prevention of crime was minimal.

Standards of Police Conduct

Although Ecuadorian police authorities had no tradition of massive or systematic human rights violations, public attention focused on police conduct during the latter part of the 1980s. Evidence was presented of torture and abuse of prisoners in the hands of the police and, in some cases, the military. A number of official and private organizations—including the Tribunal of Constitutional Guarantees (Tribunal de Garantías Constitucionales—TGC), the Special Commission on Human Rights of the Ecuadorian National Congress, and the Ecumenical Commission of Human Rights (Comisión Ecuménica de Derechos Humanos—Cedhu)—recorded and investigated human rights complaints.

According to Cedhu, the police frequently subjected detainees suspected of political infractions to violence in efforts to extract confessions and information. Common-crime suspects also suffered torture or maltreatment, especially in rural areas. Cedhu reported sixty-nine cases of torture and eighty-nine cases of brutality in 1987 and a further twenty cases of torture during the first half of 1988. Cedhu believed that police abuse was more widespread than these statistics indicated since many cases went unreported. In 1985 and

1986, five persons arrested by the police or the military disappeared and were believed to have died in custody. No disappearances had been recorded since 1986. According to Cedhu, forty persons in 1986 and thirty-four in 1987 died while in police custody. Many of these, including several of the ten AVC leaders killed by the police, were believed to have been victims of extrajudicial executions.

The United States Department of State's *Country Reports on Human Rights Practices for 1987* noted that, although mistreatment of detainees was not officially sanctioned, the government of Febres Cordero made no clear statement condemning the use of excessive force, nor were penal actions taken against police or military personnel believed to have taken part in deaths, disappearances, or torture. Upon taking office in August 1988, the Borja administration stated its unequivocal opposition to official use of abusive measures. The Department of State reported that, although some police abuse—including torture—occurred after Borja's inauguration, human rights groups hoped that over time the new president's promises of respect for human rights would have an impact on police behavior.

The TGC, an autonomous body, is empowered under the 1979 Constitution to investigate breaches of constitutional or human rights. Although the TGC had little real power to enforce its rulings, it focused public attention on human rights issues by hearing complaints of human rights activists and calling upon government officials to respond to questions (see The Judiciary, ch. 4).

Charges against members of the police were reviewed by special police courts under a three-tiered system consisting of tribunals, district courts, and the National Court of Police Justice. Although the courts were ostensibly independent, some observers called into question their impartiality, especially inasmuch as most police judges were active or retired police officers. According to a survey by two human rights groups, Americas Watch and the Andean Commission of Jurists, the number of cases involving wrongful homicide and torture was inexplicably small in relation to the number of complaints against the police in the 1984–86 period. Apparently none of the trials had resulted in convictions; all were either still pending or had been dismissed.

Narcotics Control

Cultivation of, and trafficking in, drugs was less of a problem in Ecuador than in neighboring countries. Coca cultivation, which began in 1984, had been essentially eliminated by late 1987 as a result of vigorous government action. With the assistance of the

United States, which lent two helicopters, the Ecuadorian police detected and uprooted plantings of the crop, grown mostly along the border with Colombia. The police also interdicted shipments of cocaine and other coca products across Ecuador's territory to markets and processing centers elsewhere and suppressed cocaine refining laboratories within its borders.

In early 1989, however, drug traffickers reportedly moved into the country from Colombia and Bolivia because of Ecuador's easier access to the United States market. The United States Drug Enforcement Administration estimated that thirty to fifty tons a year of Colombian cocaine were being shipped through Ecuador destined for the United States, Europe, and Asia. Cocaine had been found in container shipments of Ecuadorian frozen orange concentrate and chocolates and in air deliveries of fresh flowers. Analysts also believed that the Colombian Medellín Cartel had purchased Ecuadorian companies. Few big drug seizures had been made because of the limited resources of local authorities, although coca laboratories continued to be raided and destroyed.

In October 1988, assailants assumed to have been drug dealers murdered a superior court judge in Quito who had been working on a number of drug trafficking cases. Other judges had received death threats. Despite the fact that Ecuador has bank secrecy laws, United States officials believed that the weakness of the sucre limited Ecuador's potential to become a major money-laundering center.

In an effort to assist Ecuadorian drug-control efforts, the United States supplied a number of powerboats for patrolling rivers in the north and islands near the port of Guayaquil and supplied training by the United States Navy. It also furnished sniffer dogs to detect drugs in export shipments and baggage. In FY 1990, President George Bush requested from Congress US$1.4 million in drug-control assistance for Ecuador.

The Administration of Justice

The court system consisted of the Supreme Court of Justice, which sat in the capital; superior courts in the capitals of 10 provinces; 35 provincial criminal courts; 87 cantonal courts; and 445 parish courts. Parish judges tried minor civil matters and misdemeanors, their verdicts being subject to review by cantonal courts. Cantonal judges also could conduct preliminary hearings and make recommendations in criminal cases. Nonetheless, provincial courts were the courts of first instance in such cases, except those involving government officials. Provincial criminal judges had the authority to try criminal cases for which, according to the penal code, the punishment did not exceed three years in prison.

Criminal proceedings consisted of summary and plenary parts. The first of these usually took place before a local court and the second before a provincial criminal court. The summary assessed whether or not an offense had been committed and if a trial were warranted; the plenary determined the guilt or innocence of the accused.

After an arrest, except for minor offenses, the police were required to turn the suspect over to the judge of the local cantonal court, who would conduct an investigation to determine if there were sufficient grounds for trial. According to the law, the findings of the investigation had to be forwarded within fifteen days to the provincial criminal court holding jurisdiction over the case.

When the summary proceedings had been completed, the record was delivered to the public prosecutor so that he could prepare the accusation. If, in the opinion of the presiding judge, the information contained in the summary did not warrant a continuation of the proceedings, the judge could release the suspect on bail. Dismissal of the case would be final if the public prosecutor could not find merit in the accusation or if the judge felt the existence of an offense had not been absolutely established. If the case warranted a trial, it then went to the Tribunal of Crimes, a five-member body presided over by the judge of the provincial criminal court. Upon the completion of arguments, the tribunal retired in secret session and then announced its verdict. Except in special cases, such as those involving a breach of morality, trials were public. Ecuador did not use the jury system.

Defendants could call witnesses on their own behalf, cross-examine witnesses, and refrain from testifying against themselves, and could appeal sentences to intermediate or higher courts. Accused persons were entitled to legal counsel as soon as arrested. Although a public defender system is mandated by the 1979 Constitution, it had not been introduced as of 1988. Persons who could not afford counsel faced the longest period of pretrial detention. Detention without charge for more than forty-eight hours was prohibited by the criminal code, but the requirement was frequently violated in practice. Habeas corpus could be invoked by mayors or municipal council presidents who had the constitutional right to order the release of detainees. This power tended to be exercised liberally, regardless of the severity of the charges.

According to the Department of State's human rights reports, the judicial system was inefficient and corruptible, in part because of inexperienced and poorly paid judges. A chronic backlog of cases meant that detainees might be forced to wait two years or longer for trial. According to the Special Commission on Human Rights, approximately 50 percent of all prisoners as of 1988 had not been charged or sentenced. Time spent awaiting trial counted toward completion of a sentence, but that did not help long-term detainees who were eventually acquitted.

In the late 1980s, Ecuador recorded significant levels of urban crime. The increased crime rate, particularly notable in Guayaquil and to a lesser extent in Quito, was linked to the steady rural to urban migration. Most migrants lacked the skills necessary to obtain employment in the cities. Many, in order to provide for themselves and their families, turned to crime. The country's economic setbacks during the latter half of the 1980s created an increasingly desperate situation for adults unable to find legitimate employment. Although muggings, assaults, pickpocketing, and burglaries were the most prevalent forms of crime, since 1985 there had been an upsurge of robberies of banks and private companies by well-armed gangs, as well as of kidnappings and sexual assaults. Some robberies were connected with the AVC or the Colombian M-19, but most appeared to be the work of professional criminals.

Data reported to the International Criminal Police Organization (Interpol) indicated there were approximately 26,000 crimes committed in Ecuador in 1984. This number included 400 homicides, more than 500 rapes, almost 500 serious assaults, approximately 2,400 robberies and violent thefts, more than 6,000 other robberies, almost 700 car thefts, approximately 600 cases of fraud, and almost 200 drug offenses. Ecuador had a crime ratio of 292 per 100,000 population. Such a rate would be considered very low on an international scale, beneath that of many countries with a reputation for a low incidence of crime, such as Japan. Some observers speculated that many offenses reported to the police were not classified as crimes, or that many crimes were not brought to the attention of the police. For example, the Indian population customarily dealt with crimes within its own communities without recourse to the Ecuadorian police.

The Penal System

The National Directorate of Social Rehabilitation, a component of the Ministry of Government and Justice, continued to operate the country's penal system in 1989. The García Moreno Prison in Quito and the Coastal Prison in Guayaquil were Ecuador's largest criminal detention facilities. Quito and the capitals of all Costa and Sierra provinces also had municipal jails.

Although the laws called for rehabilitation of prisoners, few facilities had space, staffing, and equipment for education or training programs. One exception, the women's prison in Quito, provided both academic and vocational courses. Some private factories held prison work contracts. All prisoners were expected to work and were paid a minimum wage. One-third of the wages went to the prisoner upon release; one-third to pay expenses while in prison; and one-third to the court to take care of expenses incidental to the trial. During the 1980s, two halfway houses were opened in Quito from which prisoners traveled to jobs and were allowed to visit their homes.

Most prisons were greatly overcrowded, the result of budgetary restrictions and the low priority given prison construction and staffing. As of July 1986, Ecuador had 6,450 prisoners in a system whose total capacity was 2,600. The García Moreno Prison, which was built in 1875 to house 300 and subsequently remodeled to hold 640, held 1,800 prisoners who were forced to share twenty toilets. As of 1988, a new prison was scheduled to open in Quito, which would help relieve existing pressures.

According to the Department of State's *Country Reports on Human Rights Practices for 1988,* "prison conditions are so squalid and brutal that in themselves they represent cruel treatment." Guards reportedly beat prisoners for disciplinary reasons. Notoriously underpaid, guards reportedly could easily be bribed by prisoners who wanted to avoid punishment, to receive improved living conditions, to secure visits, and to obtain drugs.

According to a report by the Special Commission on Human Rights, unhygienic conditions in the prisons were conducive to skin, lung, gastrointestinal, and venereal infections. Prisons had few medical supplies and only sporadic visits by doctors. Again, the Quito women's prison was an exception to this general pattern.

The Department of State reported that guards at the Coastal Prison often mistreated detainees charged with terrorism or subversion. The Americas Watch and Andean Commission of Jurists group confirmed these observations, documenting various forms of guard brutality and the withholding of privileges, such as exercise, sunlight, visits, and recreation. This discrimination reportedly ended in 1987.

*   *   *

A number of studies trace the relationships between the armed forces and the civilian leadership. John D. Martz's *The Military in Ecuador* assesses both the 1972–79 military regime and the role of senior officers following the resumption of civilian rule. Osvaldo Hurtado's *Political Power in Ecuador* includes a concise analysis of the military's attitude toward civilian politics and its strengths and shortcomings while in power. *The Military Coup d'état as a Political Process: Ecuador, 1948–1966* by John Samuel Fitch, although based on earlier research, contains still relevant data on the leanings and social background of the officer corps. David W. Schodt's *Ecuador: An Andean Enigma* treats the role of military figures and the military establishment in both the nineteenth and twentieth centuries.

Human Rights in Ecuador, a study by Americas Watch and the Andean Commission of Jurists, contains much detail on abuses by the police, particularly in the treatment of political detainees, and on prison conditions. The Department of State's annual studies, *Country Reports on Human Rights Practices,* describe the operation of the legal system and practices of the police and prison authorities.

Up-to-date reports on the organization and operational status of the Ecuadorian armed forces are scarce. Considerable information, particularly of a historical nature, may be found in the section on Ecuador in Adrian J. English's *The Armed Forces of Latin America. The Military Balance, 1988–89,* prepared by the London-based International Institute for Strategic Studies, has data concerning weapons systems in the armed forces inventory. (For further information and complete citations, see Bibliography.)

Appendix

Table

Table 1. Metric Conversion Coefficients and Factors

When you know	Multiply by	To find
Millimeters	0.04	inches
Centimeters	0.39	inches
Meters	3.3	feet
Kilometers	0.62	miles
Hectares (10,000 m²)	2.47	acres
Square kilometers	0.39	square miles
Cubic meters	35.3	cubic feet
Liters	0.26	gallons
Kilograms	2.2	pounds
Metric tons	0.98	long tons
....	1.1	short tons
....	2,204	pounds
Degrees Celsius	9	degrees Fahrenheit
(Centigrade)	divide by 5 and add 32	

Table 2. Annual Growth Rate by Region, Intercensal Periods, 1950–82

Region	Annual Growth Rate		
	1950–62	1962–74	1974–82
Sierra	2.00	2.50	2.30
Costa	4.11	3.40	2.66
Oriente	3.98	7.28	4.95
Galápagos	4.79	1.54	1.91
ECUADOR	2.95	3.10	2.62

Source: Based on information from Ecuador, Instituto Nacional de Estadística y Censos, *IV Censo Nacional de Población y III de Vivienda, 1982—Resumen Nacional: Breve Análisis de los Resultados Definitivos,* Quito, 1985, 32.

Table 3. Population and Annual Growth Rate of Guayaquil and Quito, 1950–82

City	Population				Annual Growth Rate *			
	1950	1962	1974	1982	1950–62	1962–74	1974–82	1950–82
Guayaquil .	258,966	510,804	823,219	1,199,344	5.82	4.06	4.82	4.91
Quito	209,932	354,746	599,828	866,472	4.47	4.47	4.70	4.53

* Intercensal periods.

Source: Based on information from Carlos Larrea, "Crecimiento Urbano y Dinámica de las Ciudades Intermedias en el Ecuador (1950-1982)," in Fernando Carrión (comp.), *El Proceso de Urbanización en el Ecuador del siglo XVIII al siglo XX—Antología,* Quito, 1986, 104, 106.

*Table 4. Urban Growth Rate in the Costa and Sierra
Regions and in Ecuador by Size of City,
Intercensal Periods, 1950–82*

Region Size of City	1950–62	1962–74	1974–82	1950–82
Costa				
Metropolitan [1]	5.82	4.06	4.82	4.91
Intermediate [2]	7.71	6.24	6.13	6.76
Small [3]	5.61	3.72	5.51	4.87
Sierra				
Metropolitan	4.47	4.47	4.70	4.53
Intermediate	3.96	3.91	4.07	3.97
Small	1.65	2.79	3.42	2.52
Ecuador				
Metropolitan	5.24	4.23	4.77	4.74
Intermediate	5.51	5.07	5.21	5.27
Small	3.53	3.44	5.02	3.87

[1] More than 200,000.
[2] 50,000 to 200,000.
[3] Less than 50,000.

Source: Based on information from Carlos Larrea, "Crecimiento Urbano y Dinámica de
las Ciudades Intermedias en el Ecuador (1950-1982)," in Fernando Carrión (ed.),
El Proceso de Urbanización en el Ecuador del siglo XVIII al siglo XX—Antología, Quito,
1986, 113.

*Table 5. Landholding in the Sierra and Costa
Regions by Size of Farm, 1954 and 1974*

Region Size of Farm [1]	1954		1974	
	Percentage of Farms	Percentage of Agricultural Land	Percentage of Farms	Percentage of Agricultural Land
Sierra				
0 to 10	90.4	16.5	87.1	18.3
10 to 20	4.0	4.7	5.7	7.8
20 to 100	4.4	14.5	6.1	25.7
100 to 500	0.9	15.6	0.9	16.4
More than 500	0.3	48.7	0.2	31.8
Total Sierra	100.0	100.0	100.0	100.0
Costa				
0 to 10	63.0	7.0	67.4	8.9
10 to 20	12.8	5.1	11.9	7.4
20 to 100	19.4	23.5	17.7	32.2
100 to 500	4.0	23.0	2.9	24.3
More than 500	0.7	41.4	0.4	27.2
Total Costa	100.0 [2]	100.0	100.0 [2]	100.0

[1] In hectares.
[2] Figures do not add to total because of rounding.

Source: Based on information from Howard Handelman, *Ecuadorian Agrarian Reform: The
Politics of Limited Change,* Hanover, New Hampshire, 1980, 13.

Table 6. Organization of the Roman Catholic Church, 1986

Structure	Area *	Catholic Population	Number of Priests
Archdiocese			
Cuenca	9,672	363,000	109
Guayaquil	20,269	1,805,000	248
Quito	17,090	1,251,540	430
Diocese			
Ambato	3,844	336,200	64
Azogues	4,514	181,200	32
Guaranda	3,336	197,000	29
Ibarra	5,669	244,500	75
Latacunga	5,093	314,000	56
Loja	11,000	377,000	80
Machala	5,816	313,000	26
Portoviejo	19,000	1,050,000	86
Riobamba	6,161	507,000	62
Tulcán	5,000	135,000	31
Territorial prelature			
Los Ríos	6,521	368,000	18
Apostolic vicariate			
Aguarico	28,000	39,600	20
Esmeraldas	15,000	283,300	37
Méndez	35,000	63,700	34
Napo	25,000	52,135	27
Puyo	24,000	27,000	11
San Miguel de Sucumbíos	20,000	43,500	12
Zamora	20,000	50,400	13
Apostolic prefecture			
Galápagos	7,860	7,000	5
TOTAL	297,845	8,009,075	1,505

* In square kilometers.

Source: Based on information from *Annuario Pontificio per l'anno 1986,* Vatican City, 1986.

Table 7. Enrollment by Level of Education, Selected Years, 1967–85

Level	1967	1971	1975	1979	1983	1984	1985
Primary	897,539	1,052,484	1,254,850	1,427,627	1,677,364	1,672,068	1,741,967 [1]
Secondary							
First Cycle	106,831	161,446	256,196	345,569	405,445	438,718	452,262 [1]
Second Cycle	44,371	78,135	126,515	189,876	244,833	267,058	277,368 [1]
Total Secondary	151,202	239,581	382,711	535,445	650,278	705,776	729,630
Higher Education	19,600	45,355	129,130	225,343	— [2]	— [2]	— [2]

[1] Provisional.
[2] Figures not reported.

Source: Based on information from Banco Central del Ecuador, *Boletín Anuario*, 8, Quito, 1985, 241; and Banco Central del Ecuador, *Boletín Anuario*, 11, Quito, 1988, 243.

*Table 8. Literacy Rate among Population over Ten
Years of Age, Census Years, 1950–82*
(in percentages)

	1950	1962	1974	1982
Urban				
Males	89	92	94	96
Females	79	86	89	94
Total urban	83	89	91	95
Rural				
Males	51	63	70	80
Females	38	53	60	71
Total rural	45	58	65	76
Ecuador				
Males	62	73	79	88
Females	51	66	73	83
Total Ecuador	56	70	76	85

Source: Based on information from Ecuador, Instituto Nacional de Estadística y Censos,
*IV Censo Nacional de Población y III de Vivienda, 1982 Resumen Nacional: Breve Análisis
de los Resultados Definitivos,* Quito, 1985, 45.

*Table 9. Social Security Participation among
Economically Active Population, 1982*
(in percentages)

	Males	Females	Total
Urban	34	42	36
Rural	9	12	9
Ecuador	21	33	23

Source: Based on information from Ecuador, Instituto Nacional de Estadística y Censos,
*IV Censo Nacional de Población y III de Vivienda, 1982—Resumen Nacional: Breve Análisis
de los Resultados Definitivos,* Quito, 1985, 59.

Table 10. *Gross Domestic Product by Sector,*
1950, 1971, and 1987
(in percentages)

Sector	1950	1971	1987
Agriculture, livestock, fishing, and forestry	38.8	24.7	17.8
Petroleum and mining	2.3	−3.4	7.6
Manufacturing	16.0	17.0	17.6
Utilities	0.5	0.7	1.6
Construction	2.7	7.6	4.1
Wholesale and retail trade	10.3	17.5	15.7
Transportation and communications	4.8	6.0	8.3
Financial services	1.4	2.4	2.3
Public administration	5.8	8.8	9.3
Other services	9.3	13.6	13.0
Indirect taxes	8.1	5.1	2.7
TOTAL	100.0	100.0	100.0

Source: Based on information from Banco Central del Ecuador, *Boletín Anuario,* 10, Quito, 1987.

Table 11. *Labor Force by Sector, 1974, 1982, and 1987*
(in percentages) *

Sector	1974	1982	1987
Agriculture, forestry, and fishing	46.2	33.5	34.8
Government and community services	17.0	23.7	23.9
Manufacturing	11.7	12.2	10.8
Commerce	9.7	11.6	10.8
Construction	4.4	6.7	7.3
Utilities and transportation	3.2	4.9	4.9
Finance and insurance	1.0	1.9	2.3
Mining	0.3	0.3	0.1
Other	6.4	5.1	4.9
TOTAL	100.0	100.0	100.0

* Figures do not add to total because of rounding.

Source: Based on information from Banco Central del Ecuador, *Boletín Anuario,* 10, Quito, 1987.

Table 12. Production of Selected Agricultural
Commodities, 1983, 1984, and 1985
(in thousands of tons)

Commodity	1983	1984	1985
Export crops			
Bananas	1,642.1	1,677.6	1,969.6
Cocoa	45.0	48.7	130.8
Coffee	81.1	97.2	120.9
Sugar (centrifugal)	2,625.5	3,041.9	2,693.6
Sugar (noncentrifugal)	2,994.5	2,656.3	2,301.2
Major food crops			
African palm oil	354.2	372.5	457.9
Barley	29.6	25.0	26.7
Cassava	194.8	239.2	228.8
Corn	229.4	325.8	371.4
Oranges	355.2	272.0	230.7
Plantains	687.2	744.0	945.5
Potatoes	314.0	389.6	423.2
Rice (paddy)	273.5	437.2	397.4
Wheat	26.9	25.2	18.5
Other crops			
Castor beans	2.2	1.9	1.7
Cotton	4.2	7.8	18.9
Hemp	7.6	18.3	10.0
Soybeans	14.1	47.4	62.9
Tea	2.6	2.8	4.3
Tobacco	1.8	4.4	3.1

Source: Based on information from Vjekoslav Mardesic (ed.), *Estadísticas del Ecuador*, Quito, 1988; and Ecuador, Ministerio de Agricultura y Ganadería, *Estimación de la superficie cosechada y de la producción agrícola del Ecuador, 1983 a 1985*, Quito, 1989.

Table 13. Crude Petroleum Production in the Costa and
Oriente Regions, 1980-89
(in thousands of barrels)

Year	Costa	Oriente	Total
1980	5,503	742,219	774,769
1981	5,116	765,164	770,280
1982	5,193	765,703	770,896
1983	2,773	864,138	866,611
1984	4,171	934,626	938,797
1985	4,380	1,019,978	1,024,159
1986	4,123	1,065,824	1,069,947
1987	n.a.	n.a.	669,000
1988	n.a.	n.a.	1,240,000
1989	n.a.	n.a.	1,246,000

n.a.—not available.

Source: Based on information from Banco Central del Ecuador, *Boletín Anuario*, 10, Quito, 1987, 170; and Economist Intelligence Unit, *Ecuador: Country Report, No. 4, 1990*, London, 1990, 23.

Table 14. Value of Manufacturing Production by Sector, 1986
(in percentages)

Sector	Value
Food and tobacco processing	39.7
Textiles	22.1
Minerals and metals	12.2
Paper and printing	6.9
Chemicals and plastics	5.8
Wood products and furniture	5.6
Machinery and metal products	2.9
Other	4.8
TOTAL	100.0

Source: Based on information from Banco Central del Ecuador, *Boletín Anuario, 1987,* Quito, 1987, 154–55.

Table 15. Principal Exports, 1981–87
(in millions of United States dollars) *

Commodity	1981	1982	1983	1984	1985	1986	1987
Crude petroleum	1,560	1,388	1,639	1,679	1,825	912	739
Fuel oil	150	120	94	156	102	70	78
Bananas	216	213	153	136	220	263	267
Coffee	106	139	149	175	191	299	192
Raw cocoa	44	61	8	96	138	71	83
Processed cocoa	106	56	26	50	78	77	57
Shrimp and fish	82	128	178	167	169	315	409
Processed food	138	118	56	100	123	110	87
Industrial products and chemicals	113	102	44	48	52	61	105

* Free on board.

Table 16. Merchandise Imports, 1982–87
(in millions of United States dollars) *

Commodity	1982	1983	1984	1985	1986	1987
Nondurable consumer goods	86	52	76	85	93	116
Durable consumer goods	371	208	230	138	126	139
Fuels and lubricants	220	256	144	158	82	354
Raw materials (agriculture)	45	36	54	64	54	46
Raw materials (industry)	667	490	654	660	624	689
Construction materials	79	32	37	39	50	53
Capital goods (agriculture)	29	9	14	29	31	24
Capital goods (industry)	434	237	246	309	369	447
Transportation equipment	250	88	112	131	203	186
TOTAL	2,181	1,408	1,567	1,613	1,632	2,054

* Cost, insurance, and freight.

Table 17. Principal Trading Partners, 1985, 1986, and 1987
(in millions of United States dollars)

Country	1985	1986	1987
Imports			
Brazil	123	120	119
Italy	50	100	65
Japan	207	205	257
Spain	50	52	58
United States	575	509	575
West Germany	167	165	170
Other	566	625	675
Total imports	1,738	1,776	1,919
Exports			
Chile	44	47	31
Colombia	47	30	23
Japan	62	57	48
Panama	120	59	43
United States	1,636	1,322	1,243
West Germany	59	78	80
Other	1,088	578	561
Total exports	3,056	2,171	2,029

Source: Based on information from James W. Wilkie and Enrique Ochoa (eds.), *Statistical Abstract of Latin America*, 27, Los Angeles, 1989, 639–40.

Table 18. *Balance of Payments, 1983–88*
(in millions of United States dollars)

	1983	1984	1985	1986	1987	1988
Merchandise						
Exports [1]	2,348	2,622	2,905	2,186	2,021	2,203
Imports [2]	−1,421	−1,567	−1,611	−1,631	−2,054	−1,614
Trade balance	927	1,055	1,294	555	−33	589
Services						
Exports	340	350	418	431	444	446
Imports	−1,295	−1,573	−1,643	−1,644	−1,674	−1,692
Balance on goods and						
services	−28	−168	69	−658	−1,263	−657
Government unrequited						
transfers (net)	24	20	80	45	132	60
Current account balance	−4	−148	149	−613	−1,131	−597
Direct capital investment						
(net)	50	50	62	70	75	80
Other long-term capital						
(net)	−1,200	−896	−752	−339	83	−891
Short-term capital (net)	−1,098	−267	−287	−95	72	138
Net errors and omissions	−182	−74	77	−173	−133	192
Total monetary movement						
(net)	−2,434	−1,335	−751	−1,150	−1,034	−1,078
Valuation changes	14	22	−27	−29	−62	−23
Exceptional financing	2,473	1,327	881	1,025	936	1,026
Official financing	74	−72	−107	−47	−1	65
Changes in reserves	127	−58	−4	−201	−161	−10

[1] Free on board.
[2] Cost, insurance, and freight.

Source: Based on information from International Monetary Fund, *International Financial Statistics,* 43, No. 6, Washington, 1990, 206.

Table 19. Law-Making Process, 1989

Step	Description
Step 1	Bill is initiated by legislators or Plenary of Legislative Commissions (Plenario de las Comisiones Legislativas—PCL), the president of the republic, judicial organs, or popular initiatives.
Step 2	Text is provided to each legislator fifteen days prior to debate in Congress.
Step 3	Proposed bill is discussed in two debates on different days. After first debate, it may be returned to the originating commission, which must report on new observations to modify, alter, or change it.
Step 4	At second debate, observations may be presented only if supported by two-thirds of the legislators present.
Step 5	If the president has presented the proposed bill, he may intervene in a specially convened discussion without voting rights.
Step 6	On being approved by Congress or the PCL, proposed bill must be submitted to the president, who may approve or object to it. President may also approve it tacitly by allowing ten days to pass without vetoing it. President may object either totally or partially. If the objection is partial, the part not objected to must be adopted immediately. In that case, Congress may accept the partial objection, correct the bill accordingly, and resubmit it to the president. Congress may also insist on the original version of the proposed bill by a vote of two-thirds of its members and proceed to promulgate it.
Step 7	Final stage is promulgation, which requires publishing the law in *Registro Oficial del Estado* (Official Register of the State).

Table 20. Major Army Equipment, 1988

Type	Country of Origin	Number in Inventory *
Tanks		
M–3	United States	45
AMX–13	France	104
Armored vehicles		
AML 60/90 reconnaissance	–do–	35
EE–9 Cascavel reconnaissance	Brazil	10
M–113 tracked personnel carriers	United States	20
AMX–VCI personnel carriers	France	60
EE–11 Urutu wheeled personnel carriers	Brazil	18
Artillery		
Oto Melara M–56 105mm	Italy	n.a.
M–101 105mm	United States	50
M–198 155mm	–do–	10
MK 73 155mm self-propelled	France	10
Mortars		
Soltam 160mm	Israel	12
Recoilless rifles		
M–67 90mm and M–40 106mm	United States	400
Air defense guns		
M–1935 20mm	–do–	28
Oerlikon GDF–002 twin 30mm	Sweden	30
Bofors M–1A1 40mm	–do–	30
Surface-to-air missiles		
Blowpipe shoulder-fired	Britain	150
Aircraft		
Liaison, utility, and survey, various types	United States	21
Helicopters		
SA–330 Puma	France	3
SA–315 Lama	–do–	3
AS–332 Super Puma	–do–	4
SA–342 Gazelle	–do–	4

n.a.—not available
* Estimated.

Source: Based on information from *The Military Balance, 1988–1989,* London, 1988, 195.

Appendix

Table 21. Major Naval Equipment, 1988

Type	Country of Origin	Number in Inventory	Date Commissioned
Destroyer			
Gearing-class, 3,500 tons, four 5-inch guns	United States	1	1946; modernized 1980
Frigate			
Lawrence-class, 2,130 tons, one 5-inch gun	–do–	1	1943
Submarines			
Shyri (T–209), 1,300 tons	West Germany	2	1977–78
Corvettes			
Esmeraldas, 550 tons, each with six Exocet missiles	Italy	6	1982–84
Fast attack craft			
Quito (Lürssen 45), 255 tons, each with four Exocet missiles	West Germany	3	1976–77
Manta (Lürssen 36), 120 tons, each with four Gabriel missiles	–do–	3	1971
Coastal patrol craft			
77-foot	–do–	3	1954–55
65-foot	United States	3	Delivered 1976
Amphibious			
Landing ship, tank, 1,650 tons	–do–	1	Recommissioned 1977
Landing ship, medium, 750 tons	–do–	1	1945

Source: Based on information from *Jane's Fighting Ships, 1988–89,* London, 1988, 139–43.

Table 22. Major Air Force Equipment, 1988

Type	Country of Origin	Number in Inventory
Fighters (ground attack)		
Jaguar S, B	Britain	12
Kfir C-2, TC-2	Israel	11
Fighters		
Mirage F-1J	France	16
Light attack and jet conversion training		
Cessna A-37B	United States	7
Lockhead At-33 (reconditioned T-33)	–do–	25
Strikemaster Mk 89	Britain	6
Transports		
TAME		
Boeing 727	United States	4
Lockheed C-130H Hercules	–do–	1
C-160	France	1
BAe 748	Britain	2
DHC-6 Twin Otter	Canada	3
Ecuatoriana		
Boeing 720	United States	3
Boeing 707	–do–	2
Helicopters (liaison and sea-air rescue)		
AS-332 Super Puma	France	2
SA-330 Puma	–do–	1
Alouette III	–do–	6
Bell 212, 214	United States	3
Bell UH-1H	–do–	3
Trainers		
Beech T-34C	–do–	20
Cessna T-41	–do–	2

Source: Based on information from *The Military Balance, 1988–1989,* London, 1988, 195–96; and *DMS Market Intelligence Report: South America/Australasia,* Greenwich, Connecticut, 1989.

Bibliography

Chapter 1

Agee, Philip. *Inside the Company: CIA Diary.* Harmondsworth, United Kingdom: Penguin Books, 1975.

Aguilar-Monsalve, Luis Antonio. "The Separation of Church and State: The Ecuadoran Case," *Thought,* 59, No. 233, 1984, 205–18.

Alcina Franch, José. *Manual de Arqueología Americana.* Madrid: Aguilar, 1965.

Ayala Mora, Enrique. *Lucha política y origen de los partidos en Ecuador.* (4th ed.) Quito: Corporación Editora Nacional, 1988.

Bannon, John Francis, Robert Ryal Miller, and Peter Masten Dunne. *Latin America.* (4th ed.) Encino, California: Glencoe Press, 1977.

Bennett, Wendell C. "The Andean Highlands: An Introduction." Pages 1–60 in Julian H. Steward (ed.), *Handbook of South American Indians, 2: The Andean Civilizations.* (Smithsonian Institution, Bureau of American Ethnology, Bulletin 143.) New York: Cooper Square, 1963.

Bialek, Robert W. *Catholic Politics in Ecuador.* New York: Vantage Press, 1963.

Blanksten, George I. *Ecuador: Constitutions and Caudillos.* Berkeley: University of California, 1951.

_____. "Ecuador: The Politics of Instability." Pages 69–90 in Martin C. Needler (ed.), *Political Systems of Latin America.* Princeton: Van Nostrand, 1964.

Bork, Albert William, and Georg Maier. *Historical Dictionary of Ecuador.* Metuchen, New Jersey: Scarecrow Press, 1973.

Brownrigg, Leslie Ann. "Interest Groups in Regime Changes in Ecuador," *Inter-American Economic Affairs,* 28, No. 1, Summer 1974, 3–17.

Clayton, Lawrence A. "Trade and Navigation in the Seventeenth Century Viceroyalty of Peru," *Journal of Latin American Studies* [Cambridge], 7, No. 1, May 1975, 1–21.

Collier, Donald. "The Archeology of Ecuador." Pages 767–84 in Julian H. Steward (ed.), *Handbook of South American Indians, 2: The Andean Civilizations.* (Smithsonian Institution, Bureau of American Ethnology, Bulletin 143.) New York: Cooper Square, 1963.

Conaghan, Catherine M. "Industrialists and Reformist Interregnum: Dominant Class Behavior and Ideology in Ecuador, 1972-1979." (Ph.D. dissertation.) New Haven: Yale University, 1983.

Corkill, David. "Democratic Politics in Ecuador, 1979-1984," *Bulletin of Latin American Research* [London], 4, No. 2, 1985, 63-74.

_____. "The Politics of Military Government in Ecuador: The Rodríguez Lara Regime, 1972-1976," *Bulletin of the Society for Latin American Studies,* No. 26, 1977, 44-63.

Cueva, Agustín. *El proceso de dominación política en el Ecuador.* Quito: Editorial Planeta, 1988.

_____. *The Process of Political Domination in Ecuador.* (Trans., Danielle Salti.) New Brunswick, New Jersey: Transaction Books, 1982.

Cushner, Nicolas P. *Farm and Factory: The Jesuits and the Development of Agrarian Capitalism in Colonial Quito, 1600-1767.* Albany: State University of New York, 1982.

Davidson, David. "Good Neighbors," *American Heritage,* 35, No. 3, 1984, 104-9.

Deas, Malcolm. "Colombia, Ecuador, and Venezuela, c. 1880-1930." Pages 641-84 in Leslie Bethell (ed.), *The Cambridge History of Latin America, 4-5: C. 1870-1930.* Cambridge: Cambridge University Press, 1986.

_____. "Venezuela, Colombia, and Ecuador: The First Half-Century of Independence." Pages 507-38 in Leslie Bethell (ed.), *The Cambridge History of Latin America, 3: From Independence to c. 1870.* Cambridge: Cambridge University Press, 1985.

Drekonja, Gerard, et al. *Ecuador: Hoy.* Bogotá: Siglo Veintiuno Editores, 1978.

"Ecuador: Oil up for Grabs," *NACLA's Latin America and Empire Report,* 9, No. 8, November 1975, 2-38.

Enock, C. Reginald. *Ecuador: Its Ancient and Modern History, Topography and Natural Resources, Industries and Social Development.* London: Unwin, 1914.

Fitch, John Samuel. "Class Structure, Populism, and the Armed Forces in Contemporary Ecuador," *Latin American Research Review,* 19, No. 1, 1984, 270-74.

_____. *The Military Coup d'Etat as a Political Process: Ecuador, 1948-1966.* Baltimore: Johns Hopkins University Press, 1977.

Franklin, Albert B. *Ecuador: Portrait of a People.* New York: Doubleday and Doran, 1943.

Gibson, Charles Robert. *Foreign Trade in the Economic Development of Small Nations: The Case of Ecuador.* New York: Praeger, 1971.

González Suárez, Federico. *Historia General de la República del Ecuador.* (3 vols.) Quito: Casa de la Cultura Ecuatoriana, 1970.

Grayson, G.W. "Populism, Petroleum, and Politics in Ecuador," *Current History,* 68, No. 401, 1975, 15–19, 39–40.

Hanson, David Parker. "The Influence of Business Groups in Ecuadoran Politics Between 1959 and 1962." (Ph.D. dissertation.) Gainesville: University of Florida, 1971.

Herring, Hubert. *A History of Latin America from the Beginnings to the Present.* (3d ed.) New York: Knopf, 1968.

Howe, George. "García Moreno's Efforts to Unite Ecuador and France," *Hispanic American Historical Review,* 16, No. 2, May 1936, 257–62.

Hurtado, Osvaldo. *Political Power in Ecuador.* (2d ed.) (Trans., Nick D. Mills, Jr.) Boulder, Colorado: Westview Press, 1985.

Icaza, Jorge. *Huasipungo: The Villagers, A Novel.* (Trans., Bernard M. Dulsey.) Carbondale: Southern Illinois University, 1964.

Jaramillo Alvarado, Pío. *Estudios Históricos: Esayos sobre la Vida Interna e Internacional de la República.* Quito: n. pub., 1934.

Kantor, Harry. "Ecuador: The Politics of Regionalism." Pages 427–58 in Harry Kantor (ed.), *The Patterns of Politics and Political Systems in Latin America.* Chicago: Rand McNally, 1969.

Levy, James, and Nick D. Mills, Jr. "The Challenge to Democratic Reformism in Ecuador," *Studies in Comparative International Development,* 18, No. 4, 1983, 3–33.

Linke, Lilo. *Ecuador: Country of Contrasts.* (3d ed.) New York: Oxford University, 1960.

Maier, Georg. *The Ecuadoran Presidential Election of June 2, 1968: An Analysis.* Washington: Institute for the Comparative Study of Political Systems, 1969.

_____. "The Impact of *Velasquismo* on the Ecuadoran Political System." (Ph.D. dissertation.) Gainesville: University of Florida, 1966.

_____. "Presidential Succession in Ecuador, 1830–1970," *Journal of Inter-American Studies and World Affairs,* 13, No. 3–4, 1971, 475–509.

Martz, John D. "Ecuador: Authoritarianism, Personalism, and Dependency." Pages 381–99 in Howard J. Wiarda and Harvey F. Kline (eds.), *Latin American Politics and Development.* (2d ed.) Boulder, Colorado: Westview Press, 1985.

_____. *Ecuador: Conflicting Political Culture and the Quest for Progress.* (The Allyn and Bacon Series in Latin American Politics.) Boston: Allyn and Bacon, 1972.

_____. "Ecuador: The Right Takes Command," *Current History,* 84, No. 499, February 1985, 69–72, 84–85.

————. "Populist Leadership and the Party Caudillo: Ecuador and the CFP, 1962–81," *Studies in Comparative International Development,* 18, No. 3, Fall 1983, 22–49.

————. "The Quest for Popular Democracy in Ecuador," *Current History,* 78, No. 454, February 1980, 66–70, 84.

Mason, J. Alden. *The Ancient Civilizations of Peru.* Middlesex, United Kingdom: Penguin Books, 1957.

Mecham, J.L. *Church and State in Latin America: A History of Politico-Ecclesiastical Relations.* Chapel Hill: University of North Carolina Press, 1966.

Mejía, Leonardo, et al. *Ecuador: Pasado y Presente.* Quito: Editorial Alberto Crespo Encalada, 1983.

Mills, Jr., Nick D. *Crisis, Conflicto y Consenso: Ecuador, 1979–84.* Quito: Corporación Editora Nacional, 1984.

Morner, Magnus. *The Andean Past: Land, Societies, and Conflicts.* New York: Columbia University, 1985.

Murra, John. "Andean Societies Before 1532." Pages 59–90 in Leslie Bethell (ed.), *The Cambridge History of Latin America, 1–2: Colonial Latin America.* Cambridge: Cambridge University Press, 1984.

————. "The Historic Tribes of Ecuador." Pages 785–821 in Julian H. Steward (ed)., *Handbook of South American Indians, 2: The Andean Civilizations.* (Smithsonian Institution, Bureau of American Ethnology, Bulletin 143.) New York: Cooper Square, 1963.

Needler, Martin C. *Anatomy of a Coup d'Etat: Ecuador 1963.* Washington: Institute for the Comparative Study of Political Systems, 1964.

Nett, Emily. "The Structural Elites of Quito," *Journal of Inter-American Studies and World Affairs,* 13, No. 2, January 1971, 112–20.

Norris, Robert E. *Guía Bibliográfica para el Estudio de la Historia Ecuatoriana.* (Institute of Latin American Studies, Guides and Bibliographies Series, No. 11.) Austin: University of Texas, 1978.

Pareja Diezcanseco, Alfredo. *Ecuador: De la Prehistoria a la Conquista Española.* Quito: Editorial Universitaria, 1979.

————. *Ecuador: La República, de 1830 a Nuestros Días.* Quito: Editorial Universitaria, 1979.

Pattee, Richard. *Gabriel García Moreno y el Ecuador de su tiempo.* Mexico: Editorial Jus, 1962.

Phelan, John Leddy. *The Kingdom of Quito in the Seventeenth Century: Bureaucratic Politics in the Spanish Empire.* Madison: University of Wisconsin, 1967.

Pike, Frederick B. *The United States and the Andean Republics: Peru, Bolivia, and Ecuador.* Cambridge: Harvard University Press, 1977.

Pyne, Peter. "The Politics of Instability in Ecuador: The Overthrow of the President, 1961," *Journal of Latin American Studies,* 7, No. 1, May 1975, 109–33.

Quintero, Rafael. *El Mito del Populismo en el Ecuador.* Quito: Editorial Universitaria, 1980.

Redclift, M.R. "Agrarian Reform and Peasant Organization in the Guayas Basin, Ecuador," *Inter-American Economic Affairs,* 30, No. 1, Summer 1976, 3–28.

Reyes, Oscar Efrén. *Breve Historia General del Ecuador.* (vols. 2 and 3 as one volume, 11th ed.) Quito: n. pub., 1978.

Rodríguez, Linda Alexandra. *The Search for Public Policy: Regional Politics and Government Financing in Ecuador, 1830–1940.* Berkeley: University of California Press, 1985.

Rosenberg, E.S. "Dollar Diplomacy under Wilson: An Ecuadoran Case," *Inter-American Economic Affairs,* 25, Autumn 1972, 47–53.

Rowe, John Howland. "Inca Culture at the Time of the Spanish Conquest." Pages 198–330 in Julian H. Steward (ed.), *Handbook of South American Indians, 2: The Andean Civilizations.* (Smithsonian Institution, Bureau of American Ethnology, Bulletin 143.) New York: Cooper Square, 1963.

Salomon, Frank. *Ethnic Lords of Quito in the Age of the Incas: The Political Economy of North-Andean Chiefdoms.* Ithaca: Cornell University Press, 1978.

Schodt, David W. "State Structure and Reformist Politics: Ecuador During the Petroleum Period: 1972–1983," *Technical Papers Series* (University of Texas, Institute of Latin American Studies, Office for Public Sector Studies.), No. 52, 1986.

Scholes, W., and M.V. Scholes. "The United States and Ecuador, 1909–1913," *The Americas,* 19, 1963, 276–90.

Szászdi, Adam. "The Historiography of the Republic of Ecuador," *Hispanic American Historical Review,* 44, No. 4, November 1964, 503–50.

TePaske, John J. (ed.). *Research Guide to Andean History: Bolivia, Chile, Ecuador, and Peru.* Durham: Duke University, 1981.

Thomsen, Moritz. *Living Poor: A Peace Corps Chronicle.* Seattle: University of Washington, 1969.

Tyrer, Robson Brines. "The Demographic and Economic History of the Audiencia of Quito: Indian Population and the Textile Industry, 1600–1800." (Ph.D. dissertation.) Berkeley: University of California, 1976.

Villacrés Moscoso, Jorge W. *Historia Diplomática de la República del Ecuador.* (5 vols.) Guayaquil: Universidad de Guayaquil, 1978.

Von Hagen, Victor Wolfgang. *Ecuador.* Chur, Switzerland: Plata, 1975.

Wachtel, Nathen. "The Indian and the Spanish Conquest." Pages 207–48 in Leslie Bethell (ed.), *The Cambridge History of Latin America, 1–2: Colonial Latin America.* Cambridge: Cambridge University Press, 1984.

Washburn, Douglas Alan. "The Bourbon Reforms: A Social and Economic History of the Audiencia of Quito, 1760–1810." (Ph.D. dissertation.) Austin: University of Texas, 1984.

Weinman, L.J. "Ecuador and Cacao: Domestic Responses to the Boom-Collapse Monoexport Cycle." (Ph.D. dissertation.) Berkeley: University of California, 1970.

Wright, F.J. "1968 Ecuadoran Presidential Campaign," *Inter-American Economic Affairs,* 23, Spring 1970, 81–94.

Zevallos, José Vicente. "Oil, Power and Rural Change in Ecuador: 1972–1979." (Ph.D. dissertation.) Madison: University of Wiscon-sin, 1985.

Zook, David H., Jr. *Zarumilla-Marañón: The Ecuador-Peru Dispute.* New York: Bookman Associates, 1964.

Zuvekas, Clarence. "Economic Planning in Ecuador: An Evaluation," *Inter-American Economic Affairs,* 25, No. 4, Spring 1972, 39–69.

Chapter 2

Annuario Pontificio per l'anno 1986. Vatican City: 1986.

Bales, Fred V. "Comparing Media Use and Political Orientation among Squatter Settlers of Two Latin American Countries." (University of New Mexico, Latin American Institute, Research Paper Series, No. 4.) Albuquerque, New Mexico: June 1983.

Banco Central del Ecuador. *Boletín Anuario,* No. 8. Quito: 1985.

Basile, David Giovanni. *Tillers of the Andes: Farmers and Farming in the Quito Basin.* (Studies in Geography, No. 8.) Chapel Hill: University of North Carolina, Department of Geography, 1974.

Belote, Linda Smith, and Jim Belote. "Drain from the Bottom: Individual Ethnic Identity Change in Southern Ecuador," *Social Forces,* 63, No. 1, September 1984, 24–50.

Bilsborrow, Richard E., et al. "The Impact of Origin Community Characteristics on Rural-Urban Out-Migration in a Developing Country," *Demography,* 24, No. 2, May 1987, 191–210.

Borja M., Eduardo. "Factores determinantes de una mortalidad prematura en Ecuador." (World Fertility Survey Scientific Reports, No. 74.) Voorburg, Netherlands: June 1985.

Burns, E. Bradford. *Elites, Masses, and Modernization in Latin America, 1850–1930.* Austin: University of Texas Press, 1979.

Carrión, Fernando (comp.). *El Proceso de Urbanización en el Ecuador del siglo XVIII al siglo XX—Antología.* Quito: Editorial El Conejo, 1986.

Casagrande, Joseph B. "Strategies for Survival: The Indians of Highland Ecuador." Pages 93–107 in Dwight B. Heath (ed.), *Contemporary Cultures and Societies of Latin America.* New York: Random House, 1974.

Centro de Documentación MIEC–JECI. *Los Sucesos del Riobamba.* (América Latina Boletín Series, 11.) Lima: 1976.

Centro Latinoamericano de Demografía, *Ecuador: Estimaciones y Proyecciones de Población, 1950–2000.* Quito: 1984.

Collier, Simon, Harold Blakemore, and Thomas E. Skidmore (eds.). *The Cambridge Encyclopedia of Latin America and the Caribbean.* Cambridge: Cambridge University Press, 1985.

Commander, Simon, and Peter Peek. "Oil Exports, Agrarian Change, and the Rural Labor Process: The Ecuadorian Sierra in the 1970s," *World Development,* 14, No. 1, January 1986, 79–96.

"Conferencia Episcopal de Ecuador: Declaración de la Conferencia Episcopal Ecuatoriana ante el próximo proceso electoral," *Celam* [Bogotá], 25, No. 215, August–September 1987, 38–42.

Consejo Episcopal Latinoamericano. *III Conferencia General del Episcopado Latinoamericano: Aportes de las Conferencias Episcopales,* 3. Bogotá: 1978.

Crespi, Muriel. "When Indios Become Cholos: Some Consequences of the Changing Ecuadorian Hacienda." Pages 148–66 in John W. Bennett (ed.), *The New Ethnicity: Perspectives from Ethnology.* St. Paul, Minnesota: West, 1975.

"Detengamos la violencia: Declaración del Consejo Permanente del Episcopado," *Celam* [Bogotá], 24, No. 202, October–November 1985, 18–19.

de Vries, Lucie. *Política Lingüística en Ecuador, Peru, y Bolivia.* Quito: EBI (MEC–GTZ)–CEDIME, Editorial Abya-Yala, 1988.

Ecuador. Consejo Nacional de Desarrollo, Instituto Nacional de Estadística y Censos, and Centro Latinoamericano de Demografía. *Ecuador: Estimaciones y Proyecciones de Población, 1950–2000.* Quito: 1984.

————. Instituto Nacional de Estadística y Censos. *IV Censo Nacional de Población y III de Vivienda, 1982—Resumen Nacional: Breve Análisis de los Resultados Definitivos.* Quito: 1985.

Egginton, Everett, and Wynn M. DeBevoise. "Ecuador." Pages 343–51 in *World Education Encyclopedia.* New York: Facts on File, 1988.

Fárez, Roberto, et al. *Ecuador: Iglesia, Pueblo y Liberación.* (Colección: Diálogo Social Series.) Quito: Fundación Ecuatoriana de Estudios Sociales, 1986.

Federal Republic of Germany. Statistisches Bundesamt Wiesbaden. *Länderbericht Ecuador, 1988.* (Statistik des Auslandes Series.) Wiesbaden: 1988.

Finerman, Ruthbeth. "Inside Out: Women's World View and Family Health in an Ecuadorian Indian Community," *Social Science and Medicine,* 25, No. 10, 1987, 1157–62.

Fundación Nuestros Jóvenes. *Plan General de Investigación: el Sistema de Drogas Ecuatoriano y el Impacto de la Cocaina en el Area Andina.* Quito: 1989.

Gómez E., Nelson. *Elementos de Geografía del Ecuador: El Hombre y el Medio.* (Colección Imagenes de la Tierra Series.) Quito: Editorial Ediguias, 1989.

Handelman, Howard. "Development and Misdevelopment in Ecuador," *Journal of Interamerican Studies and World Affairs,* 24, No. 1, February 1982, 115–22.

_____. *Ecuadorian Agrarian Reform: The Politics of Limited Change.* (American Universities Field Staff, Fieldstaff Reports, South America, No. 49.) Hanover, New Hampshire: AUFS, 1980.

Harner, Michael J. "The Supernatural World of the Jívaro." Pages 347–56 in Daniel R. Gross, Jr. (ed.), *Peoples and Cultures of Native South America.* New York: Doubleday/The Natural History Press, 1973.

Hiraoka, Mario, and Shozo Yamamoto. "Agricultural Development in the Upper Amazon of Ecuador," *Geographical Review,* 70, No. 4, October 1980, 423–45.

Hurtado, Osvaldo. *Political Power in Ecuador.* (2d ed.) (Trans., Nick D. Mills, Jr.) Boulder, Colorado: Westview Press, 1985.

Kouwenaar, Arend. *A Basic Needs Policy Model: A General Equilibrium Analysis with Special Reference to Ecuador.* Amsterdam: North Holland, 1988.

Kroeger, Axel, and Françoise Varobora-Freedman. *Cultural Change and Health: The Case of South American Rainforest Indians with Special Reference to the Shuar/Achuar of Ecuador.* Frankfurt: Verlag Peter Lang, 1982.

Lernoux, Penny. *Cry of the People.* New York: Doubleday, 1980.

Levy, James, and Nick D. Mills, Jr. "The Challenge to Democratic Reformism in Ecuador," *Studies in Comparative International Development,* 18, No. 4, Winter 1983, 3–33.

Lipset, Seymour Martin, and Aldo Solari (eds.). *Elites in Latin America.* New York: Oxford University Press, 1967.

Lipski, John M. "The Chota Valley: Afro-Hispanic Language in Highland Ecuador," *Latin American Research Review*, 22, No. 1, 1987, 155–70.

McKee, Lauris. "Ethnomedical Treatment of Children's Diarrheal Illnesses in the Highlands of Ecuador," *Social Science and Medicine*, 25, No. 10, 1987, 1147–55.

Martz, John D. *Ecuador: Conflicting Political Culture and the Quest for Progress.* (The Allyn and Bacon Series in Latin American Politics.) Boston: Allyn and Bacon, 1972.

Maynard, Kent. "On Protestants and Pastoralists: The Segmentary Nature of Socio-Cultural Organisation," *Man*, 23, No. 1, March 1988, 101–17.

Meier, Peter C. "Continuity and Change in Peasant Household Production: The Spinners and Knitters of Carabuela, Northern Ecuador," *Canadian Review of Sociology and Anthropology* [Toronto], 21, No. 4, November 1984, 431–48.

Middleton, Alan. "Division and Cohesion in the Working Class: Artisans and Wage Laborers in Ecuador," *Journal of Latin American Studies*, 14, Pt. I, May 1982, 171–94.

Middleton, DeWight R. "Migration and Urbanization in Ecuador: A View from the Coast," *Urban Anthropology*, 8, No. 3/4, Winter 1979, 313–32.

Moore, Richard J. "Urban Problems and Policy Responses for Metropolitan Guayaquil." Pages 181–203 in Wayne A. Cornelius and Robert V. Kemper (eds.), *Metropolitan Latin America: The Challenge and the Response.* Beverly Hills: Sage, 1978.

Pan American Health Organization. *Evaluation of the Strategy for Health for All by the Year 2000: Seventh Report on the World Health Situation.* Washington: 1986.

_____. *Health Conditions in the Americas, 1981–84.* Washington: 1986.

Preston, David A. "Rural Emigration and the Future of Agriculture in Ecuador." Pages 195–208 in D.A. Preston (ed.), *Environment, Society, and Rural Change in Latin America.* Chichester: Wiley and Sons, 1980.

Preston, Rosemary. "Nuclear Schools in Rural Ecuador," *Geographical Magazine*, 54, No. 9, September 1982, 516–17.

Redclift, M.R. *Agrarian Reform and Peasant Organization on the Ecuadorian Coast.* London: University of London, Athlone Press, 1978.

Reid, Richard A., Karen L. Ruffing, and Howard L. Smith. "Managing Medical Supply Logistics among Health Workers in Ecuador," *Social Science and Medicine*, 22, No. 1, 1986, 9–14.

Rojas M., Milton, and Gaitán Villavicencio. *El proceso urbano de Guayaquil, 1870–1980.* Quito: ILDIS, 1988.

Ruiz N., Jaime (comp.). *Del Vaticano al Ecuador: Teología desde América Latina*. Quito: Fundación "Luis Chusig," 1984.

Salomon, Frank. "Andean Ethnology in the 1970s: A Retrospective," *Latin American Research Review*, 22, No. 2, 1982, 75–128.

_____. "Shamanism and Politics in Late-Colonial Ecuador," *American Ethnologist*, 10, No. 3, August 1983, 413–28.

_____. "Weavers of Otalvalo." Pages 463–94 in Daniel R. Gross (ed.), *Peoples and Cultures of Native South America*. Garden City, New York: Doubleday/The Natural History Press, 1973.

Scott, Robert E. "Political Elites and Political Modernization: The Crisis of Transition." Pages 117–45 in Seymour Martin Lipset and Aldo Solari (eds.), *Elites in Latin America*. New York: Oxford University Press, 1967.

Silverman, Marilyn. "Agrarian Processes Within 'Plantation Economies': Cases from Guyana and Coastal Ecuador," *Canadian Review of Sociology and Anthropology* [Toronto], 24, No. 4, November 1987, 550–70.

Solari, Aldo. "Secondary Education and the Development of Elites." Pages 457–83 in Seymour Martin Lipset and Aldo Solari (eds.), *Elites in Latin America*. New York: Oxford University Press, 1967.

Sorensen, Jr., Arthur P. "South American Indian Linguistics at the Turn of the Seventies." Pages 312–41 in Daniel R. Gross (ed.), *Peoples and Cultures of Native South America*. New York: Doubleday/The Natural History Press, 1973.

Stornaiolo, Ugo. *Anatomía de un País Latinoamericano: El Ecuador*. Quito: Ediciones Culturales BSM, 1989.

United States. Department of Health and Human Services. Social Security Administration. Office of Research, Statistics, and International Policy. "Social Security Programs Throughout the World-1985." (Research Report, No. 60.) Washington: 1986.

Vinicio Rueda, Marco. *La Fiesta Religiosa Campesina (Andes Ecuatorianos)*. Quito: Ediciones de la Universidad Católica, 1982.

Vining, Jr., Daniel R. "The Growth of Core Regions in the Third World," *Scientific American*, 252, No. 4, April 1985, 42–49.

Walter, Lynn. "Social Strategies and the Fiesta Complex in an Otalvaleño Community," *American Ethnologist*, 8, No. 1, February 1981, 172–85.

Walton, John. *Elites and Economic Development: Comparative Studies on the Political Economy of Latin American Cities*. (Latin American Monographs Series, Institute of Latin American Studies, University of Texas.) Austin: University of Texas Press, 1977.

Weiss, Wendy A. "The Social Organization of Property and Work: A Study of Migrants from the Rural Ecuadorian Sierra," *American Ethnologist*, 12, No. 3, August 1985, 468–88.

Whitten, Jr., Norman E. *Black Frontiersmen: A South American Case.* Cambridge: Schenkman, 1974.

_____. *Class, Kinship, and Power in an Ecuadorian Town: The Negroes of San Lorenzo.* Stanford: Stanford University Press, 1965.

_____. *Cultural Transformations and Ethnicity in Modern Ecuador.* Urbana: University of Illinois Press, 1981.

_____. *Sacha Runa: Ethnicity and Adaptation of Ecuadorian Jungle Quichua.* Urbana: University of Illinois Press, 1976.

_____. *Sicuanga Runa: The Other Side of Development in Amazonian Ecuador.* Urbana: University of Illinois Press, 1985.

Chapter 3

Allen, Geoffrey (ed.). *Jane's World Railways, 1988-1989.* (13th ed.) Coulsdon, Surrey, United Kingdom: Jane's Information Group, 1988.

Banco Central del Ecuador. *Boletín Anuario, 1987,* No. 10. Quito: 1988.

Bethell, Leslie (ed.). *The Cambridge History of Latin America, 3: From Independence to c. 1870.* Cambridge: Cambridge University Press, 1985.

Box, Ben (ed.). *1990 South American Handbook.* Suffolk, United Kingdom: Trade and Travel, 1989.

Burstein, John, and Alfredo Forti. "Ecuador." Pages 68-72 in *Latin American and Caribbean Review 1988.* Saffron Walden, Essex, United Kingdom: World of Information, 1988.

Collier, Simon (ed.). *The Cambridge Encyclopedia of Latin America and the Caribbean.* Cambridge: Cambridge University Press, 1985.

Conaghan, Catherine M. "Ecuador Swings Toward Social Democracy," *Current History,* 88, No. 536, March 1989, 137-41, 154.

Diffie, Bailey W. *Latin American Civilization: Colonial Period.* New York: Octagon Books, 1967.

Economist Intelligence Unit. *Country Profile: Ecuador, 1988-89.* London: 1988.

_____. *Ecuador: Country Report, No. 4, 1990.* London: 1990.

Ecuador. *Boletín Anuario, 1988.* Quito: 1989.

_____. Ministerio de Agricultura y Ganadería. *Estimación de la superficie cosechada y de la producción agrícola del Ecuador, 1983 a 1985.* Quito: 1989.

"Ecuador: The Unmasking of President Machismo," *Latin American Times* [London], 7, No. 9, January 13, 1987, 7-11.

"Ecuador's New Maturity," *World Business Weekly,* 4, September 28, 1981, 29-37.

The Europa World Year Book 1989, 1. London: Europa, 1989.
Gill, Lesley. "Ecuador: The Lion's Den," *NACLA: Report on the Americas,* 21, No. 1, January–February 1987, 6–9.
Haine, Edgar. *Railways Across the Andes.* Boulder, Colorado: Pruett, 1981.
The Heritage Foundation. "Ecuador as a Model for Latin American Development." (No. 479.) Washington: January 10, 1986.
Herring, Hubert. *A History of Latin America: From the Beginnings to the Present.* (3d ed.) New York: Knopf, 1968.
International Monetary Fund. *International Financial Statistics,* 43, No. 6. Washington: 1990.
Kaulkin, Donna. *World Aviation Directory, Summer 1989.* New York: McGraw-Hill, 1989.
Kurian, George Thomas. "Ecuador." Pages 579–600 in George Thomas Kurian (ed.), *Encyclopedia of the Third World,* 1. (3d ed.) New York: Facts on File, 1987.
Linke, Lilo. *Ecuador: Country of Contrasts.* (3d ed.) New York: Oxford University Press, 1960.
Martin, Paul. *The Airline Handbook, 1983–84,* 8. Cranston, Rhode Island: Aerotravel Research, 1983.
Martino, Orlando. *Mineral Industries of Latin America.* Washington: GPO, 1988.
Martz, John D. "Ecuador: Authoritarianism, Personalism, and Dependency." Pages 381–402 in Howard J. Wiarda and Harvey F. Kline (eds.), *Latin American Politics and Development.* Boulder, Colorado: Westview Press, 1985.
_____. "Ecuador: The Right Takes Command," *Current History,* 84, No. 499, February 1985, 69–72, 84.
_____. "Instability in Ecuador," *Current History,* 87, No. 525, January 1988, 17–20, 37–38.
Mardešić, Vjekoslav (ed.). *Estadísticas del Ecuador.* Quito: Instituto Latinoamericano de Investigaciones Sociales, 1988.
McCaslin, John (ed.). *International Petroleum Encyclopedia, 1988.* Tulsa, Oklahoma: Energy Group of Penwell, 1988.
Mendoza, Luis. *Geo-Economía del Ecuador.* Guayaquil: Nueva Luz, 1981.
Official Airline Guide, Worldwide Edition, August 1989, 14, No. 8. Oak Brook, Illinois: 1989.
Peek, Peter. *Urban Poverty, Migration, and Land Reform in Ecuador.* Geneva: United Nations, International Labour Office (ILO), World Employment Programme, 1980.
Schodt, David W. "Austerity Policies in Ecuador: Christian Democratic and Social Christian Versions of the Gospel." Pages 171–94 in Howard Handelman and Werner Baer (eds.), *Paying*

the Costs of Austerity in Latin America. Boulder, Colorado: Westview Press, 1989.

_____. *Ecuador: An Andean Enigma.* Boulder, Colorado: Westview Press, 1987.

Sennitt, Andrew (ed.). *World Radio TV Handbook, 1989.* Hvidovre, Denmark: Billboard, 1989.

Tremlett, E.I. (ed.). *Thomas Cook Overseas Timetable, March/April 1989.* Thorpe Wood, Peterborough, United Kingdom: Thomas Cook, 1989.

United States. Central Intelligence Agency. *The World Factbook, 1989.* Washington: GPO, 1989.

_____. Department of Agriculture. Economic Research Service. "Ecuador." Pages 79–81 in *Agricultural Policy, Trade, Economic Growth, and Development.* Washington: GPO, 1989.

_____. Department of the Army. United States Southern Command, 361st Civil Affairs Brigade. *Area Assessment: Ecuador.* Pensacola, Florida: 1985.

_____. Department of Commerce. International Trade Administration. *Foreign Economic Trends and Their Implications for the United States: Ecuador.* (FET 89-52.) Washington: GPO, May 1989.

_____. Department of Commerce. *Overseas Business Reports: Marketing in Ecuador.* Washington: GPO, June 1985.

_____. Department of Labor. Bureau of International Labor Affairs. *Foreign Labor Trends, Ecuador.* (FLT 88-26.) Washington: GPO, 1987.

_____. Department of State. Bureau of Public Affairs. *Background Notes: Ecuador.* Washington: GPO, October 1986.

_____. Department of State. *Ecuador Post Report.* Washington: GPO, 1986.

Valdivieso, Susana. *Estadísticas del Ecuador.* Quito: Instituto Nacional de Estadísticas y Censos, 1987.

Véliz, Claudio (ed.). *Latin America and the Caribbean: A Handbook.* New York: Praeger, 1968.

Wilkie, James W., and Enrique Ochoa (eds.). *Statistical Abstract of Latin America,* 27. Los Angeles: UCLA Latin American Center, 1989.

World Bank. *Current Economic Position and Prospects of Ecuador.* Washington: 1973.

Zumárraga, Asunción. "South America: A Statistical Survey of Ten Countries." (Library of Congress, Congressional Research Service, Foreign Affairs and National Defense Division, No. 89-552F.) Washington: October 24, 1989.

(Various issues of the following publications were also used in the preparation of this chapter: *Business Latin America;* Foreign

Broadcast Information Service, *Daily Report: Latin America; Latin American Monitor* [London]; and *Latin American Weekly Report: Andean Group Report* [London].)

Chapter 4

Alborñoz Peralta, Osvaldo. *Ecuador.* Quito: El Duende, 1989.

Americas Watch and the Andean Commission of Jurists. *Human Rights in Ecuador.* New York: Americas Watch Committee, 1988.

Arboleda, María, Raúl Borja, and José Steinsleger. *Mi poder en la oposición.* Quito: Editorial El Conejo, 1985.

Avery, William P. "Origins and Consequences of the Border Dispute Between Ecuador and Peru," *Inter-American Economic Affairs,* 38, No. 2, Summer 1984, 65–77.

Ayala Mora, Enrique. *Los partidos políticos en el Ecuador: Síntesis histórica.* Quito: Ediciones La Tierra, 1986.

Blanksten, George I. *Ecuador: Constitutions and Caudillos.* Berkeley: University of California, 1951.

Brownrigg, Leslie Ann. "Interest Groups in Regime Changes in Ecuador," *Inter-American Economic Affairs,* 28, No. 1, Summer 1974, 3–18.

Conaghan, Catherine M. "Ecuador Swings Toward Social Democracy," *Current History,* 88, No. 536, March 1989, 137–41, 154.

_____. "Ecuador: The Politics of Locos," *Hemisphere,* 1, No. 1, Winter 1989, 13–15.

_____. *Restructuring Domination: Industrialists and the State in Ecuador.* Pittsburgh: University of Pittsburgh Press, 1988.

Corkill, David. "Democratic Politics in Ecuador, 1978–1984," *Bulletin of Latin American Research* [London], 4, No. 2, 1985, 63–74.

Corkill, David, and David Cubitt. *Ecuador: Fragile Democracy.* London: Latin American Bureau, 1988.

Cueva, Agustín. *The Process of Political Domination in Ecuador.* New Brunswick, New Jersey: Transaction Books, 1982.

"Ecuador." Pages 1–37 in Albert P. Blaustein and Gisbert H. Flanz (eds.), *Constitutions of the Countries of the World.* Dobbs Ferry, New York: Oceana, June 1987.

"Ecuador." Pages 934–50 in *The Europa World Year Book, 1987,* 1. London: Europa, 1987.

Ferris, Elizabeth C., and Jennie K. Lincoln. *Latin American Foreign Policies: Global and Regional Dimensions.* (Westview Special Studies on Latin America and the Caribbean.) Boulder, Colorado: Westview Press, 1981.

Fitzgibbon, Russell H., and Julio A. Fernandez. "Ecuador: The Politics of National Revolution." Pages 177–90 in Russell H. Fitzgibbon and Julio A. Fernandez (eds.), *Latin America: Political Culture and Development*. Englewood Cliffs, New Jersey: Prentice-Hall, 1981.

Hurtado, Osvaldo. *Political Power in Ecuador*. (2d ed.) (Trans., Nick D. Mills, Jr.) Boulder, Colorado: Westview Press, 1985.

Keesing's. "The Ecuador-Peru Dispute." Pages 367–71 in *Border and Territorial Disputes*. London: Longman, 1982.

Kurian, George Thomas. "Ecuador." Pages 579–600 in George Thomas Kurian (ed.), *Encyclopedia of the Third World*, 1. (3d ed.) New York: Facts on File, 1987.

Levy, James, and Nick D. Mills, Jr. "The Challenge to Democratic Reformism in Ecuador," *Studies in Comparative International Development*, 18, No. 4, Winter 1983, 3–33.

Maldonado, John. *Taura, lo que no se ha dicho*. Quito: Editorial El Conejo, 1988.

Martz, John D. "Ecuador: Authoritarianism, Personalism, and Dependency." Pages 381–401 in Howard J. Wiarda and Harvey F. Kline (eds.), *Latin American Politics and Development*. Boulder, Colorado: Westview Press, 1985.

———. *Ecuador: Conflicting Political Culture and the Quest for Progress*. (The Allyn and Bacon Series in Latin America Politics.) Boston: Allyn and Bacon, 1972.

———. "Ecuador: The Right Takes Command," *Current History*, 84, No. 499, February 1985, 69–72, 84–85.

———. "Instability in Ecuador," *Current History*, 87, No. 525, January 1988, 17–20, 37–38.

———. "Marxism in Ecuador," *Inter-American Economic Affairs*, 33, No. 2, Summer 1979, 3–28.

———. *The Military in Ecuador*. (Occasional Paper Series, No. 3.) Albuquerque: Latin American Institute, University of New Mexico, 1988.

———. *Politics and Petroleum in Ecuador*. New Brunswick, New Jersey: Transaction Books, 1987.

———. "Populist Leadership and the Party Caudillo: Ecuador and the CFP, 1962–81," *Studies in Comparative International Development*, 18, No. 3, Fall 1983, 22–49.

———. "The Quest for Popular Democracy in Ecuador," *Current History*, 78, No. 454, February 1980, 66–70, 84.

Needler, Martin C. "The President of Ecuador," *Contemporary Review* [London], 244, No. 1417, February 1984, 57–61.

Oña Villarreal, Humberto. *Presidentes del Ecuador*. Ibarra, Ecuador: Pedidos al autor, 1986.

Ortiz Crespo, Gonzalo. *La hora del general.* (Colección Ecuador/Hoy Series.) Quito: Editorial El Conejo, 1986.

Palmer, David Scott. "Ecuador." Pages 77-80 in Richard F. Staar (ed.), *1985 Yearbook on International Communist Affairs: Parties and Revolutionary Movements.* Stanford, California: Hoover Institution Press, 1985.

Rodríguez Peñaherrera, Carlos A. *Administración pública ecuatoriana.* Quito: Instituto Latinoamericano de Investigaciones Sociales, 1987.

Saint-Geours, Yves. "Équateur de León Febres Cordero à Rodrigo Borja (1984-1988)," *Problèmes d'Amérique Latine* [Paris], 89, No. 3, 1988, 3-28.

Salgado Pesantes, Hernán. *Instituciones Políticas y Constitución del Ecuador.* Quito: Instituto Latinoamericano de Investigaciones Sociales, 1987.

Sanders, Thomas G. "The Politics of Transition." Pages 3-25 in Howard Handelman and Thomas G. Sanders (eds.), *Military Government and the Movement Toward Democracy in South America.* Bloomington: Indiana University Press, 1981.

Schodt, David W. *Ecuador: An Andean Enigma.* Boulder, Colorado: Westview Press, 1987.

Spindler, Frank MacDonald. *Nineteenth Century Ecuador: An Historical Introduction.* Fairfax, Virginia: George Mason University Press, 1987.

United States. Congress. 101st, 1st Session. Senate. Committee on Foreign Relations. House of Representatives. Committee on Foreign Affairs. *Country Reports on Human Rights Practices for 1988.* Washington: GPO, February 1988.

_____. Department of State. Bureau of Public Affairs. *Background Notes: Ecuador.* Washington: GPO, October 1986.

Vanossi, Jorge Reinaldo, et al. *Legislación electoral comparada: Argentina, Bolivia, Brasil, Chile, Ecuador, Paraguay, Perú y Uruguay.* San José, Costa Rica: Centro Interamericano de Asesoría y Promoción Electoral (CAPEL), 1988.

Verdesoto Custode, Luis. *Certezas e incertidumbres en la política ecuatoriana.* Quito: CIUDAD, 1990.

Wolter, Matilde. "Ecuador: Socialdemocracia en la Mitad del Mundo," *Nueva Sociedad* [San Salvador], No. 96, July/August 1988, 8-10.

Chapter 5

Alexander, Robert J. "Ecuador." Pages 71-74 in Richard F. Staar (ed.), *1988 Yearbook on International Communist Affairs.* Stanford, California: Hoover Institution Press, 1988.

Americas Watch and the Andean Commission of Jurists. *Human Rights in Ecuador.* New York: Americas Watch Committee, 1988.

Amnesty International Report, 1988. London: Amnesty International, 1988.

Armada del Ecuador: Una Historia, Una Epopeya, Un Reto. Quito: Secretaría de la Comandancia General de Marina, 1981.

Astudillo Romero, Jaime. *Mito y Realidad de la Seguridad Nacional en el Ecuador.* Cuenca, Ecuador: Fondo de Cultura Ecuatoriana, 1981.

Bahbah, Bishara, and Linda Butler. *Israel and Latin America: The Military Connection.* New York: St. Martin's Press, 1986.

Bustamante, Fernando. "Fuerzas Armadas en Ecuador: ¿Puede institucionalizarse la subordinación al poder civil?'' Pages 130-60 in *Democracia y Fuerzas Armadas.* Quito: Corporación de Estudios para el Desarrollo (CORDES), 1988.

Child, Jack. *Geopolitics and Conflict in South America: Quarrels among Neighbors.* New York: Praeger, 1985.

DMS Market Intelligence Report: South America/Australasia. Greenwich, Connecticut: Defense Marketing Services, 1989.

"Ecuador.'' Pages 265-68 in Gregory R. Copley (ed.), *Defense and Foreign Affairs Handbook 1987-88.* Washington: Perth, 1987.

English, Adrian J. *Armed Forces of Latin America: Their Histories, Development, Present Strength, and Military Potential.* London: Jane's, 1984.

"Equatorial Wings: Ecuador Hones Its Top Cover,'' *Air International* [London], 28, No. 1, January 1985, 14-23.

Fitch, John Samuel. *The Military Coup d'Etat as a Political Process: Ecuador, 1948-1966.* Baltimore: Johns Hopkins University Press, 1977.

Hurtado, Osvaldo. *Political Power in Ecuador.* (2d ed.) (Trans., Nick D. Mills, Jr.) Boulder, Colorado: Westview Press, 1985.

International Air Forces and Military Aircraft Directory. Stapleford Airfield, Essex, England: Aviation Advisory Services, 1989.

Jane's Fighting Ships, 1988-89. (Ed., Captain Richard Sharpe.) London: Jane's, 1988.

Keegan, John, and Adrian English. "Ecuador.'' Pages 158-61 in John Keegan (ed.), *World Armies.* Detroit: Gale Research, 1983.

Kurian, George Thomas. *World Encyclopedia of Police Forces and Penal Systems.* New York: Facts on File, 1989.

Looney, Robert E. *The Political Economy of Latin American Defense Expenditures: Case Studies of Venezuela and Argentina.* Lexington, Massachusetts: Lexington Books, 1986.

Martz, John D. "Instability in Ecuador,'' *Current History,* 87, No. 525, January 1988, 17-20, 37-38.

————. *The Military in Ecuador: Policies and Politics of Authoritarian Rule.* (Occasional Paper Series, No. 3.) Albuquerque: Latin American Institute, University of New Mexico, 1988.

The Military Balance, 1988–1989. International Institute for Strategic Studies, London: 1988.

Ortiz Crespo, Gonzalo. *La Hora del General.* Quito: Editorial El Conejo, 1986.

Schodt, David W. *Ecuador: An Andean Enigma.* Boulder, Colorado: Westview Press, 1987.

United States. Arms Control and Disarmament Agency. *World Military Expenditures and Arms Transfers 1988.* Washington: GPO, 1989.

————. Congress. 100th, 2d Session. House of Representatives. Committee on Foreign Affairs. *Narcotics Review in South America.* Washington: GPO, 1988.

————. Congress. 101st, 1st Session. Senate. Committee on Foreign Relations. House of Representatives. Committee on Foreign Affairs. *Country Reports on Human Rights Practices for 1988.* Washington: GPO, 1989.

————. Department of Defense. *Terrorist Group Profiles.* Washington: GPO, 1988.

————. Department of State. Bureau of Public Affairs. *Background Notes: Ecuador.* Washington: GPO, 1986.

Varas, Augusto. *Militarization and the International Arms Race in Latin America.* Boulder, Colorado: Westview Press, 1985.

(Various issues of the following periodicals were also used in the preparation of this chapter: *El Comercio* [Quito]; *Keesing's Record of World Events* [London]; *Latin American Monitor; Latin American Times* [London]; and *Latin American Weekly Reports: Andean Group Report* [London].)

Glossary

fiscal year (FY)—Calendar year.

gross domestic product (GDP)—A measure of the total value of goods and services produced by the domestic economy during a given period, usually one year. Obtained by adding the value contributed by each sector of the economy in the form of profits, compensation to employees, and depreciation (consumption of capital). The income arising from investments and possessions owned abroad is not included, only domestic production. Hence, the use of the word *domestic* to distinguish GDP from GNP (*q.v.*).

gross national product (GNP)—Total market value of all final goods and services produced by an economy during a year. Obtained by adding GDP (*q.v.*) and the income received from abroad by residents less payments remitted abroad to nonresidents.

import substitution—An economic development strategy that emphasizes the growth of domestic industries, often by import protection using tariff and nontariff measures. Proponents favor the export of industrial goods over primary products.

International Monetary Fund (IMF)—Established along with the World Bank (*q.v.*) in 1945, the IMF is a specialized agency affiliated with the United Nations that takes responsibility for stabilizing international exchange rates and payments. The main business of the IMF is the provision of loans to its members when they experience balance-of-payments difficulties. These loans often carry conditions that require substantial internal economic adjustments by the recipients.

sucre (S/)—The national currency. From 1971 to 1981, the sucre was pegged to the United States dollar at S/25 = US$1. Because this rate overvalued the sucre and dampened exports, the government allowed a steady devaluation of the currency throughout the first half of the 1980s. By 1985, the official exchange rate averaged S/69 = US$1. In August 1986, President León Febres Cordero Ribadeneyra (1984–88) transferred all private sector transactions to the higher free market rate and determined to close the gap between that rate and the official intervention rate through regular currency adjustments. The official rate averaged S/123 = US$1 in 1986 and S/170 = US$1 in 1987. Responding to growing external indebtedness, capital flight, and rising inflation, the free market rate climbed to S/400 = US$1 by March 1988. In response, Febres Cordero established a controlled rate for imports and exports and limited movement to within 10 percent of the prevailing official rate of S/250 = US$1. As was the case in the early 1980s, the severely overvalued official currency (the free market rate climbed to S/550 = US41 by July 1988) hindered export activity. Upon assuming the presidency in August 1988, Rodrigo Borja Cevallos (1988–) devalued the controlled rate to S/390 = US$1 and adopted a program to further devalue the currency by 30 percent per year. In May 1989, Borja accelerated this program to nearly 40 percent per year. Consequently, the official rate averaged S/526 = US$1 and had closed to within 6 percent of the free market rate.

terms of trade—Number of units that must be given up for one unit of goods received by each party (e.g., nation) to a transaction. The terms of trade are said to move in favor of the party that gives up fewer units of goods than it did previously for one unit of goods received, and against the party that gives up more units of goods for one unit of goods received. In international economics, the concept of ''terms of trade'' plays an important role in evaluating relationships between nations.

World Bank—Informal name used to designate a group of three affiliated international institutions: the International Bank for Reconstruction and Development (IBRD), the International Development Association (IDA), and the International Finance Corporation (IFC). The IBRD, established in 1945, has the primary purpose of providing loans to developing countries for productive projects. The IDA, a legally separate loan fund but administered by the staff of the IBRD, was set up in 1960 to furnish credits to the poorest developing countries on much easier terms than those of conventional IBRD loans. The IFC, founded in 1956, supplements the activities of the IBRD through loans and assistance specifically designed to encourage the growth of productive private enterprises in the less developed countries. The president and certain senior officers of the IBRD hold the same positions in the IFC. The three institutions are owned by the governments of the countries that subscribe their capital. To participate in the World Bank group, member states must first belong to the International Monetary Fund (IMF—*q.v.*).

Index

farms: size of, 76
FDN. *See* National Democratic Front
Febres Cordero Ribadeneyra, León, 4, 48, 201, 236; abduction of, xxv, 185, 214; attempt to change electoral law, 184; austerity measures under, 115; authoritarian style of, xxv, 155, 165; campaign promises of, 110; censure of, 196; crises in government of, 177, 184; devaluation of sucre under, 115, 116; dismissal of cabinet ministers under, 170; economic strategies of, 103, 116, 155; election of, 184; foreign policy of, 198, 199, 200; free-enterprise approach under, 110; friction in government branches under, 155, 162; hatred of, for Borja, 156; interference of, in military matters, 190, 230; judicial appointments by, 169; labor relations under, 119, 194; media under, 196; opposition of, to Andean Pact, 200; suppression of anti-austerity demonstrations, 237; suspension of interest payments, 199; Vargas incident, 185, 214; visit of, to Washington, 199
Federal Republic of Germany (West Germany), 202; military matériel purchased from, 222, 236
Federation of High School Students of Ecuador (FESE), 194
Federation of University Students of Ecuador (FEUE), 194, 195
FEDOC. *See* Ecuadorian Federation of Peasant Organizations
FEI. *See* Ecuadorian Indian Federation
Ferdinand VII, 16–17
FESE. *See* Federation of High School Students of Ecuador
feudal system, Spanish, 12
fiber crops, 127
fiestas, 96; *cargos* for, 94; described, 94
Finance and Credit, Ministry of, 117, 169, 242
financial institutions, private, 138
financial services, 136–37
financial system, 137–39
fiscal deficit, 113, 116, 117; control of, 114
fiscal reform, 212
Fiscal Tribunal, 161, 168, 169, 171; components of, 172; function of, 170, 172
fish: export of, 145
fishing (*see also* "tuna war"), 103, 129–30; tuna, 129; shrimp, 129

Fitch, John Samuel, 227
flood disaster (1982–83): xxiv, 107, 129, 150; emergency operations for, 232–33
Flores, Juan José, 22, 24, 157, 209; assassination attempt on, 20; battle victories of, 18; career of, 19; involvement of, in government, 158; opposition to, 20; ouster of (1845), 20; as president, 18, 19, 20
Flores Jijón, Antonio, 24; as president, 24
food processing, 134; baking, 136; as component of manufacturing, 134; flour milling, 136; rice milling, 136; sugar refining, 136
foreign borrowing, 113
foreign debt, xxiv, 103–4, 113; crisis in, 4
foreign-exchange controls, 116
foreign-exchange earnings, 106; sources of, 149
foreign-exchange reserves, 109
foreign policy: of Borja, 190, 201; of Febres Cordero, 198, 199, 200; objectives, 197–98
forestry: area, 130; problems in, 130
FP. *See* Popular Front
FRA. *See* Alfarist Radical Front
France: military influence of, 233; military matériel from, 218, 236, 237
Franco, Guillermo, 21
FRN. *See* National Reconstruction Front
FUT. *See* United Workers Front

Galápagos Islands, 5, 26, 54, 59, 129, 186, 242; administration of, 174; climate in, 59–60, 61–62; described, 58; location of, 54; military protection for, 211; tourism to, 139; United States naval base on, 30, 222, 234; volcanos in, 58; water transport to, 145
García Moreno, Gabriel, xxii, 24, 25, 26, 212; armed forces under, 209; attempt of, to assassinate Flores, 20; career of, 22–24; childhood of, 22; Conservative Party established by, 23, 180; constitution under, 158; contributions of, 23; death of, 23; involvement of, in government, 158; Liberal resistance to, 23; opposition of, to Flores, 22; religious education of, 22; Roman Catholicism under, 22–23
García Moreno Prison, 246, 247

minimum wage, 119
mining: of gold, 133; of limestone, 133
ministers of state: requirements of, 165; restrictions on, 165; missionary activities, 94
mita system: described, 13; end of, 16
mitayos, 13, 14
Mitterrand, Danielle, 202
Mitterrand, François, 202
Mobilization, National Directorate of, 215
Monetary Board, 146, 166, 215; function of, 115, 137; members of, 137
Montalvo, Juan, 23
montuvio. See mestizo
motion pictures, 141
Movement for the Unity of the Left (MUI), 187
MPD. *See* Democratic Popular Movement
MRIC. *See* Revolutionary Movement of the Christian Left
MSC. *See* Social Christian Movement
MUI. *See* Movement for the Unity of the Left

Napo Province, 199
Napo River, 59, 131
narcotics control, 243–44; coca cultivation, 243; United States assistance in, 244
narcotics traffickers, 188, 234; from Bolivia, 244; from Colombia, 207, 211, 244
National Assembly, 238
National Civil Guard, 239
National Civil Police, 239
National Communications Secretariat (Senac), 196; press freedom under, 196
National Congress. *See* Congress, National
National Coordinator of Workers (CNT), 194
National Court of Police Justice, 243
National Defense, Ministry of, 174, 215
National Defense University (Washington, D.C.), 220
National Democratic Front (FDN), 183
National Development Bank (BNF), 138; role of, 138
National Development Council (Conade), 117, 161, 162, 215; described, 165–66; restructuring of, 166

National Directorate of Civil Defense, 232; function of, 232
National Directorate for Control of Illegal Narcotics, 242
National Directorate of Intelligence, 215
National Directorate of Social Rehabilitation, 246
National Directorate of Tourism, 139
National Emergency Relief Center, 233
National Federation of Workers, 169
National Financial Corporation (CFN), 138; role of, 138
National Literacy Program, 201
National Palace, 162
National Planning Board, 165
National Police, 162, 233, 232; abuse and torture by, 242–43; conduct of, 242; development of, 239; instructional facilities, 242; members of, 239; mission of, 239; structure of, 239–42; supplementary services, 242
National Postal Enterprise, 141
National Radio, 140, 196
National Reconstruction Front (FRN), 184
National Secretariat for Public Information (Sendip), 196
National Security Act Number 275 (1979), 215, 232
National Security Council (NSC), 207, 220; established, 215; members of, 215
National Union of Teachers (UNE), 193
National Velasquista Federation, 40
National Velasquista Party (PNV), 183
Naval War College, 223
navy: bases, 221; basic training, 222–23; coast guard, 222; components of, 207; equipment of, 222; marines, 222; marine training, 223; missions of, 220–21; naval zones, 221; officer training, 223; organization of, 221–22; origin of, 220; patrols by, 211; personnel complement, 220
Negro River, 10
New China (Xinhua) News Agency, 141
New Laws (1542), 11
newspapers, 197
Nicaragua, 200, 201, 238
19th of April Movement (M-19), 211, 246
Noboa, Diego, 20
Nonaligned Movement (NAM), 200, 202
Noriega, Manuel Antonio, 201

by earthquake of 1987, 104, 110, 146; repair of, 132; volume carried over, 132

transportation: air, 143-44; under García Moreno, 23; highway, 143; infrastructure, 113; rail, 142; truck, 143; water, 145

Treasury, 117

Treaty of 1829, 18

Treaty of Mapasingue, 21

Tribunal of Constitutional Guarantees (TGC), 156, 159, 160, 161, 163, 168, 171, 172-73; appointments to, 172; Constitution interpreted by, 172; human rights complaints investigated by, 242, 243; members of, 172-73; powers of, 173; requirements for, 173; rights of, 173

Tribunal of Crimes, 145

Troop Training School, 242

tropical diseases, 99

trucks, 143

trucking companies, 143

Trujillo, Spain, 7, 10

Tumbes, Peru, 8

"tuna war," 35, 41, 198, 234

Tungurahua Province: archaeological sites in, 4

UDP. *See* Popular Democratic Union

UGTE. *See* General Union of Ecuadorian Workers

Últimas Noticias, 197

underemployment, xxiv, 118-19

UNE. *See* National Union of Teachers

unemployment, xxiv, 118-19

unionization, 192; benefits of, 80; by peasants, 74, 76

United Holland Bank, 138

United Nations, 197, 200, 201; Security Council Resolutions 242 and 338, 202

United Press International, 141

United States, 26, 36, 190, 198, 244; Alfaro's affinity for, 26; assistance of, fighting narcotics traffic, 244; Department of State, 161; Febres Cordero's affinity for, 155; Foreign Trade Act of 1974, 198; military aid, 210, 218, 234; military influence of, 234; military intervention in Panama, 201; military matériel acquired from, 223, 236, 237; military training, 234; student protests against, 237; as trading partner, 150

United States Army Command and General Staff College, 219

United States Arms Control and Disarmament Agency (ACDA), 231, 237

United States Department of State, 197; support of, for South American Development Company, 30

United States Drug Enforcement Administration, 244

United States-Ecuador relations, 198-200; basis for, 198; irritants in, 198; "tuna war," 34, 41, 198

United States Military Assistance Program, 223

United States Military Group, 234

United States National Guard, 234

United States Naval Academy, 234

United States Navy, 244

United Workers Front (FUT), 48, 193, 194

UPP. *See* People's Patriotic Union

Urbina, José María, 20, xxii, 24; emancipation of slaves by, 21, 209; liberalism under, 20-21; invasion attempted by, 23

Urbina Jado, Francisco, 27

Uruguay, 200

utility infrastructure, 113

Valdivia culture, 4

Valverde, Fray Vincente de, 9

Vargas incident: accusation by, of corruption, xxv, 185, 214; abduction of Febres Cordero in response to, xxv, 185, 214; court martial of, xxv, 185, 214; dismissal of, xxv, 185, 214; revolts led by, xxv, 185, 214

Vargas Pazzos, Frank, xxv, 185, 214; presidential campaign of, xxv; 185

Vatican: Ecuador's first concordat with, 22

Veintemilla, Ignacio de, 209; as president, 24

Velasco Ibarra, José María, 30, 33, 42, 155, 159, 183; *autogolpe* by, 40, 160, 212-13; constitution suspended by, 160; death of, 45; overthrow of, in 1935, 30, 36, 41; party organized by, 183; political polarization under, 36; as president, 30, 31, 34-35, 35-36, 40; problems under, 33; promises of,

303

Published Country Studies

(Area Handbook Series)

550-65	Afghanistan		550-87	Greece
550-98	Albania		550-78	Guatemala
550-44	Algeria		550-174	Guinea
550-59	Angola		550-82	Guyana and Belize
550-73	Argentina		550-151	Honduras
550-169	Australia		550-165	Hungary
550-176	Austria		550-21	India
550-175	Bangladesh		550-154	Indian Ocean
550-170	Belgium		550-39	Indonesia
550-66	Bolivia		550-68	Iran
550-20	Brazil		550-31	Iraq
550-168	Bulgaria		550-25	Israel
550-61	Burma		550-182	Italy
550-50	Cambodia		550-30	Japan
550-166	Cameroon		550-34	Jordan
550-159	Chad		550-56	Kenya
550-77	Chile		550-81	Korea, North
550-60	China		550-41	Korea, South
550-26	Colombia		550-58	Laos
550-33	Commonwealth Caribbean, Islands of the		550-24	Lebanon
550-91	Congo		550-38	Liberia
550-90	Costa Rica		550-85	Libya
550-69	Côte d'Ivoire (Ivory Coast)		550-172	Malawi
550-152	Cuba		550-45	Malaysia
550-22	Cyprus		550-161	Mauritania
550-158	Czechoslovakia		550-79	Mexico
550-36	Dominican Republic and Haiti		550-76	Mongolia
550-52	Ecuador		550-49	Morocco
550-43	Egypt		550-64	Mozambique
550-150	El Salvador		550-35	Nepal and Bhutan
550-28	Ethiopia		550-88	Nicaragua
550-167	Finland		550-157	Nigeria
550-155	Germany, East		550-94	Oceania
550-173	Germany, Fed. Rep. of		550-48	Pakistan
550-153	Ghana		550-46	Panama